Contents

Acknowledgements

I would like to thank Esther Whitby for encouragement in the early stages of writing the book, Masoud Yazdani and Robin Beecroft at Intellect, Lucy Kind for her excellent work in editing the manuscript, and Christine, Rosemary and Caroline for their support and patience.

The book is dedicated to my father, George Abbott, and to the memory of my mother, Gweneth (1918-1998), who died shortly before the book went to press.

Robert Abbott
28th August 1998

The World As Information

Overload and Personal Design

Robert Abbott

intellect™

EXETER, ENGLAND

First Published in 1999 by
Intellect Books
School of Art and Design, Earl Richards Road North, Exeter EX2 6AS

Copy Editor:	Lucy Kind
Cover Design:	Anne Roesler
Cover Illustration:	Yahia Badawi *

A catalogue record for this book is available from the British Library

ISBN 1-871516-75-7

* Yahia Badawi Graphic Design (ybad@btinternet.com)

Printed and bound in Great Britain by Cromwell Press, Wiltshire

1. Introduction

We have heard much in recent times about the rapid growth in numbers of publications of all kinds, documents generated by bureaucracies, broadcasts and 'media' output, sites on the Internet and its relatives, and all of these we somewhat loosely call 'information'. Statistics confirm what we already know, namely that we can scarcely cope - statistics such as that every day another 20 million words of technical information are recorded, which would take 6 weeks of 8-hour days to read, assuming a reading speed of 1,000 words per minute, by which time the poor reader would have fallen five and a half years behind[1]. Statistics such as that a weekday edition of the *New York Times* contains more information than an average person living in 17th century Britain would have been exposed to in a lifetime, or that more information has been produced in the last 30 years than in the last five millennia[2]. We are all too familiar with the notion of the information explosion, of information overload, and with such complaints as: 'We already have far more facts than we can handle'[3], or more despairingly: 'He saw there were a million things to read, a million leads to follow ... too much ... too much ... and not enough time in one life to get it all together. Snowed under'[4].

At the same time as such complaints are voiced, there is sometimes a hopeful comment to the effect that technology, principally in the form of computers, has advanced in the nick of time to rescue us from this deluge.Unfortunately, although computers can manipulate information at great speed, they cannot absorb it or understand it for us. While there is much preoccupation with the power of the hardware, the slickness of the software, and the capacity of the communication channels, there is relatively little concern with the actual material being processed - information - and with its organisation and content, and what it means to us. The arrival of the Internet and especially the World Wide Web in the media-inflamed public consciousness has at last upped the profile of information as a commodity, yet there is still an emphasis on quantity and speed over quality or meaning. As so often happens, we are seduced by technique at the expense of content, and all information increasingly comes to have the same value, or no meaning at all. Often, it appears, information is regarded as a kind of homogenous fluid, an indifferent material whose processing demonstrates the wizardry of our technology, but which in itself should concern us no more than the electricity supply that makes computing possible. GIGO (Garbage In, Garbage Out), as the computer jargon acronym would have it, might well describe how our technological enthusiasms show little interest in the personal significance of the information being processed. Little is said about real human needs or hungers for understanding or meaning, or for the desire to acquire knowledge. As usual, we have tended to dwell on the easy aspects, those amenable to glamorous technical advance.

The information explosion may be thought of as a recent phenomenon, caused by increased information productivity and by improved access and exposure to it[5], by the increased 'virtuality' of daily life, by the advent of e-mail and voicemail, by the increasing abstraction of what we do, and our reliance upon the manipulation of symbolic media. In that sense it is recent, but there is another viewpoint, that of considering everything that we see around us, everything we encounter, as information - or potential information. For information is a fundamental quality of the universe, like matter or energy. In this sense, we have always been bombarded by more than we could handle, and it is not immediately obvious how technology, or those other handy modern-day aides, the expert and the information officer, can help us. Because this is *our* problem. This book therefore addresses itself primarily to the impact of information on the individual, and to the problem of responding to the fact that we are alive in a world perceived as 'information'. It is not especially concerned with information overload as it affects life in the workplace. This is an unusual approach in that it attempts to reach back from present day information handling activities to older concerns relating to meaning and personal identity. It is by no means a conventional review of information science or information technology.

The idea of the Information Society, as an aspect of post-industrialism, is one that has become popular in recent years, aided by the works of writers such as Daniel Bell, David Lyon, Blaise Cronin, Yoneji Masuda and others, while the far reaching effects of information technology have been explored by very many other writers, including Alvin Toffler, Murray Laver, and Theodore Roszak. Effects upon domestic and working life, entertainment and leisure, finance and shopping, economics and politics, skills and employment, privacy and freedom, personal empowerment and enablement, and the creation of 'smart' environments are themes that have frequently been addressed. None of this 'sociology of information', however, really deals with information in its own right or with the individual's intimate relationship with it. These are our present concerns.

The main themes of the book can be summarised briefly as follows. We begin with the child or the adolescent trying to make sense of the world. The recognition of the state of being alive in the world can lead to problems of deciding what information to incorporate within one's own mind, or, as it were, to attach to one's personality. This is the focus of Chapter 2. Here we are speaking not only of the conventional problem of the information explosion, but a more fundamental perception of things out there in the world, as information to be 'captured' in some way. To illustrate this problem the writings of Thomas Wolfe are studied in some detail, in Chapter 3. Wolfe was peculiarly obsessed with a need to record the information content of everything he experienced. This sort of situation can have all kinds of consequences, including the craving for the capture of informational territory, and a variety of what can only be described as information pathologies. It helps to have a clearer picture of the fundamental types of information that we need to deal with, and to this end the Three Worlds model of Sir Karl Popper, a way of dividing up the information content of the universe, is described in Chapter 4. Each of these Worlds is then examined in turn (Chapters 5, 6 and 7), looking at the different species of information that there are, how they are classified and ordered, and how they impact upon the individual.

Traditional information retrieval techniques as described in Chapter 7 do not really help with the problem of personal information overload, and developments such as the Internet, while raising the profile of information as an entity in its own right, may actually make it worse. What is needed is the purposeful extraction of meaning from all kinds of documents or 'texts' already in existence, and its synthesis into coherent knowledge. The best opportunity for this, the Xanadu project, may have been lost, but there still may be other opportunities, possibly using the World Wide Web. Knowledge synthesis of this sort, leading to the utopian ideal of the World Brain, is explored in Chapter 8. Information technology and developments in society have made access to most information possible to everyone; the question now is what do we do with it, and how can this accessibility help us with the problem demonstrated in extreme form by Thomas Wolfe. The concluding chapter reviews some of the wider societal and ecological implications of the information explosion and of the new technologies, and their impact on the individual struggling to keep up.

As a species we have now grown to the point where, theoretically, everything we have ever known can be put together as information available to everyone. What is needed is more meaningful knowledge synthesis, more 'intelligence', more understanding of the information we already have, and more understanding of the reasons for personal choice. Otherwise, we may become increasingly alienated from our information resource. For the first time ever our access to information is almost unrestricted by factors such as time, geography or cost. Soon, this resource will become second nature to us, a background to our lives much as language is today. It is therefore vital that it is properly organised, despite the failure of Xanadu and the uncontrolled run-away success of the Internet. We have only just, in the last 200-300 years, found out about the contents of our world and put it all - or most of it - together, with the aid of classifications, collections, and scientific theory. It is important now, at the turn of the millennium, to take the opportunity to reject those things which are evidently bogus and to consolidate those which are true, and to extract meaning and personal significance from them.

Science, philosophy, religion and the arts developed in their various ways to try to explain the things that man saw around him and to provide outlets for expressing his reactions to the phenomena he encountered. None of these approaches, however, really helps the individual alone in a vast world of information. The recent proliferation of 'information' merely highlights and exacerbates a long-standing, insuperable problem. For this problem includes such intractable components as: how should one react to the situation of being thrust into the world for a short while, for long enough to have a tantalising insight into what is available, but not for long enough to do a great deal with it? What should the individual try and incorporate within his mind, and what should he be content to leave outside? What can he safely leave in the external world, whether it be in his personal diaries, the contents of the *Encyclopaedia Britannica* or the skyscrapers of Manhattan or other people's minds? What does he need to, in some indefinable way, bring within himself? How much should he long for the world, how much pain should it cause him, how sacred should it be for him? In short, what does the environment he finds himself in stimulate him to be, to do, to make of himself, and what does he take from it in order to make himself an individual, a character, a person? There is more to the information explosion than finding it hard to keep up with the literature on one's own profession, getting carried away while exploring Web sites, or fighting a losing battle with the e-mail or with the Sunday supplements. More than anything it is a matter of personal development and identity.

This book is therefore not only about the information explosion in the conventional sense, but about longing and nostalgia, about how it feels to be alive, and about cravings for knowledge and fame and immortality; about impossible painful yearnings for things which we can never possess and which can never last, about the cruel disparity between what we might be and what we can actually be. It is about the incongruity between man's 'circumstances and his powers', about the 'restlessness of ambition; an interminable longing after nobler and higher things, which nought but immortality and the greatness of immortality can satiate', as expressed by the 19th century Presbyterian preacher Thomas Chalmers in his first Bridgewater Treatise[6]. Such poignant feelings can lead to all sorts of reactions and responses: to discontent, despair, defeat, boredom, negativity, to anti-social behaviour or even to psychopathy, to a craving for power or a lust for knowledge or fame, to a feeling of being overwhelmed; or they can be a stimulant to creativity and to positive achievement, to specifically religious feelings, to a sense of holiness and sacredness, to the 'joy' of C. S. Lewis: 'an unsatisfied desire which is itself more desirable than any other satisfaction'[7]. This is the sort of phenomenon that in extreme form was expressed by Rupert Brooke: '... that tearing hunger to do and do and do things. I want to walk 1000 miles, and write 1000 plays, and sing 1000 poems, and drink 1000 pots of beer, and kiss 1000 girls ...'[8], the sort of impossible motivation that is sublimated by fantasies like those of Walter Mitty, only much worse. It is the sort of challenge that most typically affects the young person and then largely evaporates with full psychological maturity and social responsibility and the routine of daily life, but it may constantly affect the more obsessive type of personality. Much less romantically, and right up to the present day, there is evidence that information addiction, as well as information overload, is rife in office life. A survey by Reuters[9], published towards the end of 1997, revealed that 53 per cent of managers 'crave' information, 54 per cent of respondents claimed to get a 'high' when they found information they had been seeking, and that over a third of respondents believed their colleagues were obsessed with gathering information.

The principal character at the very centre of the main theme of this book is the American novelist Thomas Wolfe, who more than anyone else I know of personified the ceaseless torment of feeling that he had to 'do something' with the world, to make it his own, to capture it, to express it and to remake it in his own image. Wolfe was appropriately named, for his hunger for life, for experience, even for inanimate objects, was insatiable and savage. As I will show, his problem was essentially one of information processing, of trying to assimilate the information content of the world and its cultural artefacts. His painful longings of which several examples will be given in a later chapter are, for all their impossibility of ever being assuaged, an affirmation of the wonder of existence, of being alive, an affirmation bordering on religious devotion or obsessive compulsive neurosis according to one's point of view. I prefer to take the more generous view. The need for experience, for eventfulness, for capture of informational territory, may be the fire behind one's ambitions, leading one on to success in more than one area of endeavour. Hence 'Renaissance Men', like Leon Battista Alberti, Leonardo, Blake, Goethe, Victor Hugo, and Churchill, of whom it was said: 'One felt he could do anything'[10].

To try to know, do or be everything is not an illogical response to one's predicament as a thinking, sensitive, human being. It is merely an impractical one. For many, however - and we can expect more of them as education, the mass media, the seductions of superstardom and the contrasting real life scenarios of dull-employment or unemployment exert their effects - the heavy cloud of mortality hangs low, and their lust for life demands some kind of response. As we shall see, all such responses are ultimately inadequate and unrealistic because they are, besides being for the most part impossible to fulfill, tangible reactions to a feeling which is itself intangible and ungraspable. One is always left dissatisfied and longing for things which one can never quite identify. 'We want to have everything. Our tragedy is that we can't have everything'[11]. Mostly, we are unclear what 'everything' would imply, but that way lies the spur to creativity - and to all the sequelae of unfulfilled lives.

Being alive is not an easy business for any of us, but being alive in a world which is enthralling, overwhelming, never keeping still, perceived as sacred, and which we are sooner or later bound to leave, is especially difficult. But that's the way it is, and has always been. It's just that now our perspectives are wider and more poignant. We have more possibilities, more opportunities, we know more and are more self-consciously aware, yet still we are finally defeated. Awareness of this unavoidable but arguably unsatisfactory state of affairs can lead to all kinds of responses, even to insane jealousies for other people or other things, to trying to escape the limitations of one's own being, like Michael Jackson with his cosmetic surgery, only more insistently and insidiously so. Thomas Wolfe expressed a kind of jealousy, if one reads between the lines, that he could not be other people or other things: cities, Indian tribes, hotel rooms, trains. This is the pathological end state of a process found in more normal people, and perhaps in all of us. Consider the example of another superstar, Paul McCartney, who, scarcely into his twenties and already highly successful, had for the first time in his life discovered ballet, the theatre, and serious literature. In an interview he said: 'I'm trying to crowd everything in. I vaguely mind anyone knowing anything I don't know'[12].

The reasons for such a feeling are many and complex, from simple insecurity in the sudden light of public exposure right through to what I will call the Wolfean urge and the desire not to let any of life's experiences pass us by. Clearly, in a world in which information is proliferating at the rate at which it is doing, being upset by other people knowing more than oneself is an inappropriate response, especially if one tries seriously to do something about it. Equally, it is the goad to learning and achievement. Without an inferiority complex one may always remain inferior.

Although one's response to the life challenge cannot be generalised, and though it is not a new problem, the emerging concern with information as an entity in itself worthy of study prompts a new approach, as part of what might be called the sociology of information science or of information technology. The personal consequences of the information explosion and the reaction of the individual to the world as information have hardly been considered before. This book will, I hope, go some way towards rectifying that situation.

It is a little disconcerting, when well on the way with writing a book such as this, to discover that one has been pre-empted - not by another book, I hasten to add - but by a pop song which in just over four minutes encapsulates much of what one intended to say. For in 1991 Joe Jackson released a CD called *Laughter and Lust*, which I subsequently borrowed from my local library. Included on it is a song called *It's All Too Much*, which makes, very effectively, one of the main points in this book. Some of the lyrics are: 'I read the morning paper, but it all changes by the evening news; the world got so much smaller, I don't know which piece of it to choose'; 'Stay in and watch TV, 50 channels can't all be the same; maybe go to a movie, 50 films on 50 tiny screens'; and 'I'd like to get to know, all the many people I could be; if I just had the time, I'm sure I could find out which one is me'. The chorus, with variants, goes: 'They say that choice is freedom; I'm so free it's driving me insane'[13]. Curiously, Joe Jackson is one of several people from the English Midlands who feature in this book, having been born in Burton-on-Trent before growing up in Portsmouth and then moving to Manhattan and elsewhere. My own origins were in Nottingham, and we shall also meet Nicholas Whittaker from Burton-on-Trent, John Cowper Powys who was born in rural Derbyshire, and Colin Wilson, whose formative years were spent in Leicester. Maybe it is something to do with a provincial upbringing.

There are some books, like some songs, which are written as an alternative to going to see a psychiatrist. Looking again through this one I wonder whether it falls into that category. I would hope not, but I cannot deny the passions, some of them quite painful, which were the spur behind the writing, and which continue to assail me from time to time. Except for a brief section in the following chapter I have tried to keep myself out of this book, but inevitably my feelings show through. Without those feelings there would be no book. This is a young person's book, I think. Most of it reflects a youthful mad optimism that Everything is within grasp. I acknowledge straight away that this optimism is insane and impossible, but it is nevertheless real. I take the essentially young person's view that, although at some level there is a recognition of time passing and of eventual mortality, the world is a fascinating and exciting place, which can be described as a world of information, and that there is an appetite to absorb it all, personally, to make it one's own. There is a personal problem of information retrieval and overload, but there will be sufficient time, and the effort will be worthwhile. If the correct response to this situation is to go and see a psychiatrist, so be it. If not, read on. Or listen to Joe Jackson.

2. Railway Analogies

The scene will be familiar to anyone who has travelled by train in Britain at weekends or during the school holidays. At these times, at the ends of the platforms of the main London and provincial stations, and especially of the major junctions such as Crewe, Derby and York, and of those stations at the 'frontier' between different regions (such as Bristol Temple Meads, Reading, Carlisle, and Peterborough), will be found a large collection of boys and, it must be admitted, fully grown men. Stereotypically, they will be wearing anoraks, carrying duffle bags and binoculars, and be armed with biros, small spiral-bound notebooks (or in recent years dictaphones or pocket-sized cassette recorders), and be possessed with a curiously jumpy form of nervous excitement no doubt encouraged by the draughty surroundings. In a word, trainspotters. According to Nicholas Whittaker, who began trainspotting in Burton-on-Trent in 1964, the stereotype has moved on, so that today's trainspotter would prefer to be known as a 'railfan': 'a grown-up with a credit-card. He has made a Faustian pact with Dixons and comes fully equipped with camcorder, Pentax with auto-wind and telephoto, and a personal stereo on which to listen to Fleetwood Mac between trains'[1]. In the pejorative jargon of today, though, he is still 'sad', the archetypal wally.

For those not well acquainted with this peaceful, masculine pastime, the way that a trainspotter works is as follows: in his free time he travels to the busy stations mentioned above and notes down in his notebooks, or records on tape for later transcription, the number of every locomotive he sees, regardless of its age, type, location, aesthetic value or any other imaginable criteria. If he has the syndrome particularly badly he might also note carriage or freight vehicle numbers. Sometimes a group of friends will trainspot together, or parents may be roped in to assist, and this is useful at exceptionally busy stations where one person might not be able to keep up with all the train movements. Even so, the numbers spotted by this method are considered to be common property and all the individuals concerned will write them down, even if they have not seen them personally. This is acceptable practice, but to invent sightings fraudulently, the crime of the 'fudger', would be despised[2]. Trainspotting is, among other things, an exercise in self-monitored integrity.

Having made his cull of numbers for the day, our dedicated trainspotter then turns to a reference work, traditionally the Ian Allan *ABC Combine*, in which are published, in numerical order, the numbers of all the locomotives, classified according to type. The numbers that have been 'spotted' are crossed off this master list and are then of no further interest. The aim, apparently, is to see, eventually, every locomotive listed; in other words, every one that exists within the region, then within Great Britain, and then, who knows ... the world?

Although I am prejudiced, my childhood having been spent amongst noble and awe-inspiring steam locomotives rather than the seemingly characterless tinny diesel or electric sets that have replaced them, I cannot help thinking that trainspotting is a singularly useless exercise. I suspect that even when I went through the craze myself, briefly at about the age of nine, I wondered exactly what my motives and intentions were. What can a trainspotter hope to achieve? All the locomotives are known to exist; there is no chance of discovering a new one. After all, they are listed in those reference works ready to cross off, and presumably (or so a child might imagine) there is a man at British Rail headquarters who has a big book with all the details of all the locomotives in the country. They have all been seen by people at one time or place or another; one doesn't win anything for having 'spotted' them all, although there may be childhood myths to the contrary. It is easy to react to this hobby with a quick stab of 'so-whatism', but of course it is harmless and gives hours of genuine pleasure to a great many people, and that cannot be said of every youthful pastime. It doesn't create anything or prove anything or solve any problems; it doesn't reveal any great skill on the part of the trainspotter, nor does it contribute much to his education, except to the extent that it induces him to travel and to study maps and timetables. But then half the beauty of a hobby (and indeed of childhood in general) is that it doesn't have to be *for* anything. Apart from a sense of gloating satisfaction at having completed or having gone some way towards completing a self-appointed task, trainspotting is without any purpose and has no useful result or end product.

However, one can understand one of the possible motivations behind trainspotting if one takes oneself back to childhood, and tries to imagine what it was like, confronting a huge and baffling world. To collect engine numbers is to grapple with a small, but real, part of the world, with a considerable degree of control and with a reasonable chance that the self-appointed task will be accomplished. Out of all the chaos and complexity of the world, or even of a national railway network, or even of Birmingham New Street, here is something over which a tiny individual can have some illusion of mastery and control. I suppose it is the same with any kind of collecting mania, whether it be for stamps, foreign dolls, or cards in packets of tea, but trainspotting will serve as an example.

Robert Kegan has commented:

> 'The fully concrete operational child - a typical ten-year-old - is marvelously engaged with the physical dimensions of the world. This is the age of collecting, of keeping records, of memorizing baseball statistics, of the healthy obsessive-compulsive. Now that the world has lost its fluidity and plasticity there is an interest in pursuing its limits along the concrete horizon in which the child is embedded'[3].

This is the transition period between the immediacy of perception so characteristic of childhood, and the increasing abstraction, and lapsing of direct observation - possibly related to the beginning of serious reading and television viewing - in the approach to adolescence and adulthood. Hence the passion at this time of life for absorbing the statistics from the *Guinness Book of Records*, *Whitaker's Almanac*, *Wisden*, the tables of league football or the music charts, and so on.

'Mankind is a collecting animal, and the compulsion manifests itself in scores of ways'[4] and yet it is important to distinguish here between what are normal collecting habits of the young person, and the other end of the spectrum which includes various schizoid, autistic and obsessive compulsive personality disorders. There is, for example, Asperger's syndrome, which mostly affects males, and which includes amongst other features a hypertrophy of interest in such things as electronics, diagrams, and pinball machines, and excellent memory for these subjects. It sounds pretty normal to me! Nigel Whittaker is scornful of any attempt to pathologise the enthusiasm of the collector. He writes: 'Is there any human being who doesn't have some urge to make sense of their world, to enjoy it in the open air and learn about its ways, and cohabit with it to the best of his or her enjoyment?'[5]. Long ago, the great Pavlov - who evidently never salivated over mighty locos from the end of some bleak Russian platform - observed the obsessiveness of many collectors, as the psychologist Nicholas Humphrey has described. Humphrey is surprised by the worthlessness of many collecting habits, especially when what is collected is nothing more than an observation - as with trainspotting. He cites the importance to a child of merely catching sight of, say, a bird, a toadstool, a licence plate, or a pub sign, reflected in the popularity of the *Observer's books* and *I-Spy* series. He notes that the craze may not be left behind in childhood, but may continue, often with serious distorting effects on the personality, as with plane spotters who crowd the rooftop viewing galleries at Heathrow: '"The typical aero-spotter does nothing other than aero-spot", the proprietor of a shop for spotters told *The Guardian* newspaper. "He isn't married, or anything like that"'[6].

We tend to think of collecting or 'spotting' as a relatively modern trait, originating in the 19th century, but the tendency goes further back, and with just as much dottiness. Some strange examples are reviewed by Stephen Jay Gould[7], and include Willem Cornelis van Heurn, who collected the pelts of dogs, moles and pigs; Peter the Great whose collecting habits included human teeth, personally pulled; and Thomas Hawkins, described as 'eccentric and demented', who collected fossilised ichthyosaurs and plesiosaurs from the beaches around Lyme Regis. All of these were ostensibly motivated by the pursuit of scholarly research, but hovered near the edges of sanity. Helga Dittmar[8] comments that collecting behaviour is a prominent and fairly universal form of possessive behaviour in child development, and refers to studies from around a century ago showing that 80-90 per cent of children aged between 6 and 17 had systematic and extensive collections. However, she wonders if the collecting habits of children have declined over subsequent decades; I suspect that they may have been hijacked by media-perpetrated fashions.

The psychology of collecting is curious: it implies in some cases a diversion away from more normally desirable goals, especially if it is carried over into adult life - so, for example, marriage and procreation may be forfeited. What is collected or observed is confined to a definite species or type, anything else, even multiple copies of the same things, being of no interest. Humphrey considers that collectors get a mental thrill from their activity, the same sort of pleasure one derives from 'classifying incoming information: making comparisons, uncovering relationships, and imposing order on the world'[6]. Consequently such hobbies are mostly to be encountered, and are most satisfying, in childhood, when the world most needs to be ordered.

As a child there is not a lot one can do that intermeshes with the world of adult reality, but trainspotting is one possibility. It is a way of coming to terms with information about the adult world. Also, incidentally, it permits the child to know something about the adult world which the adult probably does not know in much detail. If it does not sound too pretentious, like some bogus sociological analysis of a perfectly ordinary occurrence, trainspotting is a type of information gathering exercise because, in the end, the chaos and complexity of the world is a chaos and complexity of information, and trainspotting is a valid, albeit admittedly trivial, way of trying to understand the world. The trainspotter, in his way, orders and 'captures' a small part of the confused adult world. The smallness is part of the attraction. Trainspotting has finite possibilities, especially when one's relatively small country is surrounded by water; theoretically, trainspotting is an activity that can be completed, it is 'do-able'. Ironically, according to Whittaker, 'the thing is, no one really, not in their hearts, wants to finish'[9]. In the 1950s there were more than 18,000 train numbers that could be collected, 'a lifetime's quest', but not an impossible one. The world's champion trainspotter, Bill Curtis of Clacton-on-Sea, Essex, 'spotted' around 80,000 steam, electric and diesel units in different countries over a 40 year period[10]. Locomotive numbers are just a tiny part of reality; one may assume that in time, one can collect other things, experiences, facts, information, so that ultimately one will be omniscient. This magnificent delusion leads us on, from Crewe to total knowledge!

Trainspotters come in for relentless gentle abuse. As Jonathan Meades puts it: '... the ones who want it all simple for ever, the model makers, the gricers logging locos on wintry platforms. (Never talk to a man with a vacuum flask and a duffle-bag)'[11]. Be that as it may. Trainspotting might remain a lifelong hobby, or the interest in trains might be lost altogether or modified in some way more compatible with the needs of adolescent development. One might, for instance, extend the hobby to collecting carriage numbers or wagon numbers, or develop an interest in building model railways or in railway photography or industrial archaeology or in railway maps or timetables and become an expert (or bore) on the subject of train times and connections. Nicholas Whittaker refers to his love of old timetables: 'They remind me of how I first began to discover the world, the joy of working out for myself how to get from Burton to Wolverhampton, and how to get back in time for tea'[12]. Surely we all know such people (always male), and we may smirk at their puerility and tediousness while hiding a sneaking admiration for someone who has actually got to grips with and bothered to learn such things. While it might be useful on occasion to know, the information which such people hoard in their minds seems hardly worth knowing. It is hardly worth *their* knowing, for it is all in the published timetables and can easily, or perhaps not so easily, be obtained from a British Rail enquiry office or from one of the privatised companies into which it has been forceably fragmented. Again, though, it gives some people pleasure to know these things, perhaps a sense of security and competence in handling their environment. Though easy to ridicule, these people are thoroughly at home in their world; they are in control.

So where is all this leading us? To my way of thinking collecting engine numbers or knowing timetables off by heart suggests a certain optimism about the knowability and stability of the world, an optimism which is characteristically strongest and most realistic, most justified, in childhood and adolescence, and the waning of which begins with the onset of psychological maturity, when the world destabilises and the rate of apparent change accelerates. This optimism is a kind of faith in one's existence, a faith that one has time to completely master the world, and it possibly derives from a feeling, not necessarily consciously recognised or admitted, that one is immortal. As one gets older and realises that there will not be time, the incentive to do these things decreases, and the realisation grows that engine numbers, railway timetables, and all manner of other things can be safely ignored, and kept outside one's own mind. They can exist quite happily without any personal intervention.

At this point of psychological maturity and recognition of one's personal limitations, one feels that - despite the changes and surprises characterising everyday life - one understands the world sufficiently not to have to do 'research' on it at first hand; instead, one relies on other people's knowledge and opinions about the world, and on external sources of reference. Also, at this point, unfortunately, one's world can go flat, it can pass one by practically unnoticed, and one may feel that something indefinable has been lost, something magical to do with childhood, a time when the world was more personal and 'meant much more'. As the jargon of psychobabble has it, one has become alienated. The railway timetable no longer buzzes with excitement inside one's head. One ceases, if the pun can be excused, to make connections. The timetable lies flat, bedraggled, scrawled over, and largely unseen on the station wall. A little bit of life over which one had a sense of control has been lost, and it won't be coming back.

So far, we have considered trainspotters and timetable freaks. Let us, for the purpose of thought provocation, continue for the moment to talk about railways and see how that can lead us towards information in a more abstract or general sense. Let us consider another type of railway freak. This is the sort of person, for some reason invariably male, again, who is concerned with maps. There are a number of sub-types of this species, whom I believe are found world-wide, although they probably reach their peak of obsessive typicality in Britain. This of course is true of trainspotting itself, which Whittaker believes is all tied up with patriotism and loyalty and Empire: 'propaganda on wheels'[13]. A prominent British sub-species of this kind of railway buff, who has substituted abstract information in place of actual railway reality, is the one who has memorised the entire London Underground network. Ordinary people keep this kind of information in the end pages of their diary or on graffiti-daubed maps on subway walls, and they seem to find their way around just as efficiently, or almost so. They are frequently amazed that anyone could learn what looks to them like the wiring diagram for a computer, or a complicated maze of angular spaghetti, but for a devoted adolescent it is not too difficult.

The dedicated Underground freak will make a point of travelling over as much of the network as possible, not to see what it is like, but just to know that he has done it. Not to boast about, but just to know that he, personally has been out to Amersham, Upminster, Cockfosters, Morden, round the Hainault loop, and all the rest of it. He may even try to cover the network in the shortest possible time, the current record[10] being held by Robert Robinson and Tom McLaughlin, who toured all the stations on the system on the 4th October 1994 in a time of 18 hours, 18 minutes, and 9 seconds.

The main problem is that one's existence and one's efforts remain irrelevant. All right, so you know the Underground layout. So what? So do lots of people, even a few of the people who run the system! So, one has travelled over the whole network. Well, it manages quite well without you. Even the Northern Line. See, it is running now, while you are not there. A train just pulled into Goodge Street while you weren't looking; another one left Tottenham Court Road. You cannot make any impression on the system. It goes on without you, unaware of your very existence. Psychological maturity sets in, you leave the whole business alone, and one day - sooner than you think - you will finish up, crematorially speaking, at Golders Green.

Once again, one feels that people who do this sort of thing, unless it is merely a stunt in aid of charity, are seeking some kind of control over a manageable part of an unmanageable whole. One cannot 'know' the whole world, or the whole of Britain, even the whole of Greater London, but a skeletal, self-contained structure like the Underground can be 'captured' in this way. And yet, in a real sense, it cannot. There is something wrong, some unconsidered barrier, some kind of category mistake. We will see later (in Chapter 5) how little can be done to capture the physical world.

Now, I would like to continue the railway analogy with a personal anecdote which will lead us from the problem of grasping the informational complexity of the world straight into the question of what to do with being alive, thus linking the two major themes of this book.

When I was five years old my parents took me for a week's holiday to Shanklin, on the Isle of Wight. On the return journey to our home in Nottingham we arrived at Waterloo Station where, due to a misunderstanding, I became temporarily separated from my parents - 'lost' - and had to be reunited with them, some time later, with the assistance of the railway police. At such an age, in a strange and busy place so far from home, it was quite distressing. It made a great impression on me, although it affected my parents in a different way, as they had all the issues of guilt and responsibility to deal with and had a more realistic awareness of the possible perils to which I might have been exposed (probably far fewer then, in the mid-fifties, than now). Curiously, through all my panic and distress, I had a very strong sense of knowing where I was, that this was the famous Waterloo Station, London, and a feeling that it was absolutely right, and that this was what life was like - and would always be like. Life would never be very different from Waterloo Station: all its essential qualities, the feel of life, were contained within. It was all strangely familiar, and with it there came a moment of self-observation that I had recently been born - again, as it were. There was a pleasant recognition of life, of how things are. Here it all was, waiting. Opportunity, potential. What was I going to do with it?

This type of feeling, slightly pretentious though it looks when written down, is not unique to me. Graham Greene wrote about it in his autobiography *A Sort of Life*: 'If I had known it, the whole future must have lain all the time along those Berkhamsted streets'[14]. Similarly, Susanne Langer refers to an 'artist-philosopher' who said:

'When I was a young child - before I went to school, I think - I already knew what my life would be like. Not, of course, that I could guess what my fortunes would be, what economic situations and what political events I'd get into; but from the very beginning of my self-consciousness I knew *what anything that could happen to me would have to be like*'[15].

Life has a flavour, a quality, an 'isness', which is scarcely, if ever, described, perhaps because once we are beyond early childhood it is so familiar as to be invisible and ineffable and for most purposes redundant. More problematically, but more rewardingly, life is an opportunity. We all know what life is like, so what is the point of trying to say more?

Perhaps there is no point. Waterloo Station is for me a physical reminder of the strange poignancy of being alive, and a prompter of the questions: 'what does it all mean?' and 'now that you are here, what are you going to do with it all?' Many people spend their lives working out the implications of a few episodes in childhood. Some of these episodes are desperately sad; I was lucky. My most important thoughts, in a sense, are located in, or have passed through Waterloo Station. More generally I would say that one's ambitions and one's deepest sense of meaning and identity can be rooted in childhood, and reactivated by memory.

So, using examples associated with railways - the central nervous system of my childhood - I have tried to introduce the underlying themes of this book, namely, the impossibility of coping with the world as a whole and the need to structure it and select from it; the notion that the world as perceived is essentially information in need of processing and yet is also a reality which does not need our intervention; the idea that some information about the world, in fact a great deal of it, can be stored elsewhere than in the minds of individuals; and the whole problem of what to do with the informational world as presented in all its possibilities for meaning and action to each individual.

Being alive, possessing consciousness and reflective consciousness, self-awareness, means being exposed to an environment that is, in the final analysis, information to be processed, or ignored, by the mind. We must choose, not always consciously, to incorporate our perceptions into ourselves or to recognise that we need not do so. Some part of the mind will probably incorporate them anyway, but to be really useful to us they need some kind of structuring and evaluation which the unconscious mind, for all its amazing abilities, cannot be relied upon to do, at least in a way that is convenient to handle or to access.

We are surrounded by information, both that processed by man and that implicit, potential, in the physical environment. To an increasing extent we are being force-fed predigested information, the same information to all people across large areas of the globe (due to the nature of 'news', cults, fashions, and so on), but what we choose to make of it is up to the individual. In a world where the volume of information is proliferating at an incalculable rate it seems remarkably futile to be standing on the end of a cold, windswept platform at Crewe noting down the numbers of railway engines that just happen to turn up while we are there for a few hours, but which lots of people know about already. Yet, from the opposite point of view, the view from Waterloo, as it were, it seems a great shame that following the miracle or series of miracles that we should exist at all, we are only here for 70 years or so and that there exists far more significant information than we can ever assimilate. In this light, every engine number is sacred and *must* be collected by *us*, even if it means that we can be accused of a subtle form of narcissism. Or in the words of Nicholas Whittaker, 'I like to think that one day, a hundred years in the future, it will be vital to know that the 16.24 Derby-Birmingham Sprinter was halted by a signal outside Wilnecote station and that the delay was exactly 88 seconds'[16]. It is the conflict between the tedium of total recall and the need for structure exposed by selectivity, the same conflict which assails the autobiographer. It would be nice to have collected all the engine numbers - and to have known all the butterflies, all the chemical compounds, all the books in the British Museum Reading Room, blades of grass, clouds, ants, grains of sand on the seashore - personally. If we are not going to do this, who will? Why deny ourselves the opportunity? If we are here for such a short while how can we say that we are not interested; how dare we restrict the things which we claim to be our concern? Why not try to see and know everything?

For a time, as children, the possibility remains within the bounds of an illusory reality. The child, unaware of what is supposed to be important in the world, or what the central, archetypal structures are supposed to be, sees more clearly. He sees a vivid, actual world, not a world of mental abstractions and categories. He sees the world as a gestalt, with figure and ground of comparable significance. Because of this he sees in more detail than adults, less is filtered out, and so his world is fresher and more meaningful to him, more interesting. He can distinguish between things in ways that seem almost magical to the adult - not least because to the adult they are supremely unimportant. 'And after all, which of us could easily describe essential differences between two holes dug by a child in the sand at the beach? Though the child probably could'[17].

The child may imagine that he can extend this detailed perception to the whole world and so 'know' everything. For him, there are no rules about classification techniques, no limits to what can be classified or what needs to be classified; time goes slowly and the future is boundless. A morning on holiday at the seaside can seem like half a lifetime. But unfortunately time speeds up, and with it come other interests, motivations, responsibilities and habits of thought. There will come a time when mortgages, education, sexual fulfilment, prestige and politics - things which cannot even be seen - will be more important than the Flying Scotsman racing into York, or the kitten at the corner house, or chocolate mint chip ice cream. If only children knew how mad adults really are ...

More now than at any time in the past we live in an age of information overload. The problem is not new; it wasn't new in Old Testament times, but information productivity has come a long way since then. King Solomon, as recorded in Ecclesiastes, bemoaned the fact that 'of making many books there is no end' (xii, 12) and - very relevantly, and extremely depressingly - 'for in much wisdom is much grief: and he that increaseth knowledge increaseth sorrow' (i, 18). There is much in Ecclesiastes that is pertinent to the concerns of this book. Francis Bacon (1561-1626) complained about the problem, and in 1613 Barnaby Rich wrote:

'One of the diseases of this age is the multiplicity of books, they doth so overcharge the world that it is not able to digest the abundance of idle matter that is every day hatched and brought forth into the world'[18].

The accelerating exacerbation of the problem is a relatively recent phenomenon, and yet the stuff that we call information, with which we fill our libraries, scientific journals, computers and filing cabinets, is hardly a significant increase on the information which already exists in the natural world. One might say that the atoms have just been shuffled around a bit. Ironically, much of it represents an attempt to make the natural world more manageable and comprehensible to us, even if all it seems to do at times is to give long-winded names to things. In a sense, all this hardly adds to the problem we have always had, but we feel that because it is human-processed information it deserves more of our attention than that which resides in the strictly physical world. Realistically though, we can never know in complete detail either the 'real' physical world or the world of recorded or paper-bound information; it has always been too much for us, and always will be. It can never be ours, and it goes on despite us. We are locked into our isolated consciousnesses, separated by an ontological chasm from everything and everyone else.

All active, reasonably psychologically normal members of modern society have problems trying to cope with the printed or otherwise formalised information that is thrust at them, problems of grappling with what is conventionally labelled the information explosion, but as I have said, this is a relatively minor - and one might say somewhat artificial - addition to a problem that each one of us has always had to face. The information we are concerned with has shifted its emphasis, from the sensory and the physical to the abstract and the symbolic, and especially to the printed word. However, this surfeit of formalised information forces us to examine very carefully our roles as individual sentient human beings. We would like to know 'everything' but we soon find that we cannot, and that bothers us. This need to take the information content of the world on our shoulders, a need which permeates most of our conscious life, is a great burden but, seemingly, the most valid and intense way to live. Not to have the need seems not so much of an abdication of personal responsibility as a loss, a denial of the potential fullness of life experience. At a less profound level there is continual and growing pressure to be up-to-date with every new development in one's profession, with all the latest media fads, to know and use the latest buzzwords.

Why do we as individuals need to know things which are known already? Egotistical, societal and communications needs apart, is there any point in taking the trouble to know things which many other people know already and know better, or which are more conveniently, accurately and efficiently stored in libraries and computers? We may ask, tempting the wrath of traditionalist pedagogues, why should we learn basic arithmetic when pocket calculators are so cheaply and widely available, which are quicker, and which never make mistakes (except for my wife's)? Why bother to learn chemistry when there are clearly a large number of people around who will always be better chemists than we are, or why learn history when history is already known and safely packaged away in books or on video cassettes? Or, we may argue perversely, when it has happened anyway and is all in the past. Why learn our way around the Underground when there is a map in every ticket hall? Why try and learn German when we know we will never be able to do so very well, and when most Germans speak English so irritatingly well? I am being provocative and philistine of course, and I do not seriously doubt that there are very good reasons for learning these things, but I am labouring the point that as time goes on and as recorded information expands, the crucial question will slowly crystallise out. The crucial question is this: what should we put in our minds? Management guru Charles Handy has written recently: 'The trick is not to try to transfer it all to one's brain, but to know where to find it, how to access it and what to do with it when you have it'[19]. Or as Auguste Forel once said: 'What we can put on our shelves we should not put into our brains'[20]. But how do we define the 'what'? Related questions are: 'what is the role of the human being?' (as opposed to animals or machines) and 'what is *my* particular role, what can *I* offer that is unique'?

Increasingly, in a world of expertise and closed-shop professionalism, it often seems that the individual has little to offer, and can make no impact. Let's take a look at this in quite a depressed, pessimistic way. In such a state of mind other people, organisations, computers, files, experts, always appear to know better. Whatever we do, someone or something can do it better. Professionals attend us from hi-tech parturition to straight-line-continuous-beep-EEG decease; we need experts to guide us through life and to solve all our problems from our infant's temper tantrums to fitting a new washer on the tap in the bathroom. It is easy to be cynical and self-mocking about our state of dependency on others, and there are some signs that this trend is reversing. Of course, for the most part, professional help is valuable and appreciated and it is a benefit of our so-called civilisation. And yet such aids can leave us feeling slightly redundant, emasculated, useless, and alienated.

It seems that there is little we can do which makes any impact any more, little we can do to 'effect'. We begin to feel that we have been mentally castrated. Gordon Pask and Susan Curran have written of the fear that learning will become redundant:

> 'What will be the point of acquiring knowledge when any database contains a million times more accessible information than our brain? Why try to use personally acquired knowledge when a computer can apply it more efficiently, more appropriately? Perhaps all that we now think of as knowledge will come to seem sterile and pointless to future generations'[21].

They see this 'mental castration' as leading to the loss of feelings of individual identity and worth, and ask: 'If and when machines can emulate and even surpass us in every measurable area of human endeavour, what uniquely human pursuits will be left to us?'[21].

Such concerns can provoke us into re-examining what it means to be truly human, but the danger is that the more we become reliant on external sources of information the more we expect that there will always be someone around who knows the answer, someone who will nanny us. And if there is, it does little for our self-esteem or sense of control. As Miles Kington says: 'Therefore we, personally, do not need to know.

Therefore, as information increases, we ourselves know less and less'[22]. Consequently most of us have no idea how a television set works, how to fix the car, how to make a pizza, and so on. We even have manuals telling us how to procreate, although there is no evidence that our bodies have forgotten what to do. We usually avoid confronting our ignorance by flattering ourselves that we will have to call in an expert or a consultant, or by setting up a committee or a 'working party' to 'look into' something (so tiresomely English), or by feeding the bare bones of our problem to a computer and accepting its spurious, mathematically modelled regurgitations as gospel. And yet our experts are so frequently shown up as being no wiser than ourselves, whether they are predicting the weather, advising us on what is nutritious or safe to eat, or grappling with the ethical implications of medical discoveries. In some areas of knowledge real progress is minimal, while in others, typically those amenable to the application of technology, advances have been spectacular. Such advances can sometimes leave us feeling lost, inadequate and alienated. And there is something more generally unsatisfying which underlies our era; whatever we try to do as individuals - unless we are megastars - is tainted with a feeling of insignificance. Our time seems to lack much of the stature, grandeur and respectability of former times. It could be that we are more openly self-critical and less hypocritical, but I think there is more to it than this. Ours is not a confident age.

Certainly, if we set out to impress, our success will be short-lived. The news media tire of even the greatest sensations after a day or two. Whole lives are scrunched into soundbites or sidebars. Marvels and catastrophes are soon filed away, their emotional content drained, trivialised even. The very fact of possessing knowledge, of being competent, of memorising data, frequently gets ridiculed as 'sad' in the dumbing down that goes on in our society, the diminution of ability to the lowest common denominator. The despised swot of the schooldays of an earlier generation has been replaced by the sneering reference to the anorak. What we cannot begin to cope with we banish with cheap sarcasm. But there is worse. In our rapacity for gobbling information we are doing something wrong with it; we are not digesting it properly and obtaining nourishment from it. Instead, the act of ingestion exhausts us. Information malabsorption syndrome, one might call it. The enzymes we secrete have turned against us, and eat into us like a cancer. We have forgotten how to see as children and this is something we need to re-learn. To revert to the railway metaphor, we need to remember to study the timetable more carefully.

In our world of communicative incontinence and shameless disclosure we have become bored and unimpressed and cynical; we have lost our innocence to the ready diagnoses of irony and game playing and hidden agendas, motives behind motives, scripts and scenarios. There is always someone who knows better. Even our most private little peculiarities are no longer our own. Everything which we once believed was precious and unique to ourselves we can find described and displayed in popular magazine articles, in paperbacks and on television, or at an obscure Web address: somewhere there will be an 'expert' on it. There is always someone who has already laid claim to a piece of informational territory we might have fondly imagined was uniquely ours. The world as information seems already spoken for; it doesn't really need any input from ourselves. It is just another train leaving another station. What can any one of us do that millions more cannot? What can we offer mankind? How are we uniquely human? What can we do that raises us above the redundancy of commonplace information input/output? What can we know that isn't already known, the subject of a fat thesis in a university library somewhere in deepest Illinois? What can we know that doesn't happily exist already, without us needing to be around at all? It isn't going to get any better.

Cohen and Taylor have discussed this difficulty of escaping into uniqueness and subjectivity in their book *Escape Attempts*[23]:

> 'We attempt to create free areas in which our individuality, having been wrested from society, may now enjoy a certain immunity. The ability of society to co-opt, infiltrate, and subvert those very areas which we had hoped to hold sacred for the attainment of meaning, progress and self has increased throughout this century. No sooner has a new road to the true self been encountered than it is boxed and packaged for sale in the escape-attempts supermarket, no sooner has a new vocabulary of meaning been articulated, than it is raided for concepts and slogans by calendar makers and record producers, no sooner have we begun acting in an entirely novel way than we see coming over the horizon a mass of others mimicking our every action'.

Our areas of mental privacy and potential uniqueness are shrinking, not in the sense that anyone is spying on us or deliberately manipulating us with ill intentions, but simply because more and more people are becoming interested in such matters, and this sort of probing and analysis, whether intentionally or not, tends to erode values. There is a greater readiness and openness to reveal our innermost concerns which can mean that as individuals we are of interest to others for a much shorter time than might otherwise be the case. Our script is soon read, our painful little details are soon conceptualised and chunked and compressed into easily swallowed capsules. We are growing to resemble those sad comedians who in former days could spin out their material through half a lifetime in dingy clubs and obscure theatres, but when transferred to television are drained dry in half an hour. This is another pathological side effect of The Age of Information.

It is becoming steadily harder to find ways of reserving something that is truly ours and no one else's; something which cannot be dashed by someone else's petty, sneering, know-it-all one-upmanship. 'Been there, done that', the cruel, devaluing, put-down, which we learn - actively or passively - early in childhood. Yes, but *I* want to do it anyway. I don't care if you *have* already been to Venice. *I* wanted to go there anyway, and now *I*'ve been. All it seems we can do is process information, largely the same information that is available to everyone, in different ways, making connections that haven't been thought of before, making selections and emphases in ways peculiar to our needs - perhaps needs important since early childhood - alone. The mass media, necessarily it seems, select and package information according to certain implicit assumptions and these so easily become the implicit assumptions of everyone. But they need not be, and we can learn to inject excitement back into the timetable, to make it ours again.

This approach is of course a very narrow, narcissistic and obsessive way of looking at the infinite possibilities for life's activities and the inevitable uniqueness of circumstances and personality. It would look pretty thin to someone lost in love or grief or drink or religious ecstasy, to someone battling with a problem of artistic or scientific creativity, or successfully wrapping up another sales campaign, to someone in a hot air balloon or snorkelling in the Red Sea or scoring the winning goal at Wembley... But from the point of view of life as information processing just what can we do, what can we be? What is the answer to that crucial question of what we should put into our minds?

At the crass but nevertheless important level of ambition it is harder then ever before to be 'different', because nothing remains exciting for long. Is there literally nothing sacred in a world where everything interesting is taken away from us by someone who knows better? It seems that we have to work hard to make our interests our own, and to keep and defend them in spite of other people's poses of prior authority. We have to make our own sacred objects and places, as children do unconsciously, simply because they are our own, while we remain fully aware that other people, possibly better informed and with a more objective perspective, have their own evaluations and interpretations of them too. Overload with 'news' can rapidly induce boredom and lack of personal meaningfulness, an emotional 'level playing field'. The public world is one which we react to with the same degree of indifference as the average adult does to the timetable on the station wall. The private world, the domain of subjectivity and of ordinary day-to-day life, the world we had as children, need not be so. If we could capture just a hint of the trainspotter mentality we might be less bored, less ready to dismiss huge chunks of experience because they are not particularly new or trendy or exhilarating. You have been alive 20, 50, 70, 100 years and you think you have been around a long time and you know what's what. As a species, arrogance is our most unattractive trait. What can we possibly know in such a little time? We must accept our ignorance, and in so doing we might be less ready to reject and destroy; and we might be overwhelmed. All too soon we grow from being humble, interested, excited little boys collecting engine numbers into sullen, bored, hormonally unbalanced, aggressive adolescents who have seen it all before. Generally our development stops right there. Unfortunately something seems to have gone very wrong, in most cases irreparably so.

So, having found ourselves in this odd condition called life, we come to the subject matter of this book, which is the world treated as information and our response to it. Before looking at the main types of information that there are, and how they are organised, it may be appropriate to consider first an extreme example of personal information overload, a personal 'information explosion', what we might call 'information oppression' or 'the pain of everything'. There are many examples I could have chosen - Goethe's *Faust* or *The Sorrows of Young Werther*, for instance, or Chateaubriand's *René*, and it is the kind of phenomenon encountered by Churchill in large libraries, as he recounted in his essay on *Words*:

'As one surveys the mighty array of sages, saints, historians, scientists, poets and philosophers whose treasures one will never be able to admire - still less enjoy - the brief tenure of our existence here dominates mind and spirit. Think of all the wonderful tales that have been told, and well told, which you will never know. Think of all the searching enquiries into matters of great consequence which you will never pursue. Think of all the delighting or disturbing ideas that you will never share'[24].

I could have cited Miguel de Unamuno who summarised the problem as:

'Consciousness, the craving for more, more, always more, hunger of eternity and thirst of infinity, appetite for God - these are never satisfied. Each consciousness seeks to be itself and to be all other consciousnesses without ceasing to be itself: it seeks to be God'[25].

The example I have chosen, who is the subject of the next chapter and a major background figure throughout the book, is the American writer Thomas Wolfe, who obsessively combines my two main themes of information organisation and personal development.

3. The Pain of Everything

In 1981 Andrew Smith, a consultant psychiatrist at the Greenwich District Hospital in London, wrote in the British Medical Journal:

'My problem is the compulsion to try and read and know everything. It is essential to try, but the intention to read up all about a subject is rapidly displaced by the next book, which then is itself so absorbing that its subject must in turn be pursued. In the end this is a recipe for a Jack-of-all-trades-and-master-of-none mind'[1].

Many people must have felt this kind of impulse from time to time, but imagine what it must be like to be constantly under the spell of such an urge, to have to live under such pressure. This urge may develop in the following way. We may suddenly stop and consider that out of all the vastness of space and time - and given that there is no reason man knows of why anything at all should exist - it is remarkable that we should find ourselves in our own bodies, thrown into our own lives, with our own minds and personalities, in the timespan and physical surroundings that we do. Having been born into our respective lives and into the seemingly immutable conditions that being alive in the universe demands, we may, as we develop into full self-awareness, be dismayed that the wealth of experience, knowledge and beauty which surrounds us far outstrips our capacity to assimilate, comprehend and appreciate it. An attempt to 'try to read and know everything' is, as Andrew Smith discovered, an obvious response to this difficulty.

Because of the way the mind works and the limitations of our sensory input channels, our awareness of surrounding information is always a mere fraction of what we might like it to be, or of what we feel it ought to be. There are no doubt good reasons why this has to be so, but it can be a source of frustration and psychological pain; it may be an unacceptable limitation on life. As such it can be a valuable stimulus for learning, for gaining experience, for sorting out wheat from chaff, for creativity, and for valuing the precious, all-too-short passage between unknown darknesses, that brightly lit highway that we call life. Hence a compulsion to 'read and know everything' ... and much more besides.

Despite what follows, knowing 'everything' is impossible. We cannot be entirely familiar with the universe and all its contents molecule by molecule, word by word, pixel by pixel, semiquaver by semiquaver, byte by byte. That is a ridiculous idea, and it always has been ridiculous, but the absurdity of it occasionally needs to be made explicit.

Though many people are besieged by a hunger for life and for experience, few more vividly demonstrate the anguish which can develop from such hungers as does the American novelist Thomas Wolfe (1900-1938). Wolfe's obsessive yearning was to devour everything that he encountered, to make it his own, to stop it in its tracks and to fix it in eternity. In his way, Wolfe provides us with a magnificent illustration of the pathology of information, something more profound and sinister than the excesses of the idiot savant or the juvenile information junkie or the cybernerd burning the midnight oil or, according to the popular stereotype, the midnight pizza.

The irreversible passage of time, the inexhaustibility of knowledge, and a poignant longing for landscapes both known and unknown, were at the centre of Wolfe's pain. In his writings, and primarily in his four major novels, *Of Time And The River*, *The Web And The Rock*, *You Can't Go Home Again*, and *Look Homeward, Angel*, there are principal characters like Eugene Gant and George Webber who are autobiographical projections of Wolfe himself and - together with descriptive material which he provides - they convey this sense of longing for things which can never be precisely formulated or grasped.

Apart from his writings, Wolfe himself was a living examplar of passion for life, being 'larger than life' in his physical appearance and in his appetites for food and drink, and above all in his appetite for work - at least for writing. The legend of his battle with his editor Maxwell Perkins at Scribner's in New York, over the unwieldy size and indiscipline of his manuscripts is well known, more so probably to American rather than British readers. Wolfe was just unable to stop writing; everything he saw or thought of he felt he had to write down and make permanent. One wonders what he would have made of a tape recorder or video camera. It was as though he was so in love with life that any selection on the grounds of taste, interest-value, aesthetics or readability he regarded as dishonest and unworthy. Trying to be God-like, although not in the conventional sense a megalomaniac or a narcissist, he felt that he had to include everything in his territory. Life was like it was and had to be recorded as such for fear that it would move on into oblivion without a trace, without a first hand description of how it had been and how it had looked and felt. He wanted to tell somebody about it.

Gestalt psychology has made us familiar with the concepts of figure and ground, the idea that something is only made distinct by contrast with a different background. This implies discrimination and, inevitably, discarding or downgrading a great deal in order to give prominence to the chosen object. For Wolfe, the background was as important as the highlighted foreground; the universe was his chosen object. Everything, however trivial, was precious, because it was an example of what life was like, and Wolfe could not let it go. He knew that if he did not record it, no one else would. In no way crassly egotistic, Wolfe's main concern was to record his entire life because he believed it to be so precious and wonderful; his self-appointed task might well be described as an act of worship, a religious devotion to the recording of sacred information, a diary to be read by God. This was not nostalgia in the ordinary saccharine-sentimental sense, but a special type of nostalgia for the whole of life - past, present, and future - for the whole of existence seen from a strange viewpoint, as though in some way Wolfe himself did not exist or was already dead, a viewpoint he held with a weird kind of extrasomatic objectivity and with a mature realism about his inevitable mortality. 'Wolfe was a poet of remembrance, of the hauntings of childhood and the tricks of time, of the poignancy of the moment with its freight of immortal longings'[2]. Wolfe's writings, if one can live with their tedious, post-Proustian verbosity, are pure heartache.

The example of Thomas Wolfe illustrates in a vivid and painful way the problem that each one of us - if we are concerned enough about it - may find that we have to face, namely the problem of what to take out of the world and into ourselves, what to 'tell people about', what to value and to love, and what to do with our lives. Wolfe apparently lacked any of the normal filters, even those of quality control; he was open and vulnerable to all experience. To him, life was too rare to reject any of it as being of no interest, of being of no concern to himself, although inevitably there were blind spots and lacunae in his interests and observations. Andrew Turnbull, in his biography of Wolfe, writes about his days at Harvard:

> 'He began to visualize his life as 'a vast tapering funnel' into which everything must be poured. 'I shall make one globe', he wrote in his notes, 'not of my learning but of all learning, I shall make one globe not of my life but of all life'[3].

But Wolfe, along with all other mortals, had neither the capacity for sensory input nor a suitable type of brain to make this possible, although he - like our junior trainspotters of the previous chapter - did not accept this. That he was aware of his limitations we know, because he dreamed of ways in which he could absorb more information in less time, even imagining that there might be chemical substances that would enable him to do this. He was hooked on the emotional connotations of all kinds of things, the poetry of the everyday, the ambient feeling tone of mere existence. He could have made use of the 'Mechanical Educator', proposed by Arthur C. Clarke, which 'could impress on the brain, in a matter of a few minutes, knowledge and skills which might otherwise take a lifetime to acquire'[4]. Though this remains an idea for science fiction Clarke is serious about the need for such a device to combat the information explosion. 'Soon', he says, 'we will have died of old age before we have learned how to live'. This of course is missing the point, but we know what he means. And yet, what student hasn't dreamed of learning French irregular verbs in his sleep or Shakespeare by intravenous injection or a microchip implant of the Tudors and Stuarts? So poor Wolfe had to try and find ways of cutting down the quantity of information he felt he had to absorb:

> 'He had spells and rhymes of magic numbers which would enable him, he thought, to read all of the million books in the great library. This was a furious obsession with him all the time. And there were other spells and rhymes which would enable him to know the lives of 50,000,000 people, to visit every country in the world, to know a hundred languages, possess 10,000 lovely women, and yet have one he loved and honoured above all, who would be true and beautiful and faithful to him'[5].

There is some scope for condensing recorded information, but there is no way that one's personal life can be similarly treated. No one has been here before us to digest and condense life experiences for us: only we ourselves can do that. Many people go through life letting others do the living for them, always being part of the audience and never being in the act themselves. But when one realises that one is already launched upon one's one and only lifetime (as far as we know), a realisation that typically occurs to the adolescent or the young adult, one may be provoked into trying to be part of the act. If we are not going to live our own lives to the full there is no one else who can do it for us. And in such a way one can be cajoled into a Wolfe-like passion; or into an obsessive-compulsive neurosis.

In *Of Time And The River*, Wolfe wrote:

> 'Ten years must come and go without a moment's rest from fury, ten years of fury, hunger, all the wandering in a young man's life. And for what? For what? What is the fury which this youth will feel, which will lash him on against the great earth for ever? It is the brain that maddens him with its own excess, the heart that breaks from the anguish of its own frustration. It is the hunger that grows from everything it feeds upon, the thirst that gulps down rivers and remains insatiate. It is to see a million men, a million faces and to be a stranger and an alien to them always. It is to prowl the stacks of an enormous library at night, to tear the books out of a thousand shelves, to read in them with the mad hunger of the youth of man'[6].

Wolfe could have added that it is the pain of being trapped inside one's own mind and body, of never being able to *be* anything else. One of the clichés of talks given by information scientists is to quote from T. S. Eliot's *Two Choruses from 'The Rock'*, where he asks: 'Where is the wisdom we have lost in knowledge? Where is the knowledge we have lost in information?' On such occasions Eliot sometimes gets cited as a kind of grandfather-figure or wise old man who anticipated one of the concerns of modern information retrieval. To my mind, Wolfe is a much more potent symbol of our informational problems.

Wolfe's appetite for information, or at least its affective properties, extended to all things and to all fields of activity - some of which I will consider in more detail in a moment - but regardless of the type of information which he sought, there seem to be three fundamental obstacles to the satisfying of Wolfe's craving. The first is the essential impossibility of actually taking in all the information in the world, due to the lack of time available, lack of ability to understand and remember everything, and the simple lack of capacity of the sensory organs to absorb everything. The second difficulty, rather harder to define, arises from not making clear the amount of detail that is required. With Wolfe it was not enough to have merely stayed, shall we say, in every room in every hotel in every town, but he wanted also to know about all the stains on the ceiling as well. This need to 'know' was ill-defined, and was poetical or even mystical rather than specific. Presumably he wanted to be able to visualise and remember the stains, and all the mental associations he made with them, rather than knowing their exact location, dimensions, colour, and chemical composition. The third problem, which Wolfe never really came to grips with, perhaps because it was at the core of his obsession, is that, even if it were in some way possible to have assimilated all the information that was available, because of the way the brain works, because of the nature of consciousness, it is not possible to have access to all of this at any one time. At any given moment one can only focus one's consciousness on a very few ideas or thoughts, and no matter how much else one knows, for the moment it is forgotten. One does not even have any absolute reassurance that one still does know it. It has gone for the time being, and one lacks any kind of scannable index to provide reassurance that somewhere lurking in the memory stores that particular thought or item of information is to be found. Memory is stored according to a complex logic which is as yet scarcely understood, although access to it is remarkably rapid and can be triggered by all sorts of needs and occurrences. The actor about to go on stage suffers from stage fright because, amongst other reasons, there is no way that he can be sure that he has remembered his lines, and similarly the student revising for an examination is frustrated because he can only keep a small area of thought in his mind at one time. He cannot be certain that everything he has so painfully learned up until now has not already slipped away again. There is no higher level of consciousness which can operate in a 'scanning mode' to inspect the contents of the memory; there is no 'meta-memory'. One can, as it were, 'visit' the memory, but not view it panoramically from outside. Fortunately, on demand, the mind usually releases the required information from its memory stores unless inhibited by stage fright or exam nerves, or repressions resulting from deeper psychological problems. For Wolfe it was unacceptable that the whole of his memory store was not available to his focal pinpoint of consciousness all at the same time.

'He wanted to know all, have all, be all - to be one and many, to have the whole riddle of this vast and swarming earth as legible, as tangible in his hand as a coin of minted gold'[7]. For the reasons I have suggested, this he could never do, and so his thirst for everything had to remain unassuaged. It was not that he wanted to know everything in order to be cleverer or more powerful than other people, it was not the common ambition for one-upmanship, nor even that he wanted a genuine intellectual understanding of the way the world worked. Understanding implies a depth of integration of information, or shall we say information directed to a purpose, and though this may have been one of Wolfe's unrealisable ideals, it was not really a part of his central passion. No, it was something more obsessive than that, a terrible fear that if he failed to capture something and incorporate it within himself it would be lost forever. It was a kind of collecting mania, an urge for possession and completeness, a religious mission. To Wolfe, every aspect of life was an opportunity which must not be missed, but it was life as a catalogue, not as a synthesis of knowledge or as material gathered for creative rearrangement or development.

'Quite simply, he wanted to read all the books in the world, in whatever language, on the evident assumption that this experience would put at his command all recorded knowledge'[8]. This is a frightening kind of psychological compulsion when one considers how many books there are in the world - and how many worthless, boring, unreadable books - and how many languages there are. For an adolescent this yearning for abstruse knowledge may seem highly desirable and even realistically within range, but the practical problems it involves, the sheer tedium of it, when one considers how it might be undertaken, would deter all but the most obsessional. Would a modern-day Wolfe really want to read books on the chemistry of isoquinoline derivatives, books on obsolete computer programming languages, books of statistics of mortality from various diseases, books written in Albanian, Gujerati, Laotian or Icelandic? Would he really want to read and learn the phone books for Minneapolis, Glasgow, Dortmund or Osaka? Is this a genuine craving for knowledge or merely a wallowing in the poetry of exotica? Is it trainspotting gone mad? Would he drool over the Amtrak timetable?

Wolfe sought ways of reducing his task in order to try and make it more manageable. Turnbull writes about how Wolfe would roam the Widener Library at Harvard, despairing of ever making any impact on the one and a half million volumes that were kept there. And this of course was just one library and a sane one at that compared with, say, the fantasies of Jorge Luis Borges, with his 'total library' of all possible knowledge, both real and bogus. It is probable that over 20 years Wolfe in fact read less than 6,000 books, which is less than one book per day, and that this reading, was 'more akin to rape, or at times to an athletics contest'[9] than to normal reading. Such reading habits are generally not very fruitful, and though one may be able to scan a great deal - perhaps aided by speed-reading techniques - the amount that is absorbed and retained, and amalgamated with one's existing world picture, may be quite minimal. For meaningfulness and for reliability of storage, new information must be pursued purposefully and integrated with old. Wolfe's concern was quantity, rather than content, and there is no evidence that his reading made him supernormally wise or well-informed. He was more concerned with checking off from a catalogue than with acquiring understanding. He would tell himself, fictionally or otherwise:

> '"In different editions of Shakespeare alone, English and foreign, there are almost 5,000 volumes. And you can get him all in the one-volume Cambridge edition. Very well - 1,500,000 divided by 5,000 gives 300. Ah, but you fool, they're not all Shakespeares! You have chosen the one author most numerously represented. Yes, but, curse you, 300 books is nothing. One can do a hundred times that. Consider the repetitions with Milton, Pope, Wordsworth, Tennyson, Dickens!" Whereupon he would go to one of these shelves, count the duplicate editions, and gloat if they were numerous'[9].

Meanwhile, of course, time would be passing and he would be no nearer to completing his task.

Such an attitude surely reflects a most unnatural approach to reading and is really a rather absurd way of going about the acquisition of wide knowledge or understanding. One reads for pleasure or for self-education, or ideally for both simultaneously, but one does not start at one end of a library and systematically wade through, book by book, shelf by shelf, stack by stack. Instead, one selects on the basis of one's current interests or needs, stimulated into further reading by chance comments and pointers to other references. New interests will emerge unpredictably from an interaction between internal needs and external influences. From time to time one will attempt to read all the works of a particular author, or every book available on a given - but very small - subject, but one cannot imagine even the most assiduous self-improver with what might be called a normal personality adopting the Wolfean approach to study.

One suspects that Wolfe's greatest longing was not for organised and already recorded knowledge, but for 'real' life. Like the robot called Filer 13B-445-K in Harry Harrison's *The Robot Who Wanted to Know*, who after reading 50,000 books on love and romance wanted to experience these conditions for himself, Wolfe was obsessed with the minutiae of ordinary life. It is likely that he realised that in some way books could be left alone, that they were already 'known', recorded and organised, safe, and did not need him to prevent them from vanishing into oblivion. He was reluctant to leave them to the attention of other persons, but could accept that he had less obligation to master them than he did for his own doings, the people and places of his life. People are mortal and books are potentially immortal: they capture the thoughts which will otherwise die along with their originators' brains. They preserve the products of the mind, out of the body, effectively for all time or as long as there is someone around who can read and understand. They do not need Wolfe to re-digest them. This was not so with the miscellanea of life in a small town, for example Asheville, North Carolina, where Wolfe spent his childhood, or in a big city like New York, where he lived for much of his adult life; for these, there were no systems of classification and recording available. If Wolfe failed to get them down on paper they would be lost forever. I wonder what his response would have been to the idea of the urban videoscanner, installed for security purposes, but with the potential to record everything within its range, 24 hours a day, 365 days a year.

Experiences came and went and were irretrievable except in the memory, which was unsystematic and unreliable and mortally trapped inside the skull. Places, including ones with which he was familiar and others that he had never visited, haunted Wolfe continually, and though they existed without him, his feelings for them needed to be expressed and preserved. He was infatuated with places and wanted to be everywhere at once, savouring particular local essences and qualities and atmospheres. In *The Web And The Rock* he wrote:

> 'Therefore, at any moment on the city streets, he would feel an intolerable desire to rush away and leave the city, if only for the joy he felt in being there, and for the joy of coming back to it. He would go out in the country for a day and come back at night; or, at the weekend when he had no class to teach, he would go away to other places - to Baltimore, to Washington, into Virginia, to New England, or ... a country town near Gettysburg in Pennsylvania. And at every moment when he was away, he would feel the same longing to return, to see if the city was still there ... He ate and drank the city to its roots - and through all that spring not once did it occur to him that he had left not even a heel-print on its stony pavements'[10].

Throughout Wolfe's writings there is a feeling, constant but unstated, that he is afraid that at the moment of death he will realise that there is something he has not done, something he has not known, somewhere he has not been, and now, in a last moment of anguish, the opportunity is lost forever. His supposedly fictional description of a need to be in New York and in other places at the same time is an aspect of this: a desire for ubiquity and omniscience so that there is nothing left to chance, no possibility that he will have missed anything. He wants to be everywhere at once and to know everything. And yet, as he remarks, no matter how much time he spends in New York, no matter how well he knows the city, he can make no impression on it, the city will carry on regardless of whether he ever existed or not, and his vision must forever remain that of an outsider. In some way he wanted to capture and make his own those things which are - for a short while - the objects of our attention and affections, but which will, because of the nature of existence, remain when we have passed on. Like Proust, Wolfe was trying to freeze time and to enlarge his perception until he was awed by even the most trivial, a habit that becomes quite tiresome in his novels, especially the posthumously published ones. He was setting his mental focus to see the world at its most sacred. Like Proust with his 'involuntary memory' induced by stimuli such as dunking a biscuit in tea, Wolfe was so in love with life that he wanted to celebrate all its minutiae, things which cannot be celebrated because they are so everyday, so familiar, so trivial, and so vast in number and connotation. He was in a constant Blakean ecstasy at seeing 'a world in a grain of sand', by intensifying the acuity of perceptions, by refusing to discriminate and by being able to appreciate each tiny detail in its own right, for the beauty and preciousness which it alone possessed, however commonplace in principle. For him to be completely satisfied over the sacredness of the objects he perceived he needed an appreciative audience to travel around with him, and since this was not possible his audience had to be the reading public. His was a love story: the story of being in love with the world.

'And always America is the place of the deathless and enraptured moments, the eye that looked, the mouth that smiled and vanished, and the word ; the stone, the leaf, the door we never found and never have forgotten. And these are the things that we remember of America, for we have known all her thousand lights and weathers, and we walk the streets, we walk the streets for ever, we walk the streets of life alone'[11]. There is too much to take in, too much information, life is too short, and the speed of perception and thought is too slow. As Michael Bentine had printed on a T-shirt: 'So many toys - so little time'. What can we do? Here we are, teased by this wondrous complexity of life, tantalised at being given a brief view of it, and there is nothing we can do to preserve it within us for all time, to raise it, as it were, to a totally understood and unchangeable work of art. There is not the time to take it all apart, to fuss over it and enjoy it and put it back together again. We must accept it as it is, and move on; accept that it means various things to us but that it can never be possessed by us, and soon we must say goodbye. We must forget the beginning of the story and never know how the story ends; all we know is a paragraph in the middle. Wolfe could not accept these facts, or perhaps he did and tried to counteract them - and his torments continued.

The only hope of retaining the wonder of existence, of grasping it all simultaneously, is the memory, as Proust realised. The memory is potentially the sum total of our life experience so far. If only we could spread it out like a map so that we could view it all at once, instead of having to make puny little stabs at it in the dark. Memory allows us other possibilities which are currently not in the here and now. But this only leads to further longing for that which is not actually present. Ironically, memory makes the pain worse. So, for example, we have the incident when Wolfe was sitting watching the people pass by along the Avenue de l'Opéra in Paris, when he suddenly remembered the iron railing on the boardwalk in Atlantic City, New Jersey: 'I could see it instantly just the way it was, the heavy iron pipe; its raw, galvanized look; the way the joints were fitted together'[12]. And there was nothing he could do to capture the sensation, a sensation similar to that of a youth madly in love. It had to remain as a painful longing, a heavy heartache, which could only be satisfied -

presumably - by once again travelling to Atlantic City, at the risk that by the time he had crossed the Atlantic he would be dying for some Parisian scene. The longing of course was just a state of mind, and its object was to some extent incidental and irrelevant, and certainly unpredictable. A less satisfying reaction would have been to paint the image, or to write about it, which was Wolfe's usual response. Memory, especially involuntary memory provoked by a surprise stimulus, was thus both an inspiration and a torture to him.

And places, what is he seeking there? To be everywhere at once? I think that Wolfe values places primarily as precious reminders of the wonder and strangeness of being alive. He wants them for what they are, and more than that, for some mythical significance which he has attached to them. Maybe it is something to do with the myth of writing the Great American Novel. He longs for deserted, bleak, wintry landscapes which would be far from pleasant if one was to venture out in them; he longs for American small towns glimpsed briefly from a train at night, without any feeling for how fundamentally boring such places can be; and he loves to list long strings of names of cities, states, rivers, mountains, Indian tribes, and so on. The poetry of geographical terms, the imagery of the desolate and the far away, the romance of 'the other'. And yet there is nothing he can do with these names: Wyoming, Idaho, Missouri, Virginia, Utah, Nevada, Maine ... So what? They exist. They are already listed, for example, in encyclopaedias, gazetteers and atlases, but there is nothing Wolfe or you or I could do to possess them. Wolfe tries, just by mentioning them, to elevate them to the status of poetry, to cause stirrings in the hearts of his readers, and it is by writing that he almost succeeds in expunging the mental pain that just thinking about them causes him. By trotting them out for exercise he temporarily drains them of their alterity and their emotional connotations. In a sense he is just checking them off against his memory, airing the synapses, exorcising the names and their affective associations. Because the traveller, however much he roams the earth, may feel pain at the thought of things he is never going to see again, or never going to see at all, Wolfe hopes that by listing such items he has in some way dealt with them, and he can move on to something new. But in the nature of memory he has to keep returning to them, checking that they are still there.

The 'lists' that tormented Wolfe were infinite and impossible, and straddled everything from the trivial to the profound and the - in any meaningful sense - unknowable. They '... included everything from gigantic and staggering lists of the towns, cities, counties, states, and countries I had been in, to minutely thorough, desperately evocative descriptions of the undercarriage, the springs, wheels, flanges, axle rods, color, weight, and quality of the day coach of an American railway train. There were lists of the rooms and houses in which I had lived or in which I had slept for at least a night, together with the most accurate and evocative descriptions of those rooms that I could write - their size, their shape, the color and design of the wallpaper, the way a towel hung down, the way a chair creaked, a streak of water rust upon the ceiling. There were countless charts, catalogues, descriptions that I can only classify here under the general heading of Amount and Number'[13]. We are back at trainspotting again.

The list is an emotion-provoking technique highly reminiscent of that exploited by an even more famous American writer, Walt Whitman. Many of Whitman's poems are little more than word salads of emotively pregnant objects, particularly American objects. So for example in *Starting from Paumanok* we find lists of states, occupations, Indian tribes: 'Okonee, Koosa, Ottawa, Monongahela, Saik, Natchez, Chattahoochee, Kagueta, Oronoco, Wabash, Miami, Saginaw, Chippewa, Oshkosh, Walla-Walla'; in *A Song for Occupations* we find everything in a surrealist yellow pages from fish-curing to electroplating; and in *Salut au Monde!* there are catalogues of objects in the whole world: mountains, seas, continents, rivers, ports, inhabitants of cities, nationalities, races, and all kinds of emotion-stirring exotica ranging from the tumuli of Mongolia, via Turks smoking opium in Aleppo and matadors in the arena in Seville, to Hottentots with clicking palates.

Exactly what Wolfe was craving for is hard to define, as no kind of satisfaction seems to be adequate. In his avowed desire to read all the books in the world the aim seems not so much total knowledge as a pure satisfaction obtained from the awareness that he has in fact read all the books. This is somewhat akin to the strange business of obtaining satisfaction from encountering empty cages at the zoo, which will be referred to in a later chapter. It is also slightly reminiscent of those obsessional compulsive neuroses which compel one to touch all the railings as one walks alongside the park or to avoid the cracks in the pavement - to prevent one's mother from having a heart attack, to ensure that one passes the examination, to prevent one from being in an air crash on next week's trip to Ibiza, or to postpone Armageddon.

While Wolfe wanted to know millions of faces one feels that his interest in people was not particularly deep; at the most generous his attitude was one of an inquisitive anthropologist. He would have liked to have had the time to get to know everybody and to chat casually in the corner shop (or some similarly romantic notion) but since he could not, the most he could do was to try and collect. He just wanted to know, to be satisfied, that he had seen them all, something akin to the completist aesthetic of the trainspotter. No mention is ever made of how dull the company of most people would be to a man of Wolfe's temperament and fecund imagination. It is just a poetic sentiment, a love of mankind in the abstract but a more strained affection for its individual specimens.

Apart from the vexing question of the obsession of our mass media with the ephemeral and the trivial, what in fact should we communicate, and what should we store, and where? Is anybody listening? Does anyone want to know? Wolfe wanted to preserve his every thought and emotion, but we would not normally want to do this: there isn't time, nor usually an interested audience. Why should Wolfe expect anyone to care about his longing for the railings on the seafront at Atlantic City, or his thoughts about the way a towel hung in a French hotel room? What conceit! People have got quite enough to do coping with their own event-overload to be bothered by taking him in as well, thank you very much. Wolfe's sacredness-setting of his world has seemingly been tuned to too great a sensitivity. But has it? Does anyone know the correct setting? Is it the rest of us who have got it wrong? Couldn't we all use a little more of this kind of sensitivity?

The classical approach to the problem of information overload is to conceptualise: this is so in information retrieval systems, in sensory psychology, and in the Wolfean craving for everything. By reducing the infinite detail of the world to a series of abstractions it is possible to cope, but at the price of losing touch with the reality. Wolfe was torn between the need to wallow in the local and the particular - knowing that while so doing he was ignoring many other possibilities - and the attempt to elaborate his obsessions and existential aches and pains into grand categories and stereotypes which would retain little, if anything, of direct personal consequence. His dilemma was whether to act like a professional map-maker, having a wide but superficial knowledge of many places, or like an old inhabitant, a true insider, with deep but narrow confines of knowledge, someone who knew the smell of a place but not its grid reference.

The only hope of satisfying the strange craving was that one day the puzzle of the whole world, which existed quite happily without him but which was incompletely understood by anyone, would finally be grasped, classified, ordered and nailed down within his own mind.

> 'Like an insatiate and maddened animal he roamed the streets, trying to draw up mercy from the cobble-stones, solace and wisdom from a million sights and faces, as he prowled through endless shelves of high-piled books, tortured by everything he could not see and could not know, and growing blind, weary, and desperate from what he read and saw'[14].

Nothing, it seems, can palliate this hunger for life, this nostalgia for a world which will just not stand still and be counted. 'He would come to view all life as from a speeding train - fleetingly, hauntingly, panoramically, with a never-to-return poignance. Trains, his symbol of escape to brighter worlds, plucked his heartstrings ...'[15]. One is reminded of the disturbing and obsessive symbolic presence of trains in the surrealist images of Paul Delvaux or Giorgio de Chirico. An example of this painful longing, as experienced on a train journey, occurs early on in *Of Time And The River*: 'Then the train slides by the darkened vacant-looking little station and for a moment one has a glimpse of the town's chief square and business centre. And as he sees it he is filled again with the same feeling of loneliness, instant familiarity, and departure. The square is one of those anomalous, shabby-ornate, inept, and pitifully pretentious places that one finds in little towns like these. But once seen, if only for this fraction of a moment, from the windows of a train, the memory of it will haunt one for ever after'[16].

Thomas Wolfe was to American literature what Edward Hopper was to modern American realist painting: he could select an image of a place which would itself be banal and ordinary, but could make it relate to everyone's personal experiences of places which were fundamentally the same in atmosphere. Places pregnant with the questions: what does it all mean and what are you going to do with it? Wolfe's America, like Hopper's, was - paradoxically, and despite the foreground concern with the principal characters - a country strangely unpopulated, although there is always the suggestion of people not far away, there are always the symbols of human civilisation.   The ache is for that which can never be one's own, for that which has passed, is already passing or will shortly pass, never to be seen again. It is an ache for a world which, every moment and location in time and space being unique, is sacred. 'Always he is haunted by past moments, by a devouring curiosity which makes him go to any lengths to secure a peephole through which he can view the past'[17]. It is an ache also for things not thought of since childhood, an ache for the simple sensory joys of being alive, and an ache for a comfortable, story-book image of a cosy landscape populated by immortal happy families, an ache for childhood lost.

Wolfe's obsession led him to desire things which, by their very nature, are incompatible or impossible. We have seen how he wanted to 'possess 10,000 lovely women' and yet to have one who would be above all the rest, 'true and beautiful and faithful to him'. He is neither the first nor the last person to have had such fantasies - but what a magnificent recipe for hypocritical unfaithfulness! Similarly he wanted to travel all over the world while keeping one place to return to, and to be famous and celebrated and yet to live a quiet, secluded life.

> 'In short, he would have the whole cake of the world, and eat it too - have adventures, labours, joys and triumphs that would exhaust the energies of ten thousand men, and yet have spells and charms for all of it, and was sure that with these charms and spells and sorceries, all of it was his'[18].

As he travelled around he must have longed to in some way inhabit other peoples' lives, or at least the aspects of their lives that, for some spontaneous romantic reason, seemed attractive or glamorous or moodily stylish to him.

Martin Malony has suggested that Wolfe even considered the possibility of being everybody as well as knowing everybody[19]. He appeared to possess a kind of pathological envy of people and things that were not himself: he could not accept the ontological precipice that surrounded him and which forever prevented him from being anything or anyone other than Thomas Clayton Wolfe. This is not a unique complaint, strange though it may seem. John Cowper Powys in his *Autobiography* hints at an envy of the common people he saw on his walks around the Cambridgeshire countryside in his student days[20], and J. M. Synge wrote: 'I wished to be at once Shakespeare, Beethoven, and Darwin; my ambition was boundless and a torture to me'[21].

Sometimes when people are approaching the end of their life they experience a kind of envy of younger people or other creatures, even of inanimate objects like mountains or chairs, that 'do not have to die', at least yet. Wolfe had this problem for much of his life, and though he may not have consciously admitted it to himself he was in fact jealous of New York, trees, towels in hotel rooms, long freight trains rumbling sombrely across wooden trestle viaducts over sluggish brown American rivers - and everything else besides. Not to be able to be these things was another limitation on possibility which seemed a crime implicit in the laws of nature. It was a miracle that he lived at all: surely, in a better kind of universe, only slightly more miraculous, it would be possible to be everything? A name given to this obsessional ache for everything, as displayed by Wolfe, is the Faustian sickness. Bernard de Voto, writing about Eugene Gant, the principal character in *Of Time And The River* and clearly a fictionalised projection of Wolfe himself, describes him as 'a borderline manic-depressive: he exhibited the classic cycle in his alternation between 'fury' and 'despair', and the classic accompaniment of obsessional neurosis in the compulsions he was under'[22].

While it is easy to identify this compulsion with the readily available labels of psychiatric categorisation it is nevertheless a reflection of a very real problem which we all face, albeit not so intensely as Wolfe. Why it should cause such problems for a few people like Wolfe is presumably a matter of individual psychology and cannot satisfactorily be explained on a general basis, but a feeling that one ought to absorb as much as possible of life's offerings in the short time we have here is an understandable response to our existential condition. In itself I do not see that it is an abnormal or pathological reaction to the given environment into which we are thrown, provided that it does not seriously interfere with a capacity for conducting a normal day-to-day life. Wolfe was so overtaken by his urges that just trying to cope with the problem became the essence of his life's work, and it was in the nature of the problem that it could never be satisfactorily resolved. Wolfe was an extreme case and was thus, relatively speaking, abnormal, but he was not necessarily suffering from anything worthy of a psychiatric diagnosis. A major difficulty of Wolfe's obsession was that it operated in every area of his life, and allowed him no respite. There were times when he was so torn between alternatives for action that he found it difficult to settle down and complete anything: he was like the donkey who starves to death because it cannot choose between two morsels.

In some ways, Wolfe's response to his urges does not seem to have been very intelligent. As we have seen, at times he was reduced to writing out lists of names of cities and states and railroad companies, even the names of tramps, in an attempt to 'have done' with these particular longings. It was as though some freak of memory superconductivity or memory short-circuit constantly reminded him that these things still lurked within his mind, and had not received proper attention lately from the pinpoint of his consciousness. It seems likely that they caused him actual pain, psychological or physical. It was as though the only way he could get rid of the ache and the anxiety that such promptings - presumably from his unconscious - produced, was to write out these names. What else could he do?

With a little more organisation he could, within a relatively short time, have visited all the states, principal cities, and major geographical features of the United States. That could have been achieved within a few months. Even in his short life and before the age of easy air travel he could have visited many of the most famous places in the world. When one considers the degree of familiarity with many parts of the world attained by modern travel writers like Paul Theroux, Alan Whicker, Eric Newby or Jan Morris, Wolfe seems to have achieved very little. Maybe this was partly because of his compulsion for going back over things, for reliving experiences. When he was in Paris he had a tendency to want to be in New Jersey, and when in New York City he yearned for Virginia. For all his cravings he was not widely travelled. He made seven visits to Europe, brief trips to Canada and Bermuda, but within his own country rarely ventured outside the central states of the eastern seaboard.

Because of the nature of consciousness, because we can only focus on a very few thoughts at any one time, the only practical answer to Wolfe's longings would have been to write down the entire contents of his memory, with all the logical and illogical chains of association between them, and with a detailed exploration and description of the emotions that each memory aroused. Then, from the control room of consciousness he would have been able to survey his entire world of thought and feeling. What Wolfe really needed was a map of his mind, of his memories, something permanent and outside of himself, that would reliably take him to his most treasured but unresolved feelings, to the world inside his head, and to his childhood, always so important to him.

In order to have made this map or diagram he would have needed to understand how his memory was organised, and how it was connected with the drives and desires and hidden motives of his unconscious mind. This would no doubt have been impossible to achieve in an absolute sense, although possibly some kind of not-too-detailed schema might have been achievable. If he had been alive today he might have entertained the idea of creating a hypertext model of his mind, full of associative clusters, and - even better - with hypermedia links to stores of text and imagery in sight and sound held on optical disc, with access to surrogate travel facilities stored in interactive image banks and virtual reality simulations of distant places. Virtual Virginia, Virtual Atlantic City. We will come on to hypertext and hypermedia in Chapter 8. It would be a very special introspective exercise in autobiography and could have led to the interesting situation of trying to record his efforts in autobiography within a larger autobiographical record, into a kind of infinite regress. Intuition suggests that it would not have worked at all, and would be a hopelessly wrong-headed approach, but Wolfe would have been the man to try it!

As it was, the only method available which came naturally to Wolfe was to write about his experiences and his memories, and since it was considered immodest for anyone to write about themselves and the details of their existence at such length he had to disguise his autobiography as fiction, and sublimate his emotions in that way. That it was not a very opaque and convincing disguise was shown by the anger of some of the inhabitants of his native Asheville, who recognised themselves in his writings. Later on his closest associates, including Maxwell Perkins, his editor, began to realise that their own personalities and their relationships with Wolfe were bound, sooner or later, to find their way, in a thinly disguised fictional form, into his written output. 'Perhaps Wolfe had found here the only palliative for the Faustian sickness; having set up a goal of 'allness', which exists verbally but not in fact, one is obliged to achieve the goal verbally but not in fact'[23]. To finish up in this way, cannibalising one's own life and that of one's friends to feed a hypergraphic obsession, is as absurd as it is sad. The illogical end point resembles autophagy, the act of eating one's own body. Wolfe wrote on and on, an uncontrollable avalanche of words which could never satisfy his hunger for life. One might have expected that his essentially young man's vision of the world would have matured into some kind of acceptance, that the bildungsroman that is his early work would have developed into other themes, but it never did. Wolfe's refusal to come to terms with informational limitations is his attraction and his tragedy, and his later works, put together by editors after his death, tend to repeat his earlier themes only less interestingly, although some of the outstanding passages are as good as anything in modern American literature.

Wolfe died in Baltimore in 1938 of miliary tuberculosis of the brain and was buried in the family plot in the Riverside Cemetery, Asheville. One is tempted to wonder whether some pre-existing abnormality of brain functioning lay behind his constant pain over life's experiences and predisposed him to the precise variant of his final illness. Of course it is just as likely, or perhaps more likely, that his particular psychological characteristics derived from the circumstances of his childhood, and from his relationships with his parents. A recent major biography[24] suggests this, as do some other studies of Wolfe's psychodynamics in relation to creativity and self-development. His unhappy affair with Aline Bernstein also has relevance to a consideration of his creative motivations[25].

All Wolfe's memories and longings died with him in Johns Hopkins Hospital, but he left in print or in manuscript some of the most intense, complete and evocative records of what it is like to be alive, with all its pain and nostalgia, that have ever been created. Unfortunately, because of the indiscipline and verbosity which his obsessions inflicted upon him, and because he was dependent to such a great extent on actual autobiographical events as a substitute for an invented plot, he is often denigrated. His concerns are often similar to those explored by Marcel Proust, and Wolfe's descriptions and discussions are often even more poignant, detailed and circumlocutory than those of the French novelist, and yet it is Proust who is usually regarded as the master of the subtleties of longing and of subjective feeling.

Wolfe was tormented by the information content of the environment, and though he was undoubtedly an extreme case, he was symptomatic of a tendency which we all possess to some extent, and which - given the nature of present-day society - is likely to become more prevalent. So it may be useful to look more closely at the different types and sources of information that there are in the environment at large, how they are organised, and how they relate to us as individuals.

4. Popper's Worlds

Thomas Wolfe was tormented by the world as information which surrounded him, and which he felt he had to incorporate within himself, and in some way reorganise and celebrate and tell people about. There was Wolfe, and there was the rest of the world. Combining the two, funnelling the world into Wolfe, was a major problem and, quite likely, based on a mistake about the fundamental nature of information, but it was what he felt he had to do.

When we examine Wolfe's self-appointed task of knowing everything there was to know, reading all the books in the world, visiting every place, knowing so many million people, recording his memories in print, and so on, we realise that all this information about the world falls into a small number of categories. It varies in its nature, substance, degree of organisation and importance - although importance can only be assigned subjectively, in this instance, by Wolfe himself.

Crucially, there was the division between Wolfe and the outside. It was Wolfe's aim to transfer information about the outside world into his own mind. This is a curious ambition, because as we have seen, not only does the outside world continue to exist quite happily without any intervention from Wolfe - although its details may be forgotten and lost to time - but as far as he is concerned it only exists when he attends to it, in a manner somewhat reminiscent of Berkeley's famous tree in the quad. One might even say that for any individual, the universe might as well not exist but for his consciousness; his awareness of it always remains within his own head. The macrocosm may be 'out there' but is always perceived 'in here', in the microcosm inside the skull.

Wolfe wanted to take in the outside world according to the needs of his own personality, according to his own psychological drives. He wanted to perceive and to describe according to his own subjectivity, and then to present the digested, written account back to the outside world. The intention was that his perceptions and feelings should be fed back into the world as a kind of commentary on how the world was. His need was to impose his own organisational strategy onto a world which was not already organised in any obvious way, or which was ordered in ways deficient in the poignant, sacred qualities which Wolfe found all around him.

All right, so we set out to incorporate the whole universe within our mind. When we attempt to do this we find that there are different types of information which we have available, some of which are easier to digest than others, some of which are easier to incorporate. Some information, having the potential for organisation but in fact remaining unorganised in the environment, plays hard to get.

Firstly, there is the physical realm of mountains, rivers, cities, streets, rocks, trees, planets, houses, and so on. We can know them, in the sense that we can be familiar with seeing them or using them, or we can know about their physical properties, names, uses, histories, chemical composition, etc. In order to know these things we can to some extent rely upon our own naked eye observations, but mostly we are dependent upon the observations of other people relayed to us at second-hand or - usually, even more remotely, and ever increasingly - we rely on theories and abstractions and measurements which are not self-evident to the uneducated, unassisted eye (or other natural sensory equipment). Much of our knowledge of physical things comes from books or their equivalents (teachers, films, newspapers, radio, etc.) and not directly from our perceptions of the things themselves. Importantly, we can never in any way *be* these physical things - although in certain altered states of consciousness this might seem to happen - as Wolfe would perhaps have liked, and absurd though the idea may be.

Secondly, residing in the physical realm are animate beings. In this informational context we can regard other animal species as being of the same order as rocks and trees because we cannot communicate with them on a two way basis: we know nothing or very little about the contents of animal minds. We can guess their needs, and suspect that they are aware of our habits and moods, but that is about as far as it goes. We can apply some external tests to discover, for example, whether cats see in monochrome or have full colour vision, or to establish that dolphins shut down one of their cerebral hemispheres while asleep, but we have very little insight into what it feels like to be a cat or a dolphin. We can imagine, but that will usually be some rather childish form of anthropocentric projection. Animal minds are pretty much a closed book to us.

When we come to other human beings, however, the situation is different. Knowing the surface characteristics of people is not good enough: we want to go beyond the physical, anatomical, biochemical descriptions of people and the mere histories of what they have done. Instead, we want to know something of their thoughts, their character, about what goes on in their minds, what makes them tick. We want to know something of their views on the world, how it looks from *their* inside. Except in the instance of paranormal thought transference - for which satisfactory proof that will convince everyone remains problematical - all minds are islands. There is no blurred continuum between the inside of our heads and everything else. There is what appears under normal circumstances to be an uncrossable boundary, a total barrier. All the approximately six billion minds now at large on the earth can never directly know each other, and they all have their own conception of the universe embedded within them: six billion conceptual universes each surrounded by an uncrossable moat.

Thirdly, in our classification of the environment as information, we have written language, along with its analogues in the forms of paintings, recorded music, films, videotapes, computer memories and the like, the means by which minds more or less reliably communicate with each other. Included here are the contents of the libraries that so tormented Wolfe, who was fortunate enough to die before New York City had regular access to umpteen TV and radio stations, and long before the Internet was dreamed of. Though these media are the product of man and though they are useless without human readers, listeners and viewers, once created they can survive without man (apart, of course, from ephemeral, unrecorded transmissions).

The fourth category of information which haunted Wolfe was that which was already within his own mind and which, by quirks of memory, suddenly reminded 'him' of its existence. Hence the unpremeditated longing for the railings at Atlantic City, an unanticipated replaying of a buried memory with emotional attachments as yet not worked out consciously. Within the mind there resides a vast quarry of information which is already organised in some way, even if it is only laid down in chronological sequence, but which is potentially amenable to further consciously determined organisation. Each little piece of data, each snippet of memory, has facets which may lie dormant and undeveloped throughout our lives, but which remain there, available for recall and use. Using them of course modifies them, and may drain them of their emotional freight. But there always remain limitless potential cross-sections through memory, just waiting for some unpredictable occurrence to activate them. The fact is, desperately sad to someone like Thomas Wolfe, that life keeps moving on so fast that we never have time to catch up with ourselves, to explore our feelings as they occur or our memories as they arise, involuntarily or according to will. We have to move on, leaving a good deal that is very much ourselves in a bottom drawer that we are hardly ever likely to open again. Curiously, we will never know about huge areas of our experience - the life we have lost in living, as we might call it. Most experience goes straight down a one-way street never to be revisited.

Wolfe scarcely discriminated between these four classes of information relating respectively to the physical world, to other sentient beings, to literature, and to his own mind, and he was therefore unable to make the most efficient use of the time, facilities, energy, and mental ability that he had available. Constantly he confused that which was public knowledge with that which for personal reasons had some emotional or meaningful attachment to him, and constantly he was distracted by memories which were, by definition, already a part of him, but to which he did not have continual access.

The distinction in terms of information type between the physical world, recorded information, the mental activity of other people, and one's own mental activity has surely been obvious for a long time, and a number of philosophers have, over many years, played with these ideas. Among these offerings have been the simple Cartesian split between mind and matter, the Kantian division between the noumenal and the phenomenal, or the Wittgensteinian linguistic development of this idea. What we need is something more directly suited to the structuring of information. So, we might recall Nicolai Hartmann, who distinguished between four major layers of reality: inorganic, organic, psychic and intellectual[1], or much more recently Buckminster Fuller, who chose to divide the environment - everything that was 'not me' - into physical and metaphysical, the latter consisting of 'human thoughts, generalized principles and customs'[2].

Another comparatively recent systematic attempt has been made to describe the properties and inter-relationships of these areas of experience, and to label them. An exploration of them helps us to appreciate the problems of Thomas Wolfe, and of our hypothetical trainspotter. This attempt is that of the late Sir Karl Popper, the Viennese born philosopher - of science and much else - who proposed that: 'We can call the physical world 'world 1', the world of our conscious experiences 'world 2', and the world of the logical *contents* of books, libraries, computer memories, and suchlike 'world 3'[3]. Henceforth I will capitalise this special use of the word 'World'.

Let us consider Popper's three categories in detail. World 1 includes all the physical aspects of our environment: rivers, continents, electromagnetic forces, flowers, elephants, and so on, and also the physical correlates of man's creativity, such as the biological substrate of the human brain, buildings, roads, machines, aircraft, books as printed paper objects, old-fashioned long playing records as grooved discs of black vinyl, paintings as pieces of canvas covered on one side with daubs of pigment. World 1 does not concern itself with the normal use to which things are put: as far as 'it' knows books can be used as supports for tables with legs of unequal length and magnetic tape can be used for tying parcels. World 1 is not concerned with meaning, only with physicality, rather in the same way that for a young child a book has physical properties not all that dissimilar from those of a block of wood. World 1 is not concerned with interpretations, evaluations, or human uses; it is concerned only with things as they are. As far as World 1 is concerned a brain is just an object, a slimy grey convoluted thing which could be used as a macabre form of football or door stopper. The potential for information is there, but World 1 only becomes information when man perceives, interprets, and structures it according to his own classification schemes and personal needs.

Which brings us to World 2. A dead brain apparently has no information content. Mysteriously, all this dies with its owner, unless it ascends by means unknown to the hereafter. A dead brain cannot be made to divulge the massive contents that were there until a moment before death; whether it will ever be possible to do this is, on present evidence, extremely doubtful. Fortunately, even a live brain cannot be 'played' from the outside, by attaching electrodes to it, for instance, and plugging it into a clever type of word processor. The security services would just love such a device. The most we can do at present is to observe the amount of electrical or metabolic activity in various parts of the brain, using different types of scanners and EEG machines. The information which we know the live brain holds, but to which we have no outside physical access, only 'inside knowledge', is the realm that we call the mind, and that Popper calls World 2.

World 2 is the realm of individual thought and experience, of mind as opposed to brain. In the computer jargon of the nineties it is the software, while the brain, as nervous tissue, constitutes the hardware. Although it may have some fixed location, or locations, in the brain, the most meticulous anatomical probing of the brain has failed to reveal the existence of World 2. So far there is no direct evidence of a physical basis for mind as such, only for brain activity, for processes assumed to be the physical correlates of subjective experience.

Except in the contentious instance of paranormal information transfer World 2 cannot be transmitted directly and its contents always have to be carried via World 3 if it seeks external expression. Simply, this might be ephemerally by speech, which uses symbolic language to convey messages. The sound waves are World 1, the symbolic language - whether grammatically correct sentences or inarticulate grunts - is in World

3, and what is conveyed, if all goes well, is the idea that was in the speaker's (or grunter's) head, that is, a part of his World 2.

World 3 is information in the sense that we normally think of it; Worlds 1 and 2 possess informational properties too, but we generally overlook this. World 3 is information which has been engineered, coded and manipulated by man, with the usual purpose of transmitting it to others, either immediately, or at some time in the future. So World 3 is the intellectual as opposed to the physical content of spoken language, non-verbal modes of communication (body language, gestures, grunts, etc.), books, journals, computer memories, paintings, movies, sound recordings, photographs, maps, radio and TV broadcasts and all the other recording and communicating systems which have been devised, from the cave wall painting onward. It is essentially a symbol-using medium, and unlike World 1 it is information which has already passed through or originated in the mind of man, World 2, has been organised according to man-made systems and symbolic conventions such as language, and is usually deliberately intended for consumption by other humans. It may be true, it may be deliberate fabrication. Occasionally, World 3 ideas can exist whose meaning is unknown, as in the instances of the Rosetta Stone or the diaries of Beatrix Potter, until they were decoded[4], and likewise of course in languages which we personally cannot read or in ciphers we cannot crack. World 3 can also be created now without the direct intervention of the human mind: Popper cites as an example logarithm tables generated by computer, parts of which may never be consulted by man[5]. This may seem trivial, and related to data rather than information in the sense that we normally conceive it, and an instance of an outcome of a process initially set up by man. Progress in artificial intelligence will doubtless make this kind of thing more familiar, more substantive, and perhaps more worrying. Some more examples will be considered shortly.

Popper's proposal has been taken up by many people, for example John C. Eccles with respect to the brain-mind problem, and Bertram Brookes in the context of information science. The work has also had its critics, interpreters and misinterpreters, for example David Bloor, Paul Feyerabend, Anthony Quinton, and John Horton[6,7]. I believe it provides a useful framework and shorthand for discussing information of all kinds, although I accept that it is not entirely satisfactory, as David Rudd and others have pointed out. Strictly speaking there is no justification for separating off World 3, and thereby exacerbating the existing unsatisfactory status of dualism by adding a third category. It may be - if the theory of the implicate order of David Bohm and others turns out to be true - that Worlds 1 and 2 will themselves collapse into each other. Bohm[8] considered the mental and physical realms to be aspects of a single reality, a theme developed for example in Michael Talbot's *The Holographic Universe*[9]. And there are other models that might be used, for example that of Minai[10], exploring ideas about emergence, and others representing different kinds of world views. For the time being, though, I believe that Popper's model, flawed and perhaps not ideal though it may be, is useful. My interpretation of it may strike some as highly idiosyncratic, but it suits my purposes.

From the Wolfean perspective, then, the intention is to transfer the contents of Worlds 1 and 3 to World 2, and then to represent them again in World 3. For Wolfe, the conversion of everything he perceived into World 3 was his life's work. Colin Wilson comments pertinently on this matter: 'Man labours impersonally at this gigantic edifice that is World 3: that is his home'[11]. Well, maybe for some.

Worlds 1, 2 and 3 interact in the individual's experience as follows. A human mind, one of six billion (6×10^9) similar but discrete, isolated, island universes, comes into being surrounded initially by World 1 only, and then, as learning increases and a - possibly innate - capacity for the understanding of symbols is activated, by World 3. At what stage World 2 begins no one knows, but from conception onwards it is potentially there, like the plastic lead-in on a blank magnetic tape which has not yet begun to record. Soon, however, genotype heads towards phenotype, the nascent World 2 is modified by exposure to World 1 and then to World 3, and begins to include within itself miniature replicas, as it were, of those other Worlds. Its mother's face, domestic surroundings, words and songs, odours and textures, will slowly gel together; repetition will lead to familiarity and ultimately to a sense of self-identity. Sometime during childhood, awareness of internal mental states develops along with a realisation that the mind's contents can be viewed or listened to or otherwise privately explored (albeit inefficiently without an index - hence Wolfe's problem) with no external stimuli present. The child learns to see in his 'mind's eye' and to hear in his 'mind's ear', and develops consciousness of self. Though this is a truly momentous human activity and a development of mental activity beyond that of all, or most, other species, we take it very much for granted. World 2 is not logically dependent on the emergence of true self-consciousness, but it is difficult to see how it could develop effectively without it.

After a while, as a result of stimulation by the outside world, and once the rudimentary capacity for communication has been acquired, World 2 may have become sufficiently developed to the point that it has something to say to the world, something it wants to offer to the realm of culture, in the broadest sense. Let us assume that we have now jumped ahead from early childhood and have reached a creative stage in late adolescence or early adulthood. In order to express the message that one wishes to convey, from World 2 into World 3, that is from the mind to the intellectual-aesthetic-symbolic-cultural realm, World 1 materials have to be used, such as keyboard and VDU, pen and paper, paint and canvas, or guitar, microphone and tape machine. This of course reduces the creative process to a skeletal banality but it does help to illustrate Popper's concept. All kinds of creative loops and aerobatic manoeuvres between Worlds can be envisaged. For example, an artist might be so moved and excited by exposure to some scenery that he decides to paint it in his own style. Here, World 1 makes an impact on World 2, and the result is given in World 3 for the edification - as they say in music hall banter - of other World 2s. Alternatively our artist might be excited by someone else's painting hanging in a gallery and be stimulated into producing something himself, not a copy, but something of his own triggered off by, or influenced by, the original painting. In this instance we have a World 3 object, made of World 1 materials, itself the result of the impact of World 1 on someone else's World 2, making an impression on another World 2, already influenced by exposure to World 3 theories and evaluations, and the final product emerging once again into World 3, albeit made from World 1 materials. Evidently, this soon becomes rather silly and complicated, and is a long winded way of describing the obvious, but at this stage I think it is useful to have a clear understanding of Popper's Worlds, and how they interrelate. Arguably, it is only common sense.

As a final example let us consider a scientist whose mind, World 2, has been suitably prepared by education, by exposure to scientific literature, and by practical experience, in other words by exposure to World 1 materials - chemicals, electronic equipment, for example - which are the objects of scientific study or experimental tools, and to a World 3 scientific picture which attempts to explain and predict World 1 behaviour. Thus prepared, our scientist performs an experiment, in World 1, and sees certain results, out there in World 1 but interpreted according to World 3 theories and expectations, and perceived and understood for their significance in World 2. He goes away and mulls over (in World 2) his experiment, which he then writes up in World 3 and manages - with luck - to have published in a respected journal. In turn these results might encourage other scientists to do further work, standing on the shoulders of his own creativity. And so it goes on, working towards ever more complete knowledge, at least according to the Kuhnian[12] model, towards what is currently held to be 'the truth'. As Popper says: 'All work in science is work directed towards the growth of objective knowledge. We are workers who are adding to the growth of objective knowledge as masons work on a cathedral'[13].

World 3, for most purposes, is what we ordinarily think of as information or culture or collected knowledge. It is a uniquely human creation, dependent on human language and thought for its existence, and though it is the consequence of the mind of man it has a life of its own, acquires an extra-human autonomy, and becomes a foundation for further intellectual manipulation, for criticism and for evaluation. As in the case of the scientist stimulated by work already completed it permits the process known as emmorphosis to take place. Emmorphosis has been defined as: 'the process of change within the human mind (or image) caused by the receipt and integration into the image of a structured message received directly or indirectly from some human source'[14].

No matter how elegant the concept of the scientist, or how beautiful the image in the mind of the artist, they are of no use until they can be shared with others, thus requiring the creation of a World 3 artefact. Then, and only then, can the image be appreciated, rejected, or ignored. World 3 lives on without its creator and for this reason we still have the music of Beethoven with us. World 3 is our best bet for immortality. Without World 3 human civilisation would find it very difficult to get off the ground from one generation to another. In a sense, then, taking cultural civilisation as the greatest collective purpose of mankind, World 3 is more important than World 2. Individuals with all their faults and problems come and go, but their greatest achievements survive. As long as there is someone around capable of the interpretation, World 3 outlives and transcends its creator. If a neutron bomb - that cold war cliché of futuristic clean combat - or chemical or biological warfare were to destroy all but a few members of the human race, the survivors, if they were sufficiently intelligent and appropriately motivated, would in principle be able to reassemble most of the patterns of knowledge and culture as far as they had been developed. However, a weapon which selectively destroyed paper, magnetic tape and other recording media but left people intact would effectively eradicate most of the foundations of our civilisation.

The written word, and analogues of language in other forms, can transcend time and mortality and perpetuate the human mind after death. If the purpose of human life is the development of thought and understanding, then World 3, in the form of libraries, art galleries, record collections and so on, is man's greatest creation, his greatest offering to his gods and his greatest contribution to coming generations. But of course other people will say that there is much more to life than the concretisation and recording of thought, and they would be right.

Most importantly, the existence of World 3 allows us to pore over and consider other people's thoughts, to interpret them and modify them in various ways, to integrate them into what we know already, according to our needs and our subjective peculiarities. The availability of World 3 media permits us to consider and discuss problems, ideas, and stimuli for new areas of thought which would otherwise be difficult to grasp and to evaluate efficiently. This activity is something which stems largely from self-awareness of the type which as far as we know only man possesses. If some animal species possess it - dolphins for instance - they cannot tell us. Popper writes:

> 'animals, although capable of feelings, sensations, memory, and thus of consciousness, do not possess the full consciousness of self which is one of the results of human language and the development of the specifically human world 3'[15].

An equivalent of World 3 in the animal world would be the built artefacts such as birds' nests, spiders' webs, and the honeycombs of bees, and also, in a more abstract sense, the sometimes complex social organisations of, for example, ants, and the not-so-primitive animal languages such as the dance of bees. However, because no animal species systematically records its activities in any form analogous to writing, in a medium which is amenable to self-conscious rumination, evaluation, and manipulation, these animal artefacts cannot be considered to be World 3 in the true sense. World 3 implies self-conscious or reflexive structured thought which goes beyond spontaneous, instinctive and pre-programmed activities and responses.

World 3 takes on a life of its own, which far outstrips the mental capacities of individual men and women - and trainspotters - and even those with a Wolfean hunger for knowledge. Mere mortals cannot compete. Thomas Wolfe certainly cannot. As Popper says, it is 'superhuman', for 'it transcends its makers'[16]. 'Its impact on any one of us, even on the most original of creative thinkers, vastly exceeds the impact which any of us can make upon it'[17].

World 1 exists without man: one can easily imagine a universe in which no conscious or self-conscious life had evolved. There would be no problem about it existing but there would be no one to know it, except perhaps for God. Such a universe is plausible but sounds rather lonely and pointless, unless that smacks of anthropocentric conceit. When one thinks of existence in this way, the need for humans to know things seems quite superfluous and trivial. What does Jupiter care for the puzzlement of human astronomers over its big red spot and its intense radio noise? These things just are, and it doesn't matter very much in the long run if a few folk on planet Earth understand why they should be. Jupiter will be around long after you or I, have no fear. Or consider the metabolic processes occurring in that wonderful organ, the liver. Although I have studied biochemistry I have very little idea how my liver works. In fact I am not entirely sure where my liver is. Indeed, I have no direct evidence that I possess one. As far as I know there is no memory trace in my brain which will tell me how to operate my liver - say, how to metabolise a bottle of wine - in the way that there is a memory trace which tells me how to get from Oxford Circus to Heathrow Airport. But my liver, fortunately, so far, has had no problems in knowing just what to do - it consistently gets all its chemical formulae and metabolic pathways exactly right. It is a first rate, Grade A biochemist.

Somehow, this isn't enough. We are not entirely happy that Jupiter and my liver are so good at what they do. *We* want to know these sort of things, we want to know consciously, up there inside our skulls, even though it is not necessary for us to know. As astronomers, biochemists, doctors and other intelligent human beings we want to understand, even though our understanding is surplus to the uneventful performance of a liver or of the planet Jupiter. Nicholas Humphrey comments: 'Magnets do not need to do physics. If they did - if their survival as magnets depended on it - perhaps they would be conscious. If volcanoes needed to do geology, and clouds needed to do meteorology, perhaps they would be conscious too'[18]. Wanting to know and to understand is a very significant part of what makes us human; it is our privilege, and our curse.

World 3 cannot be understood by World 1, or vice versa. World 2 is an essential intermediary, it 'becomes, on the human level, more and more the link between the first and third world: all our actions in the first world are influenced by our second-world grasp of the third world'[19]. If we accept Popper's model it is not possible to reduce Worlds 1, 2 and 3 to each other. World 1, the physical world, would exist anyway, without us - unless we are fanatically solipsist - as we have noted. World 2, thought, depends on the existence of World 1, on the existence of the physical world. As far as we know it needs the biological structure of the brain and its supporting anatomy and physiology to operate (although we must accept that its exosomatic existence as soul or spirit is possible). Whether conscious experience is reducible to physical processes is of course highly problematical; the Popperian model treats it as being non-physical.

World 3 depends on World 1 for its actual physical form, and it needs World 2 for its creation, its structure and its understanding. Without World 2, World 3 is meaningless and can have no influence.

'There is a give and take between brain-stored culture and the external World 3 culture, and it is useful to develop the technique of putting as much as possible into the external World 3 ... if we are ourselves active and producing something, then it is quite insufficient just to work it out in our minds: although this is a very important stage, it is insufficient. We have to write our ideas down, and by writing them down we typically find problems which we had previously overlooked and which we can then think about'[20].

But the paradox remains that without the continued intervention of mind, World 3 is valueless other than as an unvisited museum of the imprints of human thought.

World 2 can interact directly with World 1, by perceiving physical matter and causing actions to be performed upon it, and Worlds 2 and 3 can interact directly, as in reading and writing, but Worlds 1 and 3 cannot interact directly. One can imagine computer-controlled devices which would cause the printing of messages upon the detection of certain phenomena, or one can posit, for example, a radio-controlled bomb triggered by the input of a particular piece of music, a very obvious World 1 effect apparently resulting from World 3. But even these instances require human intervention, the only unusual factors involved being time delay, some sophisticated robotics, and an element of unpredictability.

The relationships between Popper's Worlds are clarified in the diagram below :

WORLD 1
(PHYSICAL)

perception via $\Downarrow\Uparrow$ physical activity
sense organs   initiated by mind

WORLD 2
(MENTAL)

creativity using $\Downarrow\Uparrow$ understanding mediated via sense
World 1 materials   organs and previous knowledge/
                                                                                                          memory

WORLD 3
(INFORMATION)

When we consider the individual being alive in the world, and his problem of what to partake of the world and what to do with it, we are concerned with the interaction of Popper's Worlds, regardless of whether one's informational needs are of Wolfean proportions or not.

The crucial question arises of what properly belongs in each World and what can, or ought, to be transformed or transferred from one World to another. Should we try and know everything? Should a machine be built which contains all known facts? Should our entire lives be videotaped or even recorded in a form suitable for three-dimensional holographic projection? What would it mean to analyse our physical, cognitive and emotional behaviour and to simulate it in animated virtual reality? How do we feel about developments in artificial intelligence which indicate that, not only will machines be able to store vastly more information than can our brains, but that they will be smarter than we can ever be - at least in some respects - in the ways that they can manipulate and utilise that information? What about those attempts, like the CYC project associated with Douglas Lenat and others, based in Austin, Texas, to build artificial intelligence engines that are taught common sense concepts and codified so that increasingly they simulate an understanding of the world and its contents and interrelationships?

When everyone is drowning in unmanageable information saturation, we need to examine what we should put into our minds, and what we need to 'tell the world'. Our mass media are often accused of peddling trivia, while at the same time not making enough of real advances and fundamental issues. The more information that is transmitted, the less it seems we understand; each generation - at least in the UK - seems more ignorant than the last.

World 3 is primarily intended to be for the benefit of other people - it is public knowledge - but it can be used for our own purposes too. We can have our own private domains of World 3, our diaries, family snapshots, unpublished autobiographies, private notes, and so on, and we are increasingly developing personalised electronic databases to help us cope with our need for back-up memory, to assist our poor overburdened brains.

Meanwhile, aspects of World 3 become relatively autonomous and to some extent unavailable to man. They get locked away in libraries in Washington or in computers in Basingstoke, computers that we have no idea how to get into. No longer within the mind of one man, or all men, they inhabit an obscure semi-public domain outside of mind altogether, a domain sometimes too dull even to qualify for entry into something worthy of the glamorously nerdy name of cyberspace. Just ... a mainframe in Basingstoke. Huge chunks of recorded knowledge are not known to individual minds, and there may well be parts that are not known to anyone at all. Arguably this is just lowly data, below the status of information or knowledge, and in any case unworthy of cortical representation, of human ownership at all. For example, mathematical and statistical tables, telephone directories, the financial accounts of large corporations, the amino acid sequences of vitally important proteins such as insulin, the genomic sequence, the program for our word processing package, the unfathomable hyperlinked complexity of the World Wide Web, and yes, railway engine numbers. These are all in some sense known, are a valid part of World 3, but except perhaps in a few eccentric cases (of trainspotters and assorted freaks and memory men) they are not known in detail or in their entirety by anyone, even the people who created and compiled the information, and it is not intended that they should be.

Since it is so difficult and unpleasant to try and memorise data of this sort we can perhaps safely conclude that these things are valid candidates for storage in World 3. Partly the reason for the reluctance to memorise these types of data is because one knows that they can so easily be looked up in books or elsewhere, and partly it seems that the brain/mind is structured in such a way as to show a facility for handling analogue data, particularly that with a rich emotional, logical, spatial or associational content, but a minimal ability for processing what might be called digital or semantically unstructured information. Even mathematical geniuses and memory men often have to resort to the use of odd, but more meaningful, number associations - synaesthetic imagery, for example - to help them in their tasks. Perhaps this realm of very dull data gives us the beginning of an argument about what we should put into our minds and what we should exclude. What should be part of us, and what should be part of Basingstoke. If Wolfe could have known about Popper's Worlds, and been able to recognise what can happily reside within each one of them, and what the essential transfers between Worlds are, rather than everything having to go into World 3, he would not have had his problem ... and we would be the poorer.

More and more information is being generated which has never passed through the mind of man. We have come a long way from producing log tables on electronic calculators: artificial intelligence techniques will lead, or may already have led, to World 3 acting directly upon itself. This is a direct consequence of the information explosion. Usama Fayyad and colleagues, from the Jet Propulsion Laboratory at the California Institute of Technology in Pasadena[21] have written: 'The explosive growth of many business, government, and scientific databases has far outpaced our ability to interpret and digest this data, creating a need for a new generation of tools and techniques for automated and intelligent database analysis'. In the general sense this is known as knowledge discovery, but in its most well-developed aspect it takes the form of data mining, an essentially statistical technique for the examination of data already available to an institution[22]. Using techniques such as neural networks, rule induction, decision trees, and data visualisation it is possible - given favourable circumstances - to extract from existing statistical data information on associations of events, sequences of events linked over time, the classification and clustering of items, and the prediction of the future values of continuous variables, such as sales figures. This is essentially a purely World 3 activity, set up by human minds of course, usually with an eye to a business opportunity, but with an unpredictable outcome. Because of the almost infinite ability of computers to make comparisons and correlations such systems are quite capable of generating entirely spurious 'intelligence'.

World 3 is going off on its own in other ways too. Personalised agents, smart environments, avatars acting as electronic ambassadors of ourselves in cyberspace (a concept explored fictionally in such works as William Gibson's *Idoru* and Neal Stephenson's *Snow Crash*), and Web-crawling 'spiders' - inhabitants belonging more than anywhere in World 3 - are in their infancy, but are being intensively reared. As this happens we can be grateful that we are being released from having to handle so much uncongenial data, but at the risk of alienation from the real world, the physical world, and of being increasingly dependent on the so-called wisdom of other authorities, human or machine. We will return to this in the concluding chapter.

Information science has its roots in many places, in library science, communications and organisation theory, as well as having philosophical, linguistic, technological, societal and practical components. It is now driven more than anything by technology, by the public fascination with computers and especially with the Internet, by problems of information overload in the workplace and elsewhere (problems made more visible by the success of the Internet), and by the commercial ambitions of the broadcasting and entertainment industries. One may judge that it has come of age, or perhaps that the public world has caught up with the information professional - and in some respects by-passed him. So far as information science can be considered to have developed as a subject in its own right, independently of librarianship, taxonomy, computer science, linguistics, and so on, it is traditionally concerned with World 3, with the objective organisation of recorded information. However, when we look at the universe in which we find ourselves, in its totality and rawness, when we consider our strange predicament from the viewpoint of being alive, or from that of Thomas Wolfe, we have to accept that information is potentially in both Worlds 1 and 3 and also, very importantly, within our own minds. Information is what we do, as a species. We are all information specialists now.

A fully respectable information science must concern itself, at least in principle, with all kinds of information. In the following three chapters we will be concerned not only with information as it is usually thought of, the World 3 sense, but also with the informational aspects of the physical world and of the mind. In turn, we will examine each of Popper's Worlds and see how the individual trying to find meaning and trying to cope with the overload of events, sense impressions, facts and fictions which threaten to engulf him, can respond to the stimuli of these three Worlds, how he may or may not be able to control them, and how they can challenge him into pursuing his life's activities. We will look then at some recent developments in information technology, and how they may or may not help the individual grapple with the problem exemplified by Wolfe's life and work.

5. Dürrenmatt's Absent Lemur

The physical world, World 1, includes everything in a physical sense in our external environment and - presumably - our own bodies as physical objects. Excluded is the information or meaning content as evolved by man. Books, paintings, magnetic tapes, sculptures and buildings would merit inclusion in World 1, but not - in the abstract sense - literature, art, music, science or aesthetics, for example. In our highly print- and media-saturated society the difference is sometimes obscure, since our interpretation of the physical world is so dependent upon the theories, discussions and representations which have been generated around it. To take the title of this book, the notion of the world as information is becoming ever more prevalent: this is not merely because text, pictures and sounds become digitised and measured in megabytes but in other ways too. For example, the human genome, the blueprint for the species, becomes essentially a code, a text, an informational instruction; so does money, no longer a tangible entity but an invisible transfer of digits, a long way from a bartering transaction with proferred produce, or precious metals, banknotes or cheques. Much of what we do, think, and are, can be reduced - not very usefully in some cases - to the collection, storage and dissemination of information.

Unlike Popper's World 3, World 1 has no structure imposed upon it by man. It just is. By and large it has no obviously intended meaning, although in the instance of manufactured articles there will be implied messages of purpose or style, for example. The world of nature does have meaning for those who can extract it, of course, but as far as we know the meaning is not deliberately put there. Clouds often mean impending rain, but the deduction is secondary. With familiarity and usage World 1 does acquire meaning in the form of styles and symbols and deducible, predictable, cause-and-effect sequences. In other contexts - geography, for example - it has therefore sometimes been called the 'semiosphere'. But if this happens then arguably such interpretations reside outside of World 1, directly in World 2, sometimes with the aid of theorisations which have found their way into World 3. World 1 just is, and what we can do with it is limited.

A broad generalisation of the difference between Worlds 1 and 3 is as follows. In World 3, information is synthesised and formalised according to socially agreed codes or languages or patterns so that a message can be reliably conveyed. There will be plenty of room for misinterpretations, but normally a World 3 stimulus is expected to produce a specific response in the recipient.

For World 1 there is no such socially agreed code, although there may be widely held opinions about the aesthetics of physical objects, and conventions of what is beautiful and what is ugly. In this instance we are projecting a World 2 feeling out on to World 1, which is fundamentally fallacious although we do it all the time. The perception of World 1 is distorted by the opinions, knowledge, needs, moods and tastes of the beholder: the reaction that ensues is entirely his business. The physical environment has an existence which is objective and, in a world devoid of people, completely lacking in qualities. But it also has properties which can be determined - once observers are allowed in - by scientific or other means, with a high degree of objectivity, properties such as history, chemical composition, dimensions, and colour. And it has personal messages which can only be uncovered subjectively by individuals motivated to do so. At all levels this can be lumped together as information.

Small areas and facets of the world we can make our own, in a way, by personal attachment, discovery, residence, ownership, or by intense mental activity to a degree that we become popularly associated with them - although in this sense personal territory would be more usually related to a World 3 activity. So, Larry Adler is the harmonica man, Ravi Shankar is the sitar man; more physical would be the associations between Cézanne and Mont Sainte-Victoire or between Sir Edmund Hillary and Mount Everest. Yet physical objects infuriatingly insist upon remaining indifferent to our longings and our intellectual or creative struggles over them. They cannot reciprocate our feelings and therefore they will never be able to satisfy us in the Wolfean sense. After all, the Wolfean problem is not theirs but ours, inside our heads. There is always more than we can ingest; as Tintoretto said in the context of painting, 'the sea always gets larger'. More infuriating still is the way that objects are inexhaustible in the things they mean to different people at different times and under different circumstances: their permutations of meaningfulness are endless - simply, of course, because it is we, not they, who supply the meaning. As Maurice Merleau-Ponty expressed it: 'every object is crisscrossed with a multitude of significances which can be traced out perceptually but never exhausted ... every perceptual experience is filled with inexhaustible dimensions of meaning'[1]. This is a truth which the theory of information science has yet to adequately take on board.

From this point on I will consider the physical world from two aspects, the first being the question of what it consists of and how it may be thought to be structured, and the second being the effect of the physical environment on the individual and his response to it in terms of possessing, using, and travelling about in it, and in terms of his life ambitions. In other words, what World 1 is, and what we can do with it.

The Classification of World 1

Making sense of World 1 involves in the first instance naming it and classifying it, and the two activities go very much together. You don't name something without first distinguishing it from something else. The way that World 1 is classified depends on the nature of the subject matter concerned. Though there is no classification inherent in nature some parts of the physical world seem to be self-evidently classifiable because they have an obvious structure, visible or otherwise, perceptible to the human scale, whereas for other areas we classify more according to our practical needs, because of our prejudices, habits of mind, historical or geographical circumstances, or for other more or less arbitrary reasons. Lest it be thought that the classification of the physical world is something that only professional classifiers have to worry about, it should be pointed out that it is something that we all have to do in order to cope with the everyday world, whether we are infants just beginning to find out what is what, or whether we are buying or selling food, using a library, deciding what to watch on television, socialising at a party, or running any kind of business. For the most part this act of classification is done at a subliminal level, based on long experience and making use of perceived similarities and dissimilarities between objects, but it can be more complicated and more deliberate than this. The most natural division is between 'I like it' and 'I don't like it'. Much of our life follows on from that intuited hedonic dichotomy.

Association, that is, perceived resemblance or analogy, is the key to classification but the associations used for classifying World 1 are far from consistent. Maps of the different subject areas can be made, but the parameters chosen for constructing them (in World 3 of course) will often vary between types of subjects. Some of the principal parameters involved are time, space, physical and chemical composition, size, shape, colour, process, function, style, and ideas of developmental or evolutionary stage. Classifications, then, depend on the nature of what is to be classified and though they may take various forms, for example attempting to be natural or being deliberately artificial, they will reflect something of the perceived underlying structure of reality.

Classification depends partly upon language, partly upon habit, and partly upon the dominant world view or local paradigm of how reality - whatever that may turn out to be - is constructed. The classification schemes of so-called primitive peoples who have escaped the one-tracked mind - what Blake would call the 'single vision' of post-Renaissance European culture (and especially of Anglo-American 20th century culture) - can be very different from our own. They are not wrong, even if we do not attach much significance to them. They may, however, lack the scope for wider application. Every such scheme reflects its circumstances and its reasons. There are no God-given classifications of the physical world; however, some schemes may have deeper foundations and greater power and applicability than others, and some may be more convenient and efficient to operate. Vickery[2] has reviewed how the sciences have been classified down the centuries, with each age having its own characteristics. For example he refers to the Aristotelian and Platonic classifications, those of the early Latin culture of Europe which included within the 'seven liberal arts' the trivium of logic, grammar and rhetoric and the quadrivium of arithmetic, geometry, astronomy and harmonics, and how these seven were added to by medicine in the 7th century and by the mechanical arts in the 9th century. In the 10th century the Turkestan philosopher al-Farabi, also known as Alpharabeus, produced a classification of the sciences which included logic, physics (sub-divided in the Aristotelian fashion and including the biological sciences), and mathematics, which was divided into seven parts, namely arithmetic, geometry, music, astronomy, optics, statics, and mechanical devices. New sciences such as algebra, astrology and agriculture were introduced three centuries later by the Persian Nasir al-din al-Tusi.

A substantially new classification was proposed by Roger Bacon, covering grammar and logic, the quadrivium of mathematics, natural science, and metaphysics and morals, with the natural sciences including the old Aristotelian physics, plus optics, astrology, statics, alchemy, agriculture and medicine. In the 17th and 18th centuries further classifications were proposed by Leibniz, Thomas Hobbes, Johann Heinrich Alsted, and others, and then we are into an essentially modern period in which numerous proposals, based increasingly on rational theoretical principles, have been proposed. Such classifications do not remain static for long: now, for example, we have molecular biology, spherical trigonometry, chaos theory, organometallic chemistry, and many much more narrowly focussed specialisations.

Some aspects of nature inherently require a greater depth of abstraction in order to derive a useful pattern of categorisation than others do, simply because they are more opaque to our natural way of seeing things, but whatever we do, we cannot entirely escape some theoretical component in our classificatory schemes. 'We cannot avoid theory. Every scientific activity has its theoretical basis. Even the most empirical fact-searching must be guided by an idea of what one is looking for'[3]. At the same time we must remember that because the very act of naming implies classification, the extent to which that name holds an obtrusive significance reflects its importance in our classificatory scheme of things. The existence of well-established names tends to preserve classificatory principles even after they have been superceded, as is illustrated by the history of change of biological taxonomies from the Linnaean to Darwinian and post-Darwinian eras[4].

Let us consider a few of the principles used in the classification of different kinds of things. Geography, location as a World 1 entity, most obviously, can be mapped onto World 3, but even here we need an abstract, theoretical underpinning: the intuitive awareness of spatiality is not enough. We cannot produce a useful map without knowing the names which are attached to geographical features, and naming involves the making of distinctions for reasons which are not always obvious and sometimes complex. Again, to produce accurate two-dimensional maps we need to have a theory of map projections which is far from obvious, and the mathematical techniques to handle that theory. Though geography perhaps classifies more naturally than any other subject, in its simplest form according to spatial distribution, it does require some theory, and it requires the existence of names, which in turn implies other classifications and abstractions.

History, too, has a pretty simple ready-made classification because of chronology, the arrow of time, but it is further complicated by a need to specify spatial location, that is, by secondary geographical (and hence political) classification, for example English 19th century history as opposed to French 19th century history. Of course once dimensions such as economics, politics, and sociology are brought in - as the structuralist approach of Fernand Braudel would require, for instance - it can become much more complicated.

So far, in the subject areas of geography and history, we have been able to classify things and events according to where they are, or where and when they were. Next, we may want to know what they consist of, and this is not so easy, and not just because of the complexities of chemical analysis. A satisfactory categorisation of substances had to wait until a plausible atomic theory had been devised, at least in a basic sense, along with an understanding of the difference between chemical elements, compounds, and mixtures, and in fact until the observations that had been made - by John Dalton,

William Odling, Johann Döbereiner and others, on the principle of atomic weights - which made possible the construction of Mendeleev's periodic table of the elements in the mid-19th century.

Until the time of Mendeleev it was of course possible to classify substances according to their texture, colour, use, physical properties, believed spiritual or magical attributes, simple chemical reactions, place of discovery and so on, and such classifications were useful and had a basis in common sense and common experience. This form of classification or *bricolage,* however, was no great advance on that employed by children or by primitive or ancient man, and it was not helpful in promoting the understanding necessary for the growth of the chemical industry, which in the early 19th century was just beginning, in Britain, Germany, the United States, and elsewhere. Although it was possible to define an element as a substance indivisible by chemical means, ideas were so confused that entities such as air, water, fire or blood might be considered elemental. Chemistry depends a great deal on theory which cannot be deduced directly from common sense or naked eye observation. Common experience alone would not tell us that water is a compound of two gases, or that oxygen and sulphur are chemically similar, or that carbon and tin have anything in common, or even chlorine and iodine. Common sense would tell us that sodium and phosphorus should be grouped together because they both readily ignite in air, or that sulphuric acid and sodium hydroxide belong together because of their caustic, corrosive properties, but a deeper chemical understanding tells us that these similarities are superficial and that there are more substantive reasons for not grouping these substances together.

That deeper understanding had largely to wait until Dmitri Ivanovich Mendeleev (1834-1907), who in about 1869 established that all the chemical elements can be placed into a single ordered system, the periodic table, and showed that if they are arranged according to their atomic weights they fall naturally into groups with similar chemical properties, for example the alkali metals (including lithium, sodium and potassium), and the halogens (principally fluorine, chlorine, bromine, and iodine). Mendeleev cleared up a problem that had been baffling scientists for a long time, who were convinced that there was some kind of relationship between the atomic weights and the properties of the elements (John Newlands had, for example, recognised the 'octaves', the periodic repetition of similar properties of the elements) or that all the elements were composed from combinations of a single, common substance. At that time, the periodic table contained many gaps, for elements which had not yet been discovered (for example hafnium, lutetium, rhenium, and the inert gases - helium, argon, neon, krypton, xenon and radon), or which do not occur naturally and had to await developments in nuclear physics before they could be synthesised (promethium, technetium).

Mendeleev was in some cases able to predict the physicochemical properties of elements yet to be found, with some accuracy, as he did for what he called eka-boron (later to be called scandium) and eka-silicon (which we know as germanium). These predictions (and there were others which were less accurate) tended to confirm the validity of Mendeleev's proposals but it was not until the end of the 19th century and the early part of the 20th century that the major components of the atom (protons, neutrons and electrons) were discovered, providing a more satisfactory underpinning of his theory. Mendeleev's scheme is fully compatible with modern atomic theory, and with more recent discoveries and classifications of families of subatomic particles (hadrons, baryons, fermions, leptons) and with the concept of families of different kinds of quarks at an even more fundamental level. So the classification of what things are made of is very firm indeed but based upon abstractions which are very far from intuitively obvious.

In all cases, classification depends both upon our perceived needs and upon what we know - or think we know. Constantly, though, we are looking out for deeper and more general theories which more powerfully and more logically connect things together. At the same time these theories may well grow further and further away from features that appear to be obvious but which, as it turns out, are merely surface phenomena. Chemistry, for all its abstruseness, has provided us with a reliable and comprehensive framework for the classification of all substances, whether they occur naturally here or on another planet or in a star, or whether we synthesise them in our laboratories (including elements, the so-called transuranic ones, such as curium, plutonium, and americium, which are entirely man-made and were not foreseen in Mendeleev's original scheme). This classification scheme, though theory-based, is completely non-controversial. It is perhaps the most all-encompassing, natural, logical and certain classification system that we have ever devised, and it seems unlikely that it will ever need radical modification although it may be added to, if and when new transuranic or superheavy elements are found or created, following on from recent syntheses such as seaborgium and meitnerium. As such it provides a consistent system as good as those based on time or location. It has the additional advantage of providing us with an unambiguous, although admittedly daunting, language by which we can name any chemical substance, however complex, such as 7-chloro-2,3-dihydro-l-methyl-5-phenyl-lH-1,4-benzodiazepin-2-one, which we may prefer to call Valium or even diazepam, or alpha-(5,6-dimethylbenzimidazol-1-yl) cyanocobamide, with which we are probably more familiar as vitamin B_{12}. So-called trivial or unsystematic names survive because of their obvious convenience. Chemical classification and nomenclature, for all their perceived complexity, are now on very solid ground.

When we come to the classification of living species, though, the situation is rather different and rather less satisfactory. The standard hierarchy is to classify in the following sequence of increasing specificity: class, order, sub-order, family, sub-family, genus, species and sub-species. One might expect plants and animals to be classified according to their gross physical characteristics, with some reference made to their habits, habitats, natures, and finer details of their structure (for example eye structure, dentition, claw formation, numbers of petals, means of reproduction), and partly this is so. For sub-species it is not quite so simple and classification tends to become more of an exercise in trivial naming rather than in hierarchical taxonomy. One would also expect that any classification scheme would allow for borderline cases, and this may be more difficult than it sounds. It is sometimes virtually impossible to assign some species to particular categories; sometimes there seems to be a spectrum of types to be found in different parts of the world, so that one sub-species blends continuously into another and it is hard to say where one variety ends and another begins. This is arguably more of a problem of naming than of classification and under the constraints of such a system a reliable taxonomy is possible only within small geographical areas, for a species may spread across the globe and evolve towards a convergence with other named species. So, for example, the herring gull in Britain, if followed westwards round the Arctic regions, changes gradually through Greenland, northern Canada, Alaska and Siberia, so that by the time Britain is reached again it has changed so much that it is now the black back gull. An analogous difficulty is that occasionally there may be plants or animals in different parts of the world which bear remarkable similarities to each other, and yet which are held to be unrelated from a taxonomic point of view. An example of this would be the parallelism between the emerald tree boa from South America and the green tree python found in northern Australia and Papua New Guinea. For the most part, however, biological classification is relatively straightforward.

Modern biological classification begins with Carl Linné (1707-1778), also known as Carolus Linnaeus. Linnaeus was the first to propose the principle of dividing plant and animal types into genera and then into species, with each example being given two names referring to the genus and to the individual species. He presented this scheme in various publications, notably the *Systema Naturae* of 1735, the *Species Plantarum* of 1753 and the fifth edition of *Genera Plantarum* in 1754. Linnaeus' classification of plants was based mainly on flower parts, which tend to remain unchanged during the course of evolution, but even at that time he recognised that it was an essentially artificial system. In fact his scheme was so successful that it actually hindered the introduction of more natural schemes, and besides classifying the plant and animal kingdoms he also devised classifications for diseases and minerals.

Linnaeus and his emulators paved the way for the great collectors who travelled the world and furnished national and local museums, zoos and botanical gardens with magnificent displays of prehistoric bones, brightly coloured minerals, exotic shrubs and curious animals. These collections can be thought of as the first systematic attempt to capture World 1, and though we tend to think of them as essentially Victorian, they had begun much earlier, with, for example, the collection which Elias Ashmole presented to the University of Oxford in 1682, thus founding the Ashmolean Museum, and Sir Hans Sloane (1660-1753), whose collections of 100,000 specimens and 50,000 books, manuscripts and drawings provided the nucleus of what came to be the British Museum, founded in Bloomsbury in 1759. The natural history collections were subsequently transferred to Alfred Waterhouse's new building in South Kensington in 1881, which we now know as the Natural History Museum. And still the World 1 capturing exercise goes on, so that, for example, this one museum alone now has some 100,000 specimens of Himalayan plants, 180,000 minerals, 100,000 rock specimens, and over 1,000 meteorites, and its major role in identifying and classifying species continues. There are now more than one million known species of animals and nearly half a million plants, with some 25,000 new species being discovered each year[5].

The classification of species has, fortunately or unfortunately, been greatly influenced by Darwinian evolutionary theory[6], on the assumption that the theory is correct and that species have indeed evolved from each other. Attempts have been made to show with mathematical precision just how closely species are related to each other, and modern techniques of DNA sequencing and genomic mapping lend credence to this approach. At present there are three principal techniques for biological classification[7], which each have their strengths and weaknesses. These techniques are numerical phenetics, which is based on notions of overall similarity; cladistics, first enunciated by Hennig in 1950, in which the criterion for grouping species together is the closeness or relative recency of common ancestry, giving an unambiguous, hierarchical, nested structure of relationships and overcoming the sort of difficulties we encountered with the black back or herring gull; and evolutionary classification, to produce what is called a phylogram, recording the points of branching and the degrees of subsequent evolutionary divergence. All this is fine if the theory of evolution is true, and while most scientists would say that it is, at least in most of its details, the recent heated debate, centred on the southern United States, between the evolutionists and the creationists, illustrates how undesirable it is to have a classification based on what is in fact an unproven - though widely accepted - hypothesis, and which is vulnerable to creeping or revolutionary paradigm shifts in our understanding.

Perhaps classification schemes which acknowledge the involvement of man, mind and theory are more honest, even if less objective or fundamental than we would like them to be. Classification of qualities like colours, tastes and odours has to be highly subjective, or one should say intersubjective, to be of much use, despite the existence of their physical correlates such as wavelength or molecular structure, and knowledge of the topology of receptor sites. In the softer sciences such as psychology, sociology, and economics, and in literature and the arts, where World 3 productions are considered almost as World 1 materials for study, classification revolves around similarities of style or purpose or method, around perceived activities or qualities or around prominent individuals or groups of people ('movements'), with some common features and usually some focus in time and/or place. Problems arise with works which fall into no obvious genre, or which transcend the usual categories. Much of this sort of classification comes to us as second nature, as common sense, but the question remains as to whether it is ideal. So much is embedded in natural language and in tacit usage that to suggest alternatives is virtually unthinkable, virtually meaningless.

With man-made artefacts classification tends to be more arbitrary than that of naturally occurring specimens, and depends very much on chance factors of geography, history, cultural grouping, purpose, design, style, usage and so on, and as we move more and more into the world of man as opposed to the world of given physical things so our classifications become more complicated, more need-oriented, and more subjective. At this point we can begin to see how the classification of World 1 becomes confused with that of World 3; we are no longer classifying things as they are but as we intellectually (World 3) and subjectively (World 2) believe them to be. We are classifying our theoretical model rather than the real world, but this confusion seems unavoidable if one is to adhere to the rigid demarcations of Popper's universe.

Because there are no God-given distinctions between things in nature, and even though common sense soon suggests seemingly obvious and useful distinctions, all things possess latent multiple qualities any of which might be useful as a basis for classification. This means that we can never escape our intentional subjective involvement in classificatory activity: Worlds 1, 2 and 3, in the context of classification, are already blurred.

Information science is not especially concerned with classifying the physical world. It has tended to appropriate widely accepted classifications of World 1 within itself, not for the primary purpose of accepting them as taxonomy in its own right, but with the intention of employing them in the classification of World 3 material. Ideally there should be no conflict between scientific and bibliographic classification[8], but sometimes there is. Classification is based upon a witches' brew of reliable facts, scientific hypothesis, commonsense observation, subjective interpretation, convenience, convention and need. It is not a structure of divine creation but one reflecting human psychology, language and culture. But here we are moving away from World 1 and into World 3.

Capturing World 1

Given that we can classify World 1, and that we can capture it on paper, film or magnetic tape (as World 3) or actually imprison parts of it in enclosures like museums, zoos, safari parks, theme parks and national parks, and that we can designate bits of it 'areas of outstanding natural beauty' or 'wilderness zones' or 'listed buildings', what can we do with it? How does it affect our individual lives?

Here we must return to the subjective viewpoint, that of the individual thrown into the world, trying to absorb information and at the same time trying to develop a personality and to achieve ambitions. How do Worlds 1 and 2 interact? As individuals there is, in a practical sense, very little of the physical world with which we can intermesh, still less that we can possess, and this is essentially because of the ontological chasm between Worlds 1 and 2. Our relationship with World 1 is mostly via the organs of perception and the mental representation of the external world within the mind. There is not a lot that we can capture directly, and if we do, it hardly counts as a transfer of information. We can own property, obviously. If we are royalty or head of state we can make some dubious claim to 'own' a province, country or empire including its inhabitants, but that ownership is of very suspect quality. We can win the allegiance of the populace by persuasion, affection or force, we can claim a right to buildings, land or products, but where is the satisfaction? The very idea of trying to possess things - other than in the sense of legal ownership, for example this is my house, this is my record collection - seems intrinsically mistaken. Yet many people evidently do derive great satisfaction from this kind of ownership, whether it is an expensive music centre, designer labelled air shoes, or a pot dog from Pwllheli. The satisfactions of materialism can be very real. But I wonder what this really means. Probably it is to do with status and buying power, as well as with nostalgic associations, reminders of the love and affection that others have for us. Perhaps the most we can expect is sentimental or aesthetic pleasure from the things that we say are ours. The capture of World 1 is problematical; a few things, which we classify as foods, we can eat, which is a kind of possession, albeit a destructive kind. On occasion, as we shall see towards the end of this chapter, during certain types of mystical experience or altered states of consciousness we may feel that we are fused with our surroundings, that all is one and that we are a part of everything and that we know everything. In reality there is not a lot that we can possess; the satisfactions come from the associations made with the fact of possession.

We can confront some aspects of the physical world, some extremes, and demonstrate that we are equal to them. Hence sporting records, climbing Mount Everest notoriously because it is there, and participation in the kinds of activities publicised by Richard Branson or recorded in *The Guinness Book of Records*. In fact, these are variations on the London Underground record that we discussed in Chapter 2. These are perhaps the classic ways of trying to come to terms with World 1, by breaking little bits off at a time.

Clearly the quality of our relations with the physical realm, rather than just the naked fact of physical possession, is important. A satisfying ownership demands legitimacy, a right to ownership, something that we have put into it, money or the effort of collecting. In this context I am reminded of an incident when I was at school, in my mid-teens, when someone's stamp album had been stolen, presumably by another boy. The headmaster addressed the assembled school and, failing to embarrass or intimidate the culprit into confession (although making many other pupils, myself included, feel acutely guilty), asked what kind of pleasure he would ever derive from gloating over that stamp collection in private, never being able to show it to anyone, always remembering the guilty secret. Clearly, it could be no greater than the satisfaction obtained by one of Nicholas Whittaker's 'fudgers', who had abdicated that unverifiable personal honesty that the rules of trainspotting imply. Of course, the headmaster naïvely overlooked the probability that the stamp collection might be sold, or its contents swapped, or taken apart and reassembled and absorbed into another collection, but the point is that mere possession is no guarantee of satisfaction. This episode all seems very innocent compared to the antics of some of today's youth, who evidently obtain satisfaction from, say, riding around in expensive cars which do not belong to them. Theft as another kind of possession. As with trainspotting, it all depends on adherence to one's self-imposed code of conduct. Always the real world is something other than ourselves, and we have to supply the meaning, the significance, the value[9].

A satisfactory relationship with the environment implies much more than crude ownership. Rather, it implies that the physical world is converted within us into a world of thoughts, or in other words, that Popper's World 1 becomes mediated by World 2, developing in the process meanings and significances from which we derive satisfaction and a sense of belonging in the world. Meaning and information have to be extracted from the physical world by the application of science, social coding, imagination or a sense of wonder. We can possess meaning and information; we can derive comfort and pride and social identity from our possessions, but we cannot possess physical reality itself.

Often our motivations in this respect are obscure, even (or especially) to ourselves. Frequently we feel goaded into checking things out just for the sake of completeness, not even to be able to say that we have 'done them', but because we are afraid we might miss something and feel anxiety if we leave a self-imposed information gathering task uncompleted. As Whittaker notes[10]:

> 'Consumerism is loaded with 'trainspotting' overtones - the must-have item, the desire for a complete range, whether it be PG Tips cards or kitchen utensils or 'Great Composers' cassettes. The urge to collect, to tick off, to underline, to have the 'full set' is in us all'.

Apart from the more obsessive motivations there is an aesthetic component to obtaining a complete set, whether it be a set of stamps, a range of glassware or porcelain, the obscure recordings of a rock'n'roll dinosaur or the complete collection of Maigret stories. Fulfilling such needs, for missing items, is also big business.

Possessing and collecting are two ways of interacting with World 1, but they do not necessarily imply any concomitant selective growth of World 2. Preserving old buildings does little for us unless they have a personal meaning for us, and so it is for the rest of the physical realm. So why have the same furniture, the same white goods, the same electronic toys, the same books and records and prints on the wall as everyone else?

The completist tendency is a species of informational anxiety. We will walk miles round some hot foreign art gallery in a city that we will never visit again, glancing unseeingly at hundreds of paintings which hold not the slightest interest for us (especially as we are thinking about where to get a drink or what to do tomorrow) and which we will immediately forget all about, the moment we step out into the sunshine again. But the paintings are by Rubens or Rembrandt or somebody else famous that we in our infinite ignorance have just about heard of, and so we have to make sure that we clock them all. At the zoo - if we find the time in our busy lives to visit one - we may even obtain satisfaction from seeing the labels with their Latin names and little maps partly coloured red (perhaps they subliminally remind us of the British Empire), even if the cage is manifestly empty[11], or the anti-social occupant is having a snooze round the back, out of sight. Miles Kington has observed this sort of non-event in his 'franglais' study called *Au Zoo*[12], and has even invented a naturalist called Dürrenmatt, who specialised in collecting such invisible animals, the example quoted being Dürrenmatt's Absent Lemur, which is 'toujours somewhere else'. It is a matter of common experience that if the animal isn't there it saves us time and we can get on to seeing something else that isn't there that much quicker, and ultimately to reach the exit turnstile happy that we have 'done' everything. Hopefully we do obtain some pleasure from seeing some of the occupants and feel that we have had our money's worth. And then on to the next thing.

Helga Dittmar, in her study of the social psychology of material possessions tellingly subtitled *To Have Is To Be*[13], comments extensively on the symbolic meanings that consumer products possess, in the way that they help to define our identity, our status, and as a way of communicating with others. Some possessions are of course practical aids to making life easier, more comfortable or more pleasurable, but others act as an extension of our personality, and even, where there is some inadequacy, as a substitute for personal development - shoulder pads as a surrogate for natural assertiveness, having a mobile phone instead of having something to say. She also notes, however, the pathology of 'consumption disorders', which range from compulsive eating to compulsive buying, and the detrimental effects of 'the psychology of more' in a world of finite resources and increasing pollution, and of the 'throw-away mentality' arising from the social imperative to consume and to move on. Because identity is no longer guaranteed by being a member of a group we have to invent and achieve our individual identity, and the accumulation of possessions and wealth contribute to this. Possessions form a kind of collage representative of our lives, a relatively permanent backcloth in a changing world, and we may even wish to confirm the validity of that pattern by handing on our possessions when we die. To my niece, the pot dog from Pwllheli. All this can be regarded as an information territory marking exercise, the colonisation of information space, a stage beyond trainspotting in making the world one's own. There are of course many other ways of looking at this type of activity.

Travel as a Wolfean Activity

Geography represents another Wolfean challenge. Which bits of it are we going to 'collect' in our lifetime? Are we going to try and make all of it our own? As individuals we all inhabit different geographical worlds. Though we may live in the same city, or even in the same street, we all see things slightly differently, and we have different private geographies of places we visit, places that we like or dislike, places where relatives and friends live, places where we go for our holidays. Our individual repertoires in informational geographical space are unique, but are again subject to influences encouraging uniformity more strongly than ever before. Telecommunications and computer networks meanwhile erode the significance of geographical space.

   This uniformity is perhaps paradoxical considering that, as individuals, we now travel - in terms of total miles per lifetime - far greater distances than our ancestors, even our immediate ones. This results from the socioeconomic conditions that enable most people in the industrialised countries to have greater mobility, from the ubiquity of the internal combustion engine, from the growth of cities necessitating long distance commuting, from the development of international business and tourism and - more than any other reason - from the invention of the aircraft and the availability of flights priced so as to be within the purchasing power of most people for at least part of their lives. For various reasons long haul flights are not significantly more expensive than short haul ones, at least from a British perspective. While travelling to Australia may once have been an unrealistic option, a mere dream, we can now decide whether we want to go or not, or whether - with a limited holiday allowance - it should take preference over Devon, Lanzarote, Greece, or Florida. Our personal travel is growing, if not exponentially, then close to it. Buckminster Fuller, famous among other things for his unusual habits of quantification, estimated[14] that since 1913 he travelled some 3,500,000 miles, including 47 round the world flights, which he considered, however, 'a paltry mileage for any senior Pan American Airways pilot'. Pre-1913 man, on the other hand, would only cover 30,000 miles in an average lifetime. But then again, does hurtling through the stratosphere at 600 m.p.h. equate to seeing the world, and does it prove anything about oneself other than one's ability to pay the fare and to endure hours of discomfort?

What is intriguing in terms of life challenge and Wolfean ambition is why some people choose to visit certain places just because, Everest-like, they are there. The sort of person who does this is largely unmotivated by the advertised attractions of places and of their snob value. Rather, he seems to be responding to an inner need, something deep within him, another variant of the informational collecting urge or perhaps something like the 'Russia' or 'Africa' of the mind as described by Laurens van der Post, which he feels that visiting these places can satisfy, a topographical itch which can be touristically scratched. The Atlantic City boardwalk as imagined from Paris.

Thrown into the world, where do we go? Do we try and cover the whole world? Do we try to visit every country, every historical or scenic attraction, every metropolis or megalopolis? What exactly is the point in doing so when we have images of them all readily available through television, films, books, and an instant - if inaccurate - recall in our minds? For some reason we need to go and see these places for ourselves.

Tourism becomes ever more the checking out of certain well-known features: districts, monuments, buildings, streets, paintings, atmospheres (often urban villagey, arty ones: Montmartre, Trastevere, the Jordaan, Greenwich Village). We leave home with a pretty good idea of what they are like, we sample them and savour them, we find they are or are not like we had expected and we return home, happy to have run them through our synapses. The Grand Canyon will be bigger or smaller than we had expected - but so what? Soon, we forget 'our' impression and revert to stereotyped images we had before we went or to a photographic image we collected while we were there. If we are very lucky, we might retain a recollection of some moment of self-observation we had while we were there. None of this is scarcely more exciting than the non-observation of the aforementioned Dürrenmatt's Absent Lemur. The satisfactions it provides are minimal, the sense of personal significance almost non-existent.

It seems that whether or not we are Wolfean in our appetites most of us crave a first-hand experience of certain world-famous objects, and the direct transference of them, via perception, from World 1 to World 2. However, the tendency nowadays is to transfer as much as possible of our experience to a World 3 format and to neglect the direct experience of the World 1 - World 2 interchange. We have become cerebral rather than feeling creatures, abstracters rather than wallowers; one might even say digital rather than analogue beings. We try to make permanent that which we know can never be permanent, namely our memories of experiences of places, persons, objects and events. Rather than relying on memory and intensity of observation we would rather record a scene and wait till we get home to look at the photographs or the videotape. And this is becoming an attitude which is increasingly pervasive in all of life's activities. Don't bother to experience it now, record it for later. Photocopy it, tape it, timeshift it. File it, hoard it, forget about it, move on. But at least we can say that we have been there.

Throughout our lives we record our appearances and activities in photographs and on movie film or videotape and audiotape. Since the birth of photography and of the early cinema it has become unthinkable that major events - expeditions, wars, ceremonies - should not be recorded in this way. A wedding is scarcely felt to have occurred and been legitimised unless the photographer has captured it, and now there is a feeling of disappointment unless Uncle Dave brings along his camcorder too. In time perhaps, we will demand the ability to recreate the event in 3D holography, or as a high definition graphical simulation in virtual reality. Once again, it is the conversion of experience into information; passion into binary digits. There is nothing wrong in all this - except narcissism and a blunting of our habits of observation and memory. Our memory is spared the clutter, and what was an amorphous changing experience floating precariously, once-and-once-only, on the flux of time becomes crystallised, fossilised, into selected images, which with luck we may remember. Sadly, we have become impatient of the repetition from which meaning may be extracted; we are too ready to move on to something else which we will find equally lacking in nutriment. The railway timetable remains unread. We assume that we can go back to it later, if we need to. Rarely do we go back, however. Malabsorption syndrome again.

We seem over-anxious to convert our existence into an unchangeable indestructible World 3 record. We consume and document experiences rather than enjoy them from the inside, as it were, chewing over them and redigesting them years later. To borrow the terminology of Erich Fromm, we operate more in the having mode than the being mode. The more we document the less we want to examine the documents. The more books we buy the less we look at the old ones. We listen to the latest record for a few days and then hardly ever again. We cannot be bothered to read that journal article now so we photocopy it, file it, and never do read it; similar is the fate of the videotaped time-shifted television programme. It is yet another sub-species of Dürrenmatt's Absent Lemur. We allay our informational anxiety by checking off totally empty non-experiences.

If we react to the world in the Wolfean way our feelings are much different; if we look at the world from the point of view of our deep and genuine life interests and ambitions it is possible to have a much closer relationship with the physical world so that it becomes a personal possession in a deeper sense. Instead of feeling that one has to possess it or classify it or merely travel about in it, the physical world, and especially the geographical environment can provide a strong feeling of permanence and of personal meaning and value.

The awareness of the strangeness that anything should exist is, on the face of it, a pointless and redundant observation, but it can be a spur to a deeper sensitivity. When we forget how strange being alive actually is, even though paradoxically it is the most familiar condition of all, we are liable to lapse into a kind of sleepwalking existence, the sort of state that Gurdjieff warned against. John Eccles has written: 'Is it not true that the most common of our experiences are accepted without any appreciation of their tremendous mystery ? Are we not still like children in our outlook on our experiences of conscious life, accepting them and only rarely pausing to contemplate and appreciate the wonder of conscious experiences?'[15]. Attention!

Most of us will have known moments when our environment has taken on a new quality, moments of hyperaesthetic awareness imbued with feelings of sacredness and permanence. Alcohol or falling in love may induce such states, but the causation can be less tangible. Such moments are accepted for themselves, without any conventional aesthetic evaluation or classification. Moments as banal as when Proust wrote of savouring the odour emanating from the public lavatories on the Champs Elysées[16]. Although uncommon, such moments are not exactly rare, and are typically triggered by certain World 1 or World 3 stimuli. Works of art, perhaps most notably music, are frequent triggers. We might find such moments occur on hot summer days (like on Goethe's famous 'Italian journey'), at the start of a holiday, or while we are at a place of acclaimed beauty, but surprisingly they can occur in settings which are far from beautiful. It is hard to know whether something in the surroundings triggers the ecstatic state, whether our thoughts lead to a mood so that what is perceived seems more beautiful than usual, or whether there is mutual feedback between the two. A heightened arousal and expectation and a positive mood can affect one's reactions to the world to an exaggerated degree. The result is that we are put back directly in contact with World 1 with an immediacy forgotten since childhood.

The nature of the experience has been described by many writers. Among the most important of them are Abraham Maslow with his 'peak experiences'; James Joyce, who called such memorable - but in a sense trivial - moments 'epiphanies'; Wordsworth, with his famous 'spots of time'; John Cowper Powys, who depicted many such moments both real (autobiographical) and fictional; Marion Milner, alias Joanna Field, who described several such experiences and some very Wolfean cravings for everything in her work of self-exploration called *A Life Of One's Own*; and Marcel Proust, who was stimulated by the specific process known as involuntary memory. Many autobiographies contain references to ecstasies and other moments of self-awareness, often recalled from childhood and adolescence. They are undoubtedly highly significant events in the lives of many people.

A good example of a peak experience, or what Aldous Huxley would call a feeling of 'all rightness', is given in Lawrence Weschler's biography of the Californian painter Robert Irwin. Irwin had just flown back from Japan and arrived home at midnight, expecting to sleep for the next two days, but he found that he was so 'jagged and hyper' that he could not sleep. Instead he cruised around the Los Angeles freeway system in the middle of the night, stopping for Cokes and hamburgers.

> 'I was driving over Mulholland Pass on the San Diego freeway, you know, middle of nowhere at about two o'clock in the morning, when I just got like these waves - literally. I mean I never had a feeling quite like it - just waves of well-being. Just tingling. It's like I really knew who I was, who I am'[17].

According to Abraham Maslow, who 'discovered' peak experiences, the 'peak experiences of pure delight' enjoyed by his subjects were 'among the ultimate goals of living and the ultimate validations and justifications for it'[18]. From the point of view of pondering one's being alive in the informational vastness of the world it is interesting to look at some of the situations and stimuli that trigger these kinds of experiences, and they illustrate one way in which we can obtain spiritual nourishment directly from World 1. Two of the most relevant authors here are John Cowper Powys and Marcel Proust.

A couple of decades or so ago Powys, for long ignored, became something of a cult figure, partly perhaps because of his earth mysticism and partly because of the reprinting of much of his vast literary output by the Village Press. His two most substantial works are his *Autobiography* (described by Kenneth Hopkins as the greatest autobiography in the English language[19]), and the novel *A Glastonbury Romance*. Throughout most of his works there are gems of observation of what it is like to be alive, and these are usually descriptions of scenes which ecstatically portray a sense of place and of 'rightness' in the natural world. He calls these moments 'vignettes of memory', and though they are similar to Proust's moments of involuntary memory, they are tinged with an earthier and more mystical kind of longing.

Powys claims that: 'There are moments in almost everyone's life when events occur in a special and curious manner that seems to separate that fragment of time from all other fragments'[20]. One of Powys's obsessions is with the 'look' that things have, that peculiar sense of 'isness' which becomes most obvious under certain conditions of light and weather, and during certain moods of the observer. It is a type of perception which is also more prevalent during childhood. There is something slightly frightening or sinister about the visual form of many things, when experienced as 'aesthetic frights', but for Powys they are usually a source of mystical exhilaration. So for example in his *Confessions* he refers to how 'the peculiar and special look of a grassy bank against the sky' thrills him[21]. In Popperian terminology this is the intimate interaction between Worlds 1 and 2, an enmeshing of mind in the physical world as - since childhood - we had forgotten it could be. Powys was surprised that there was no recognised name for such moments of delight, actual or remembered. He refers to Wordsworth's 'pleasure which there is in life itself' and specific sensations such as that of a feeling of freshness in the air, but rightly says that there are no words to describe 'the continuity of sense-impressions which are flowing over us all the while and receding from us all the while'[22]. In other words the very feeling of being alive.

For Powys the triggers were usually simple, natural, or even childish things, often those things which are conventionally held to be the very opposite of aesthetic. Even the ugliest sight is a symbol of existence and may act as a surprising reminder that one is alive, a fact which in its obviousness we may have forgotten among the distractions of 'living'. It is part of the interconnected informational matrix of the world and thereby - to the appropriately tuned mind - it becomes just as sacred as everything else. To others of course it is as uninteresting as everything else.

Proust was the supreme introspective novelist and he described ecstasies over familiar and commonplace scenes, and memories activated by the observation of minutiae. Unlike Wolfe, who was exhausted and driven to distraction by the elusive detail and 'isness' of the world, and unlike most adults, who simply ignore it, Proust would seem to have found a way of directly absorbing, digesting and benefiting from World 1. The Proustian memory or involuntary memory contributes a strong sense of being alive, of being oneself. Esther Salaman believes that the experience of involuntary memory is universal[23] and I suspect for many people it occurs with great frequency, but few have been so obsessed with it as Proust, who ironically chose to detach himself from the so-called real world of the Parisian society which he described in order to recreate that world in fiction, in World 3. Involuntary memories are often very vivid because, being of trivial things, they have not been mulled over and distorted down the years; they are still fresh, having resisted the impersonalisation of classification or of being otherwise attenuated by the medium of language. It is the World 1 - World 2 interaction again in almost animal intensity.

Proust's triggers are well-known: dunking a madeleine in camomile tea; stepping on uneven flagstones; hearing the sound of a spoon against a plate. Such banal events are capable of releasing a whole flood of emotions and memories as though they somehow encoded them, for as Margaret Mein has commented of Proust and Nerval: '... memory and emotion attach themselves to the apparently trivial and to the periphery of human experience'[24], rather than to what might be described as central consciousness. This hints at a technique for creating, albeit erratically, one's very own personal world of special places and objects.

Once one begins to feel deeply in this way, then questions concerning the strangeness of existence soon arise. Questions about the meaning of existence suddenly become overlaid mentally on to images of places and scenes, as I described in Chapter 2 when talking about Waterloo Station. Soon one may begin to ask those irritatingly fundamental questions like: Why do things have to be the way they are? Why do they exist at all? But this questioning is done in a new light of personal feeling. One starts to marvel, as did Dorothy Richardson, at the simplest, most trivial things in life. All the more spectacular things follow. As John Rosenberg records in his biography of Dorothy Richardson:

'The existence of quite hackneyed objects - a bar of soap, a scrap of linoleum refracting the light - would at times strike her as almost miraculous, harking back to her own childhood wonder that anything at all could exist'[25].

Or:

'It was 1957, and she was in her eighty-fourth year. On a fine afternoon when Rose came to visit her, she led the way out of the house - not into the neatly laid-out garden but into the wilder little patch of kitchen garden, to sit by a compost heap; and suddenly, in exactly her old tone of remarking that something was good, she exclaimed, probably for the last time in her life, on what a miracle it was that anything existed, and how beautiful the world was, as she gestured round this little wilderness surrounding the compost heap'[26].

This is the aesthetic peak experience, and it is the very opposite of 'informational malabsorption syndrome' - and admittedly impractical on a regular basis. It seems that an ability to have such experiences and to find wonder in the world is a major ingredient for a sense of inquisitiveness and subsequent creativity, and a force for motivating oneself.

There is not, when all said and done, a great deal that one can do to capture or possess World 1. Any explanation, exploration or possession of the physical realm, and any meaning which may be attached to it, whether satisfactory and convincing or not, is entirely subjective and lies within the mind, which is where we turn to next.

6. The Universe Within

The least amenable to study of Popper's Worlds is undoubtedly World 2, the realm of the mind and of all inner, subjective experiences. There is not too much that can be said about this in the present context, and therefore this chapter will be a short one. Quite where mind is located, and whether it is synonymous with brain or not, is not crucial to the Popperian model, but its elusiveness does not make its study any easier. It is perhaps necessary to emphasise, although it is surely obvious, that everything that happens that you are aware of - and much that you are not aware of - also happens in your mind. During your lifetime your mind is your window on the universe; without your mind the universe could still exist, but as far as you are concerned there would be nothing. Obvious though this is, it is supremely important. Though consciousnesses are two a penny, each one is unique because it can only be experienced from within, the microcosmic window on the macrocosm, and cannot be accessed from outside.

We have come to take it for granted in Western society that the development of the individual, and the individual's mind, is a desirable goal, while recognising the side effects that this emphasis can have. Not all societies cherish this promotion of the individual as an end in itself, and oriental societies look much more to group interests and satisfactions[1]. Abraham Maslow, guru of individual self-actualisation, tried towards the end of his life to define what a 'high synergy society' might be - something like that described in Aldous Huxley's *Island* perhaps - in which everyone would self-actualise in such a way that they could develop maximally as individuals but in so doing help to 'actualise' others.

The self-actualising society is a desirable goal, but it is utopian in the sense that it is as far away from fulfilment as ever. It can perhaps follow from the more general self-fulfilment of individual members of society; individual satisfaction probably has to be achieved first. Though the individual has a commitment to society at large he has to decide what he is going to do with his own life, and a very great part of that problem lies in deciding what are going to be the important contents of his mind, what his information input is going to be, and what his territory will be. This assumes that he is going to try and live an authentic existence rather than one dominated by fads and fashions, facile social pressures, socioeconomic anxiety or suburban conformism, and that he will not succumb to passivity, lethargy or easy fatalism. To individuate, to use the Jungian term, is to invite isolation and rejection by society and to carry the world on one's shoulders[2]. It can be a great burden - it means staring mortality, inadequacy and impermanence in the face - but it can also be a road to great happiness. Only a few can live this way, 'making' - according to Heidegger and quoted by A. J. Ayer - 'the prospect of death a spur to their self-realization'[3]. Without individual 'realisation', a happy society is unlikely.

So, once again, what should one put in World2? Man cannot absorb all the information there is about the universe, but throughout his life he is working at the interrelationships between the outside world and his mind. What takes place in the carving of an authentic personality is a core of something unique and vital but also a large contribution from that which is common to the outside world, and common also to the human psyche - in effect, common knowledge, and also common emotions, common hang-ups, and common defects. Carving the unique part is an aspect of Jungian individuation: this is increasingly important, for 'resistance to the organized mass can be effected only by the man who is as well organized in his individuality as the mass itself'[4]. How to be true to oneself, without knowing what that is supposed to be, and while bombarded with the products of the mass media: that is quite a challenge. But we all do it effortlessly and, in a sense, we are all authentic, even if aspects of our behaviour are not.

Norton, in his study of *Montaigne and the Introspective Mind* wrote: 'The whole man is one who faces the reality of an inner and outer existence ... To become whole is to achieve, then, a reconciliation of the inner and outer man'[5]. In the present context this means not just a rapprochement between the conscious and unconscious levels of the mind, but with everything outside in Worlds 1 and 3 as well. As Norton says, individuation is 'the only valid way for man to live his life, for it is the path by which he strives to become what in fact he is'[6]. To develop in this way involves becoming in a sense spiritual. 'Instead of fleeing from realities and shutting himself up in an abstract world, a spiritual man is constantly facing up to it'[7]. Pleasure comes from a feeling of being able to cope with the environment, and part of that is the information environment.

In Wolfean terms, the reality to be faced up to and successfully grappled with is the entire world as experienced. In practical terms it means interpreting the outside world in a special, personal way. An example of this approach is provided by a quotation from Goethe which Edward Hopper used to carry in his wallet:

> 'The beginning and end of all literary activity is the reproduction of the world that surrounds me by means of the world that is in me, all things being grasped, related, recreated, moulded and reconstructed in a personal form and an original manner'[8].

Few have the talent of Goethe, or Hopper, or even a fraction of it, but the process operates to a greater or lesser extent in all of us. In all cases, though, the currency with which our minds operate is information. The Wolfean problem is that of cramming everything in the billions of cubic miles of the universe - throughout eternal time - in the form of information, into a few hundred cubic centimetres inside the skull, and of then being able to review and enjoy these brain contents from some kind of homuncular control room or viewing gallery, continuously and simultaneously. This seems to be impossible, within the time constraints imposed, at most a few decades, demanding as it does some very peculiar features of those 1400 or so grams of brain tissue. While it is true that, per unit volume, the human brain is the most complex and information-rich domain in the universe (the most 'eccentric space' to use Robert Harbison's phrase), there must be limits to its capacity. External information sources are proliferating and there is no evidence that the brain's storage capacity has increased significantly during recorded history. It seems obvious that the universe at large must contain many times more items of data than can exist within the cranium of one man.

There are arguments against this. One may claim that the mind has no physical basis, that thought is not subject to the restrictions of space and time. This is a tricky one. More useful is the notion that most of the matter in the universe is not intelligent in the way that we usually think of the word, whereas mind has a tremendous ability to conceptualise, to store generalities and to throw away the details. One can, for example, think of the entire universe containing myriads of atoms, in a single moment and with little mental effort. One can, in a sense, capture the whole universe using a relatively small number of neurons or brain circuits or whatever the physical basis of thought eventually turns out to be - if it has one. It is all a matter of detail of course. Conceptualising in this way is economical of brain space but it does not leave us - or Thomas Wolfe - very satisfied either. Curiously, it has been estimated that the number of possible interconnections between all the brain cells exceeds the number of atoms in the universe, so there may yet be hope for the really dedicated Wolfean. But we need to know about the contents of other minds too.

What, then, is the brain's capacity ? Logically, there would seem to be a limit. No one knows for sure, because we do not know how thought is processed, how many neurons are needed per thought, whether they are re-usable or tied down by old memories, or how neurological architecture is used to encode memories. Some recent work suggests that temporal coding of nerve impulses is used for encoding information in the brain, so that the memory capacity is phenomenally greater than a mere neuron-count would suggest. Each neuron can receive inputs from as many as 10,000 other neurons[9]. Estimates of the number of neurons vary between 15 and 100 billion, with nervous electrical impulses travelling at between 2 and 200 miles per hour[10, 11]. Taylor[12] puts the number of synapses (inter-neuronal junctions), at 10^{14} while figures for lifetime memory storage range from 10^{11} to 2.8×10^{20} bits. Elizabeth Loftus[13] thinks that larger memory will mean less efficiency and more errors, so that old memories are relegated to 'rear dusty mental files' (where?) and 'only the memories that are biologically useful or that have personal value and interest need stay alive and active'. Boulding[14] puts brain capacity at 2 to the power of 10 billion bits, assuming 15 billion neurons. To write out this number at the rate of one digit per second would take 90 years; if some unlucky person had to do this would he or she then run out of brain space? It seems pretty unlikely, since the brain can work as a kind of operating system rather than just a memory store. Rucker[15] puts the number of possible mind states, whatever that means, at one gigaplex, or ten to the billionth.

These sort of approaches strike me as dubious. No one has ever run out of brain capacity - except perhaps in severe degenerative organic brain diseases. It just doesn't work like that, and an efficient memory is arguably more useful than one that is merely huge. The examples of famous memory men throughout history have shown not the slightest hint of a ceiling to memory capacity: mnemonists like Shereshevskii, intensively studied by Luria, or Ben Jonson, who could repeat everything he had ever written and recite whole books by heart, or Themistocles who knew by name more than 20,000 citizens of Athens[16], or Professor A. C. Aitken of Edinburgh who, besides being a lightning mathematical calculator, also possessed a phenomenal memory. He once complained that learning the first one thousand digits of pi was a 'reprehensibly useless feat had it not been so easy'[17]. And perhaps it was: Hiroyuki Goto of Tokyo memorised pi to more than 42,000 decimal places. Such feats, however, represent a miniscule amount of memory storage compared with what we take in effortlessly through our senses every day. It is just that the storage is more deliberate and more accurately accessible to conscious recall.

Joseph Pelton[18] has proposed the concept of the TIUPIL, which stands for Typical Information Use Per Individual Lifetime. For a person of average lifespan, literacy and cultural exposure this works out at about 650 million words or 20 billion bits of linguistic information. Ian Pearson, of British Telecom, estimates that over an 80-year lifespan we process 10 terabytes of data[19]. A terabyte is a million million (10^{12}) bytes. Large - and meaningless - though such figures are they compare favourably with the capacity of modern telecommunications and computing equipment. As Shereshevskii found, and as Jorge Luis Borges once exploited in a story, being unable to forget is a tremendous burden, but no one has ever reached the point when no further information could be absorbed by the mind without pushing out existing memories. This would be the Sherlock Holmes view of memory, and it has no substantive basis. The mind seems not to work like that. It is not a library of finite size in which books have to be withdrawn to make room for new accessions. (At least it might be, but the building is vastly greater than the number of books that will ever have to be stored.) Rather, it appears to be a process with more or less competence at storing and retrieving information; the problems are not with the capacity but with the quality of the original input (in terms of observational accuracy), the indexing at the time of acquisition, and with the output and access mechanisms.

We do not yet know whether thought itself is entirely describable in terms of physical events and whether memory is chemical or electrical in nature, or indeed whether at the microscopic level concerned the two are synonymous. We are used to telephone network or computer analogies of brain mechanisms and recent ideas in the fields of artificial intelligence and virtual reality simulation offer further suggestions, but we do not really know. A more adventurous model of the brain is that based on the hologram, in which all information is stored throughout the cerebral cortex, but this analogy is as inadequate as the others, and is only valid up to a point. Our models for mental activity are hobbled by the technologies familiar to us, in much the same way that what we know and how we know it are limited and dictated by the nature of mind itself and the properties of our sensory perceptual input devices - eyes, ears, skin, etc. - and from which it is more than a little difficult to escape. We do not know comprehensively how memory is organised and stored, how thoughts are created and passed over, how non-conscious bodily functions can sometimes be influenced consciously, what the unconscious mind is and what the nature is of the control gateway to and from consciousness, what the mind knows of the needs and contents on either side of that gateway. In short, despite intensive research in the neurosciences, we are profoundly ignorant of the nature of mental processes. There are two main reasons for this: conceptual or philosophical reasons in that it is difficult to think about thinking and we are too enmeshed in traditional approaches to mind-brain interactions to be able to assess the problem properly; and technological reasons, by which I mean that the brain is so constructed as to be extremely difficult to examine from the outside. Introspection and the describing of subjective states have for most of the 20th century been scientifically taboo, but are now beginning to emerge into respectability. Techniques such as electroencephalography, tomography and autoradiography have enabled us to detect the presence and location of physical events which apparently correlate with mental activity, but we still lack a 'cerebroscope' which could directly monitor thoughts - and for this we should be grateful. Research is, however, pursuing this approach, with the long term goal of direct mind-computer interactions. The Wolfean science fiction scenario would be of microchip implants which would permit rapid scanning and retrieval of knowledge or memories, as we shall see later.

For the time being, we do not know in any general sense where particular thoughts, memories or emotions are located, or where the pinpoint focus of consciousness is situated - if indeed it is localised. So far, thought has not been precisely linked with any material physical substrate, but research is getting closer all the time. The evidence has often been conflicting, from early experiments by Wilder Penfield suggesting that detailed memories are located in precise locations right through to other work indicative of a spread of memories across the brain, rather in the manner of the image on a hologram. Howard Gardner suggests that the frontal lobes are a likely candidate for the location of 'consciousness'[20], but the evidence is meagre. Areas like the hippocampus and temporal lobes seem to have roles in the release of memories and emotions, and the amygdala appears to tinge memories with emotional affect, thus improving the chances of their recall. Conversely, Professor John Lorber of the University of Sheffield has found, from studying brain scans of patients with hydrocephalus[21], that there was little correlation between mental activity and the mass of the cerebral cortex. Some people, it seems, like Pooh Bear, can perform with amazingly little brain. David Lorimer[22] has reviewed the intriguing possibility that the brain is merely a kind of transceiver and that mind is located elsewhere outside of space-time altogether, and is thus non-material. This would be a basis for an explanation of paranormal experiences, which presumably demand properties of mind that defy the known physical laws of matter and energy. Further intriguing possibilities are that other parts of the body can 'think', for example, the nephron, the basic functional unit of the kidney, or blood cells, or the acid-secreting parietal cells of the stomach[23], even that insulin has a role to play. The whereabouts of World 2 are more than a little mysterious.

Much of our mental functioning goes on without our awareness of it, to the extent that we might hesitate to call it thinking, yet all the time we are awake we have some sort of awareness of things going on outside or within. 'I', the sense of self, is like a monitor or filter, a detector or sensor on the surface of the deep ocean that is the mind. This state of being, consciousness, is notoriously difficult to describe although we all know exactly how it feels. We have a continuously dynamic highlight of consciousness, a focussing of thought and perception that is ever changing while around it is a penumbra of half-formed thoughts. Beyond is the realm labelled 'currently unavailable'. We may feel that we have too little consciousness for the size of our brains, too small a visual display unit on which to examine the contents of the computer, and (pun intended) too few 'windows' to point at and click on at any one time. Or, in the metaphor of the year 1911, when Evelyn Underhill's *Mysticism* was originally published:

> 'It is as if one telegraph operator were placed in charge of a multitude of lines: all may be in action, but he can only attend to one at a time. In popular language there is not enough consciousness to go round'[24].

This is part of the reason for Wolfe's problem. In order to think, the subject of thought has to be brought within the area of focus, but how we dredge up thoughts or the precursors of thoughts is not known. Although we imagine that we can think consciously, the process is actually carried out elsewhere, out of sight or - indeed - out of mind, and we are presented instead with a kind of screen display; the thinking process itself remains hidden. So much of our mental activity seems to be controlled from somewhere which we recognise as a vital core of our being, and yet one which we have never directly encountered. Most of our thoughts and our bodily control processes lie completely outside the scope of volition (yogic and biofeedback techniques notwithstanding); they are as involuntary as a knee jerk. Both the unconscious mind that all this represents, and the homunculus-like whatever-it-is that watches the VDU, are parts of Popper's World 2.

So a crucial difficulty with World 2 is that not only is most of it inaccessible at any one time, but that it operates outside our control: 'one does one's thinking before one knows what one is going to think about ... thinking, then, is not conscious'[25]. In mental arithmetic, for example, the processing is as hidden and mysterious as it is using a pocket calculator. Only the result flashes up on the little liquid crystal display screens of the mind.

In some mysterious way the visual display unit is alerted only to what we need to know. The unconscious mind somehow senses that which is significant and pertinent, and presents it to us: 'Somehow the brain works by cutting out the irrelevance all the time' [26]. The unconscious, by way of a backwards analogy, is like one of those Web personal assistants or agents that knows our interests and goes off to look for things that we might want to know about, and informs us at just the right moment. So in fact consciousness is only a tiny part of mental activity. Julian Jaynes has likened it to directing a flashlight around a darkened room. What we see is illuminated so that we tend to conclude that there is light everywhere; similarly 'consciousness can seem to pervade all mentality when actually it does not'[27].

We can even carry on this sort of processing for long periods of time without the unconscious mind bothering to tell us. A dramatic example of this is quoted by Guy Murchie, concerning the pianist Arthur Rubenstein, who told an interviewer: 'At breakfast I might pass a Brahms symphony in my head. Then I am called to the phone, and half an hour later I find it's been going on all the time and I am in the third movement'[28]. Daniel C. Dennett, referring to Lashley's comment that 'no activity of the mind is ever conscious' asks:

'what is consciousness for, if perfectly unconscious, indeed subjectless, information processing is in principle capable of achieving all the ends for which conscious minds were supposed to exist?'[29].

So much escapes us - for now, at least. Ernest R. Hilgard has written: 'The unity of consciousness is illusory. Man does more than one thing at a time - all the time - and the conscious representation of these actions is never complete'[30].

It seems likely that what we experience or know about is actually a minute proportion of what our brain handles, and for our sanity this has to be so. If we had to consciously deal with everything we needed to we would start to break down within seconds. Something like this happens when the 'doors of perception' are opened during psychedelic drug experiences, when the normal filters are chemically dissolved. Kornhuber estimates that the information flow through the peripheral sensory channels is in the order of 10^5 bits per second while the flow of conscious information is only about 10 bits per second. 'Thus', he comments, 'the wisdom of the body is broader than the wisdom of our conscious mind'[31].

The Wolfean problem is especially acute and tantalisingly poignant because of the architecture of mind. There is no index, plan, or catalogue of mind contents which can be browsed through or glanced over: '... we cannot be all of ourselves all at once. The narrow light beams of perception and of recollection illuminate the present and the past in vivid fragments'[32]. And yet, as an information storage and retrieval device, the mind is extraordinarily efficient. We just go to the thought we require - unless blocked by stage fright or repressed memories - without the slightest inkling of how we do it and even without being aware that we are doing it. Words just come, thoughts just go. Where they come from and where they go back to is a mystery. We do not know their address. They are retrieved and re-filed effortlessly, by multiple indexing parameters. Occasionally, for no obvious reason, they fail, when we 'forget to remember' something (typically someone's name as we are introduced to them), or when we experience the comment provoking and irritating tip-of-the-tongue sensation. Generally, the pathways between the unconscious and conscious aspects of the mind are astonishingly efficient in their own way and rarely fail to respond to our most excessive demands.

Given the incompatibility of the intrinsic qualities of the human mind with the Wolfean ambition, we can legitimately ask, once again, what should we try and input? We recognise that the mere ability to remember or to mentally process may be pathological, as in the idiot savant with a subject specific supernormal memory, or a 'grand calculateur'. What is the use of an ability like that of Zerah Colburn of Vermont, who could factorise any number up to one million instantly; or those abilities demonstrated by the character Raymond Babbitt, played by Dustin Hoffman in the film *Rain Man*; or like cases of the savant syndrome reviewed by Darold Treffert[33, 34]? We may ask, is there any point in being a 'trivia freak' or an 'information junkie' like a student described by Elizabeth Loftus[35] who memorised facts about America, such as the congressional districts, election results, or city populations. Children and adolescents often like to learn such statistics, as we have noted, akin to trainspotting. This desire for concrete, reassuring information about the world gives a type of satisfaction rarely found again later in life. Learning this sort of thing probably does no harm except that these facts are often inaccurate, out of date, and only of parochial value and applicability. We can use them to impress, to show off, perhaps as a substitute for a body of in-depth and well-integrated knowledge which we lack, or as a compensation for not being smart enough to get by without having to absorb mere facts. Such items form part of that ill-defined background to our lives which goes by the name of general knowledge, a background which ironically seems to be diminishing in extent and seriousness and solidity as the popularity of quiz shows, competitions in magazines, and games like Trivial Pursuit increases. There is an analogy here with the difference between knowing discrete facts and the deeply ingrained knowledge that Michael Polanyi called the tacit dimension, those skills and types of understanding which are so fundamental to our being that we scarcely realise we have them. The question of why we should bother to learn anything at all when books or computers or experts can handle it all so much more efficiently is a question about our personal design.

One of the answers is that, though we cannot in any sense possess the world, the acquisition of knowledge helps us to recreate the world according to our own special needs and circumstances, and according to the peculiarities of our own personality and subjective modes of thought. Colin Wilson asks the very reasonable question: why does the brain bother to store every trivial memory, since most of it will never be used, and it will all decompose within a few minutes of death? His partial answer is that in moments like peak experiences or in what I have called Wolfean longings various odd memories can group together to give a powerful sense of meaning. Probably this is a right hemisphere activity.

'What is so striking', he says, 'is that these memories can blend together and connect into something much bigger. The tarry smell of the sun-warmed fence is connected with the smell of grass, and an odd cold sensation that seems to be a memory of water, which in turn brings back the cold of a winter day and the sogginess of melting snow .... And at this point, it becomes difficult to pinpoint the sensations because they seem to be spreading outwards ...'[36]. This is a plausible explanation - I do not think it is a complete one - but in truth we do not know why memory is as good and bad as it is, and how the brain filters and connects. Nor can we be sure if the brain *does* store every trivial memory, or if it does, and both input and retrieval are imperfect, in fact grossly so, what is the point of this facility.

The mind, seemingly one's most sacred possession, is paradoxically anything but uniquely one's own, and to most of it we have no direct access. Large parts of it are more or less faithful copies of the outside 'real' universe and as such are shared with the rest of the population, or are properties of mind in general. Deeper down in the unconscious mind are responses common to all individuals or even common to many species, responses which are archetypal and have more to do with biochemistry and physiology than with psychology. Pre-programmed into the mind, or hard wired into the brain, according to whichever metaphor one chooses, are reactions to extreme situations like ecstasy, fear, intense pain, and imminent death, reactions involving a large biochemical component, and with features shared by most or all people. These rituals of the unconscious and of biochemistry are genetically transmitted as part of the average human condition, along with livers and kidneys and arms and legs. The classic illustration of this type of phenomenon is the calm experienced by some, possibly many, people at a time when imminent death seems inevitable and unavoidable, and when they might be expected to be suffering extreme pain and anguish. It has been speculated that this process is mediated by the group of substances called the endorphins, the brain's own inbuilt opioids, although it is not known precisely how this would work. Something of this sort may have happened on the famous occasion when David Livingstone was attacked by the lion[37]. The near death experience is a more extreme and perplexing variant.

From the Popperian point of view it is difficult to know how to regard such processes; one hesitates to include them in World 2 because they are not consciously willed events at all, but they are clearly pre-programmed and result from an informational template at some kind of genetic or physiological or biochemical level. Descartes[38] said that the mind seemed to receive some ideas from outside itself, to invent some others, and to have some that were innate. Indeed it does seem to be that this is so and that there are three corresponding levels of understanding: that of biochemistry and its associated genetic and immunological control; that of the unconscious or intuitive mind; and the conscious/self-conscious mind which is essential for giving us awareness of being alive. Only the last of these three can we deliberately do very much about.

To summarise, when we wonder about the mind, about World 2, from the Wolfean point of view we are concerned with such matters as memory, learning, attention and the perception of detail. This leads us directly to the problem of personal information overload, which contains several facets, of which some of the most important are: that the volume of published information is increasing exponentially (or maybe even asymptotically) and is far in excess of what an individual can hope to perceive, process, assimilate, and make use of; that individuals do not have a clearly defined structure of knowledge into which they can readily slot new pieces of information; that trying to assimilate information imposes a sometimes intolerable burden on the learning process and on memory, at least if we try to cope with the quantity of information now being generated; and that the focus of conscious attention and short term memory span are so small - according to conventional wisdom we cannot recall more than seven (plus or minus two) items without prior rehearsal or resort to mnemonic tricks. We may be able to go a little way beyond the unfortunate Gerald Ford, of whom it was said unkindly that he was incapable of walking and chewing gum at the same time, but certainly our window on the world is a small one.

Mental Maps

Although each of us has just that one window on the world, for everyone the view is different, and consequently the structure of the perceived world is different for each person. Thus there are some six billion World 2s currently in existence. In order for there to be mutual comprehension between them one has to make the assumption that large chunks of World 2 are widely or even universally shared, in that their content is similar and overlapping, although the experiencing of them necessarily remains separate and discrete. Exposure to World 1 and World 3 leads to the possession by individuals of a tacit groundbase of information and experience which becomes assumed as second nature and is essential for the meaningful transfer and receipt of more complex information. Language is of course a crucial part of this.

With respect to the kind of knowledge with which information science is primarily concerned, that is, World 3 knowledge, one can imagine that World 2 is an inferior, patchy version of this, with blank areas of ignorance, downright errors and misunderstandings, prejudices, obsessions, specialist knowledge, peculiarities and distortions of emphasis and so on. For an expert in a field, one would suspect that his World 2 picture would closely correspond to the World 3 model as generally accepted - however that might be derived - and perhaps also to relate reliably to World 1. This suspicion might be ill-founded. However, for someone without expertise, the picture would be very much more sketchy, or even totally empty of content. Large areas of World 2 will have no obvious correlates in Worlds 1 and 3, being the flux of transient and half-formed thoughts, the stream of consciousness, the continuous rollercoaster of minor emotions that make up so much of the mental life of any individual.

There is an interesting analogy between trying to map World 2 (which necessarily has to be done in World 3) and some of the work that has been done on the subjective perception of the environment, or on 'mental maps' as the subject is frequently called[39]. This recently fashionable area of research seems to me to be very relevant to the investigation of Popper's Worlds, for it illustrates how World 2 can be studied and mapped.

The subject really began in 1960 with the publication of a book called *The Image of the City*, by Kevin Lynch of Harvard. Lynch[40] asked sample groups of the inhabitants of three large American cities to list the features of their city that they were aware of, and to draw maps of the city. Although the inhabitants undoubtedly knew that there was a correct layout of the city, as found in reality (World 1) and in published street plans (World 3), the maps they drew were highly selective and distorted. Typically, people had a good idea of their own locality and some idea of the prominent, public, famous features of their city, usually to be found in the downtown area, but there were huge areas of ignorance and vague confusion. Their knowledge of the city was dependent upon education, economic circumstances, and mobility, among other factors. Generally, Lynch found that people observed five major types of features in their environment: landmarks, nodes, edges, paths, and districts. Analogies can be pushed too far, but I think it is easy to see how this work on the geographical aspects of World 2 also bears some relation to World 2 knowledge in general, with its errors, distortions and areas of expertise and ignorance. There is a tenuous analogy with the way in which we make associations between ideas, with the way that we recognise 'islands' or 'districts' of knowledge or of ignorance (so-called 'anomalous states of knowledge' to use Belkin's term), and with the way that we match these 'districts' when we answer questions. According to our circumstances we select, emphasise, or remain in ignorance of different subjects (districts), and perhaps have some idea of how they relate (paths). If we are concerned with a specialised field we may know of a number of significant events or major personalities, or publications or keywords (nodes) relating to that subject, or we may recognise some outstanding features which are not in fact functionally very important (landmarks), such as a first publication on a subject or a commemorative lecture saying nothing new - or in history that Alfred burnt the cakes, or in chemistry that H_2S smells of bad eggs. We may also be able to tell whether a particular fact is relevant to our present concerns: we can define subject edges. We would expect that correlation with the objective or 'official' picture of a subject would increase with one's knowledge of that subject, but this may not always be the case. As with Lynch's city dwellers there will often be a specialised subject knowledge (comparable, say, to the home neighbourhood) and a more general background of common knowledge (corresponding to a lesser familiarity with the city as a whole).

It may be of interest in passing to note the superficial similarity between Lynch's geographical work and the diagrams of relationships between scientific papers as established by co-citation analysis or 'scientography', of the sort practised by the Institute for Scientific Information in Philadelphia. These diagrams show how particular publications or authors are cited by others, and very clearly demonstrate clusters of interrelated work, the routes between them, their peripheries, and isolated communities of research work. Also striking is the similarity between Lynch's terminology, with its emphasis on navigating one's way, and the principal features of hypertext systems - which will be discussed further in Chapter 8. Simon Shum of the Department of Psychology at the University of York has reviewed the whole subject area of cognitive mapping[41] in the context of information spaces.

Since Lynch's original work, mental maps have been constructed for many cities and regions of the world and - despite some criticisms of Lynch's methodology and his interpretation of the findings - broadly similar results have been obtained. Mental maps could presumably be constructed for other subjects besides geography to reveal areas of consensus agreement - or ignorance - among sections of the population, and perhaps they would reveal some interesting prevalent misconceptions. For example, it is known that there is a widespread ignorance of simple human anatomy (the whereabouts of my liver, referred to earlier, being an instance of this). It might be possible to produce a consensus picture of what the human body is thought to look like. This would perhaps be quite odd and amusing, but it would be an example of a World 2 cognitive map. Such maps might also tell us something about the way that memory is organised, revealing for example the 'landmarks' of memory, those bizarre but unimportant details which we have already noted and which stand out across the years. They would be a step on from studies of commonplace errors, such as a recent investigation which found similarities in examination howlers in students in the UK, North America and English-speaking Africa[42].

Another possible area of investigation of consensus misconceptions would be language: words which are in some way so regularly employed in unorthodox ways that their misuse is considered normal. Included in this area might be commonly mis-spelled words (separate/seperate; Piccadilly/Picadilly; all right/alright); pairs of frequently confused words (flout/flaunt; flammable/inflammable; embarkation/disembarkation); words which are regularly (according to the dictionary) mispronounced, such as anemone, asphalt, and dachshund; and words which have acquired popular but incorrect meanings (schizophrenia to mean split personality, nubile to mean having shapely breasts, chronic to mean really bad). There is scope here for all kinds of fascinating research!

What emerges from all such studies is a discrepancy between the World 2 version of events, and the 'real' picture, out there in Worlds 1 and 3. This sort of discrepancy has been studied in many areas of science, and notably in physics. For example, Michael McCloskey[43] of Johns Hopkins University, has shown that although Newton's laws of physics are well known, many people believe that moving objects behave otherwise. In particular they seem to hold views similar to the essentially Aristotelian 'impetus theories' popular before Newton's time, and put forward by Philoponus in the 6th century and by Jean Buridan of Paris in the 14th century. There is a discrepancy between physical reality and what is intuitively believed to happen. For instance many people believe that if a man walks along carrying a heavy object which he then releases while still walking, it will fall vertically to the ground, or even take a backwards trajectory. In fact its path is approximately parabolic, the object landing some way in front of the point of release. Another widespread faulty intuition was that an object twirled around one's head on a piece of string and released would follow a curving trajectory whereas its actual path is straight, namely a tangent to the circle of orbit.

McCloskey considers that educational benefits could result from identifying such intersubjective fallacies, but states that 'studies by several investigators suggest that the intuitive ideas are difficult to modify'. He considers that 'the errors are not random but systematic'. They arise from a general, coherent theory of motion that adequately guides action in many circumstances, but ultimately is incorrect. One is reminded of Piaget's observation of consistent errors in young children's understanding of, for example, the conservation or continuity of matter. Rosalind Driver of the University of Leeds is one of several workers who have studied the alternative frameworks which people hold about various aspects of physics, biology, the concept of the earth, etc., and in a popular review[44] of the literature on children's ideas about natural phenomena notes that these are at variance with scientific theory, can persist into adulthood and are cross-cultural. She also comments on the educational consequences of a better understanding of these tenaciously held, commonsense but incorrect notions. All these erroneous beliefs inhabit an intersubjective World 2 version of events at odds with physical reality (World 1) and with orthodox theory (World 3). Though these beliefs are fundamentally incorrect their study might give us a more rounded picture of knowledge as actually possessed and used, which could be useful for sorting out problems of faulty communication between experts and laymen, for example between doctors and patients, or the myths surrounding nutrition[45], or the problems that arise because of discrepancies between our mental models of the world and the design of everyday objects, the easy operation of which so often eludes us.

The 'deviant' aspects of World 2 will become increasingly relevant to the creation of 'intelligent' information retrieval systems, and this is especially so with respect to the understanding of language. From the point of view of information retrieval a major source of variability and uncertainty in World 2 results from the sorts of associations an individual makes in response to certain words, that is, with a private sense of meaning and understanding. This is not so significant for scientific and business communities (there is not much that one can get the wrong end of the stick of about carbon tetrachloride or the Dow Jones Index, assuming that one understands them at all) but is very relevant to information retrieval in the humanities. Looking to the longer term developments in information technology even some of the more offbeat associations of words are clearly going to be important when it comes to automatic indexing of texts, machine translation, or 'intelligent' question-answering systems. At present, as we will see in the next chapter, information retrieval is primarily document retrieval, and to progress from this to retrieving relevant evaluated facts, in other words to report-generating question-answering systems, there will have to be - apart from much else - a much more subtle understanding of the use of natural language. There will have to be a more profound awareness of the subjective nature of tacit understanding, of fuzzy spreads of meaning, of comprehension by default, of the use of metaphorical analogies and of the fact, noted for instance by Umberto Eco and George Steiner, that all utterances potentially have different significances for each individual. This of course presents one of the central problems for cognitive science research.

Such cognographic studies of the subjective and everyday use of language - and of geography, physical laws, or other phenomena - cast light on the way that people actually think, as opposed to the formal structure of reality, and can thus claim to be scientifically valid as far as they go. They lead to what we might call an objective picture of subjectivity, or more accurately an intersubjective or consensus view of perceived reality. We get very used to the idea that there is a given or correct way of classifying and labelling the contents of our world, but in fact there are many, not just because of cultural and linguistic differences, but because of individual subjectivity, from what we may consider to be normal, via the syncretic or paleological thinking of the child or the 'primitive' and the novel conceptual linkings of the creative artist or scientist, to the paranoid or delusional constructs of the mentally ill. Most of these systems go unrecorded and do not have a terminology to capture them, which does not necessarily imply that they are without value. As Chiari said: 'Subjectivity can be a source of true knowledge only if it transcends the personal and the ego, which are isolating and limiting, and connects with intersubjectivity or the absolute'[46]. If some way of incorporating the known qualities of intersubjective informal understanding into more rigid knowledge structures could be achieved, it could aid the clarification of meaning when computer handling of text is involved - as in automatic indexing or machine translation, for example. If this mapping of World 2 were to be done, then the product would necessarily lie in World 3.

And it is to World 3 that we now turn in our brief tour of Popper's Worlds. The easiest way of holding the informational world at bay, of filtering it out from our minds while ensuring that nothing is lost, is to record it in a physical medium in some way, to preserve a record of our thoughts and experiences in a way which is accessible to consultation and which can be contemplated and modified by further thought. This record of our thoughts is essentially what we mean conventionally by the term 'information', and it is to this usual meaning of the so-called 'information explosion' that we must now address ourselves.

7. World 3

According to Christopher Evans, writing in *The Mighty Micro* in the late Seventies: 'The truth is that one of the main problems - perhaps *the* main problem - of the time is that our world suffers from information overload, and we can no longer handle it unaided'[1]. World 3 is the home of the conventional problem of the information explosion. So, what is the size of the problem? How do we tackle it?

The Information Explosion

Estimates of the current volume and growth of information are probably meaningless as well as inaccurate. Arguably more important is the value of information, which is notoriously difficult to determine in either monetary or semantic terms: knowing the six winning numbers of the National Lottery has a value several million pounds less after 7.30 on a Saturday evening than before; a picture is worth a thousand words; a raised eyebrow may tell us more than a 500-page report; it takes less time to recite the Lord's Prayer than to transmit a TV commercial for dogfood. Well, so what? Valuable information is information that you can make use of now. According to traditional (Shannon-Weaver) information theory, information is that which reduces uncertainty, i.e. it tells you something new. Whether that is a philosophy of life or the virtues of a pet product depends upon your immediate concerns. Where meaning and value are at stake, size doesn't matter.

Whatever figures for information growth are arrived at, there are the regrettable truths that as information productivity grows the individual become relatively (but hopefully not absolutely) more ignorant, and the more info-junk there is. Television and the tabloids so often emphasise the trivial, creating an information realm populated by fruity pseudo-facts about pseudo-personalities and pseudo-issues, part of the so-called hyperreality of Baudrillard. The more information we have, ironically, the less useful it may become. We may reject it, become alienated from it. Apart from 'the world as information' this may happen on the local scale, at work, when the burden of e-mail, the virtual in-tray, starts to overwhelm us. Quite simply, we may just not want to know about it. We may develop info-fatigue, knowledge burn-out, the symptoms of stress. As Kathleen Woodward questioned the situation:

> 'We speak of an information explosion that triggers an ever-accelerating growth of information. The process is figured as being continuously fed by positive feedback, and the production curve of information charts a constantly increasing abundance. To many, this is a utopian vision, but to others, the information explosion means violence, destruction by information fallout'[2].

The growth of literature is not necessarily the same thing as the growth of knowledge. It is not enough to have snippets of disembodied information: they must be embedded within meaningful structures and backgrounds, and they must be understood by human minds and assimilated for use, action and the growth of wisdom. Their mere collection and storage is of little value. This shows up, for example, in the growth of the Internet, a maze of hyperlinked but disorganised pieces of information. It also shows up in scientific research. As research advances so does its level of difficulty; it becomes unreadable and inaccessible to all but a few specialists. There is even a worry that eventually new knowledge will become impossible because it will take longer than a lifetime's education to reach the frontier of existing knowledge and because science at its leading edge will encompass concepts too difficult for any one mind. This scenario has been refuted effectively by Sir Peter Medawar[3], but it is illustrative of a real trend. It emphasises the need to build in contextual links so that these new concepts are approachable, and it also explains why the arcana of quantum chromodynamics or immunology or cosmology aired on the pages of *Nature* or *Science* will never make the slightest impact on all but a tiny fraction of the population. They might as well be written in Venusian.

One of the 20th century's most symbolic psychological plagues was that of alienation, the feeling of being cut off from one's roots, a feeling of personal meaninglessness and lack of control over events. The mushrooming of the volume of information is only part of the problem, and a part which may be amenable to at least partial solution by the appropriate application of the techniques of information science and technology. It may be an easier one to crack than some of the other facets of alienation, such as those stemming from undemocratic political systems, from the methods of so-called Theory X management and automated production in the workplace, and from the mass consumption of depersonalised consumer items. But still there are the information rich and the information poor, the haves and the have nots, and we must assume that those who are underprivileged in terms of wealth or education are also denied access to many sources of information. This is a situation which is likely to worsen. Jean-Marc Lévy-Leblond of the University of Nice has written of how we have had to abandon the Enlightenment dream of complete sharing of knowledge by all, and instead of the ideal of absolute knowledge 'it is a reality of relative ignorance with which we have to deal'[4]. Similarly, Jean-Pierre Dupuy has written '... ours is a world about which we pretend to have more and more *information* but which seems to us increasingly devoid of meaning'[5]. Information overload affects us all to a degree, but operates according to a kind of Matthew principle whereby those who have are given more and those who have little will have that taken away from them (Matthew xxv, 29). Ironically, it is those who already have the most information who want to know more, and it is they who suffer most from information overload. The informationally-disadvantaged carry on blithely without worrying about it. But we all need better ways of structuring the information we already have, and bolder discriminatory abilities to home in on the most useful items. Admitting the limitations on our ability to know will be an issue for the new century.

So let us, Wolfe-like, consider an attack on the shelves of the world's libraries. What is the immensity of our task? The estimates are derived in various ways and are sometimes contradictory. Never mind, the answer - even if wildly inaccurate - will be a daunting one. The number of copyrighted items is perhaps in the region of one billion, or about one item for every five people alive today, and growing at a rate of 3 per cent per year, or half as fast again as the growth in population. This equates to around two million bits per second (a million times the birth rate), or 7,000 scientific articles per day. For a child born in 1980, by the time he or she leaves college, there will be four times as much knowledge available as there was then[6]. This is all part of the acceleration of change popularised by Alvin Toffler as 'future shock'.

There have been several attempts at quantifying information growth in other ways, one of the most famous being that by Derek de Solla Price[7], who produced graphs for the growth of various kinds of literature and stated that the number of scientific articles increases ten-fold each half century, with abstracting journals tending to follow the same way. Whatever the precise figures, we cannot keep up. Bernard Lonergan[8] writes:

> 'an account of knowing cannot disregard its content, and its content is so extensive that it mocks encyclopaedias and overflows libraries; its content is so difficult that a man does well devoting his life to mastering some part of it; yet even so, its content is incomplete and subject to further additions, inadequate and subject to repeated, future revisions'.

As long ago as 1968 Harrison Bryan, Librarian at the University of Sydney, reviewed the subject, in particular Library of Congress and United Nations surveys, and came up with a growth rate of 4 per cent per annum[9]. Even earlier, in 1963, John Senders[10] estimated the number of publications stored in the world's libraries as somewhere between 75 million and 770 million - an uncertainty of a factor of ten. Assuming an average of 100,000 words per volume, five letters per word, and 12 bits per letter, the information contained in all this was between 4.6×10^{14} and 4.6×10^{15} bits, increasing at around 2×10^6 bits per second. Not very meaningful. Senders estimated that the printed material was replicated some 40 times in libraries around the world, and various estimates put the number of different volumes at 75, 220 or 490 million. That says nothing of the redundancy resulting from the duplication of information between publications. Kevin McGarry[11] in 1981 estimated that there were about 80,000 regular scientific journals in existence, a figure projected to reach 400,000 by the end of the century; this estimate already falls short of the true situation. The annual output of books is about 300,000, of which around 90,000 are in English, and at any one time about three million titles are in print. This compares with a total of approximately 30,000 titles and editions of books produced in Europe up until the time of Gutenberg, and eight million during the 19th century. By 1985 the number of documents in existence was doubling every 5 years, but by 1997 it was doubling every 9 months, with over 90 per cent of new documents now being created in electronic format. Some estimates of the growth of the Internet are given in the next chapter.

There are various ways to illustrate the growth of information: statistics in terms of bits or bytes are perhaps not very meaningful but numbers of publications are, and time elapsed for a number of publications to appear even more so. So, for example, we find that it took 32 years from 1907 for the first million papers to be recorded in Chemical Abstracts, 18 years for the second million, eight years for the third million, under four years for the fourth million, and at present the rate is almost a million papers a year. Thankfully the publication is now available on-line and on microfilm; the bound volumes occupy well over 300 feet of shelf space, and grow at the rate of about 13 feet per year.

Durack[12] has provided a highly tangible way of looking at the growth of literature. Selecting the medical literature - surely as hyperactive as any type of literature for proliferation of publications - he determined the weight of printed output as represented by Index Medicus. This publication has existed since 1879, under various titles and auspices, and indexes the biomedical literature by subject matter, author, title, and bibliographic reference. It is now issued by the National Library of Medicine, located near Washington, DC. From 1879 until the mid 1930s the weight of the publication remained steady at about 2 kilograms per year. Then, a phase of exponential growth began, so that between 1935 and 1955 the weight doubled to 4 kilograms, by 1965 it had reached 15 kilograms, and by 1974 it had doubled again to 30 kilograms. There are factors which blur the validity of such figures, such as the trend towards multiple authorship, increased depth of indexing and increased average length of papers, but the rate of growth is none the less impressive. By 1988 the rate of growth seemed to have slowed down slightly, the weight of the publication for that year having reached 44 kilograms[13].

Some arbitrary but spectacular examples suggest that knowledge is beginning to outstrip the real world that it attempts to describe and explain. The accumulated engineering drawings for a jet aircraft may weigh more than the aircraft itself[14]; for a Boeing 747 laden with its essential documentation the weight exceeds normal maximum take-off load. It brings us back to the fundamentally Wolfean problem of hotel towels and stains on ceilings, of how much we need to know about anything, since clearly there are no limits to detail. The problem is analogous to that encountered by Benoit Mandelbrot, contemplating what it means to measure the length of the British coastline. Use a four-mile-to-the-inch road atlas and you get one result, measure it on Ordnance Survey Landranger series maps and you get a larger figure, pace round every headland and harbour and you get a still larger one. Then if you try to track around every pebble on the seashore, every shifting grain of sand, every molecule of silicon dioxide, the result becomes impossibly large and meaningless. The World 3 representation begins to exceed World 1 reality, which on the face of it seems ridiculous. Mathematically this is a question of fractal geometry, a concept which is very relevant to the way that the Wolfean craving encounters ever more detailed layers of incompleteness of description. We finish up with a map at a larger scale than the territory it represents, a Borgesian absurdity. There has to be a more meaningful, in-between, human scale. So it is with our handling of information - we have to learn to skip some of the detail, to conceptualise, to be prepared to gloss over.

The first scientific journal was the Royal Society's *Philosophical Transactions* which appeared in 1665, and its creation transformed the science of the time because it meant that new discoveries could be published rapidly without the need to present sufficient information to fill a book[15]. In the early days there was no need for indexes, but by the 18th century indexes were necessary, and then cumulative indexes. By 1750 there were still only ten scientific journals. We have come a long way since then; by 1978 Lancaster estimated that there were approximately 50,000 science and technology journal titles published worldwide, with an annual growth rate 4 per cent[16]. UNESCO publishes an international listing of scientific and social science periodicals, and this now comprises almost half a million titles. The British Library subscribes to fewer than 20,000 of these[17], which is worrying, although it can borrow from other libraries when necessary. In the area of chemistry alone, Chemical Abstracts covers 9,000 publications, to feed its current total of over fifteen million references.

The problem of the growth of information is not restricted to learned medical and scientific journals. Despite the costs of publishing, books continue to be produced in large numbers. In 1977 the Library of Congress in Washington housed over 18,000,000 books and pamphlets[18]; now there are a total of more than 108 million catalogued items including manuscripts, microfilms, maps, prints and records[19], and the collection is growing by more than seven million items per year. The contents of the Library of Congress have been estimated as equalling some 16 terabytes[20].   The British Library holds about 18 million books. James Martin, author of *The Wired Society*[12], claims that by the year 2040 there will be 200 million different books, requiring some 5,000 miles of shelves and a card catalogue (a now strangely anachronistic device) with three quarters of a million drawers. This would surely be more than enough to drive a Thomas Wolfe to despair. The problem is a worldwide one of course: the Lenin Library in Moscow has nearly 12 million books and, as might be expected, Japan suffers from information overload too. In Japan there are some 125 daily newspapers (compared with over 1,600 in the USA) which sell a total of 68 million copies, some 28,000 scientific and journal titles, and - as a direct symptom of the problem - a 10 per cent annual growth rate in new book and article titles[21] related to the study of information. Many similar statistics could be quoted. Less impressive are the statistics which show just how small a percentage of scientific articles is actually read or cited. Way back in 1958 an American study found that only a half of one per cent of articles published in chemistry journals are read by any one chemist, while in 1993 French researchers estimated that nine tenths of primary journal articles do not have a single reader, and that probably 25-50 per cent of journal articles are never cited subsequently[17]. More recently, Sidney Redner of Boston University has found that of scientific papers published between 1981 and 1997, 47 per cent were never again referred to in the scientific literature[22].

Such figures force us to look at ways of making data more manageable, useful and digestible. Substituting graphics terminals or microform as an alternative to print materials cuts down on storage, but does not help the consumption of information by man. More realistically, ways have to be considered of pruning the volume of information that needs to be attacked, by providing simplified overviews of subject areas or by offering ways of reliably discarding material of no interest. Editorial criteria for controlling what is published have the benefits of quality control and the demerits of censorship, but are essential. Naturally, as the body of literature grows, so individuals can only absorb the same amount (although modern man absorbs astonishingly more than his ancestors did), and this means being more selective in choosing what is read or otherwise input. We fast forward and we channel surf, and the more manically we do so, the less it means. Attention deficit disorder is truly the symbolic affliction of our age. Using efficient alerting and retrieval techniques the intake of useful information need not suffer greatly, but it is hard work trying to keep up, and in the context of both total and specialised information published we all become relatively more ignorant with respect to the total output. So specialisation increases and new interdisciplinary hybrid subjects with long names are created, ever more rarified journals are designed accordingly, and with them may come feelings of alienation and overall meaninglessness. There is only time to stab at the most important literature; it is all rather unsatisfactory. The people who should be best informed, the leaders of government and industry, often have the most superficial acquaintance of all with what they ought to know.

The acquisition of an overall grasp of knowledge thus becomes ever more important, while retaining one or more specialisations. Unfortunately, even general knowledge is now such an enormous and rapidly changing field that it is unrealistic to assume that much of it can be retained by anyone. Constantly the rate of change accelerates. Gone are the days when one could lazily learn the names of the countries of Africa, the name of the Chancellor of the Exchequer, or that of the world's tallest building - although I am sure that many kids still try to do just that. For children of today there is a pressure to absorb the ephemera of pop and TV. Facts seem to change more rapidly, to be less stable, to have more blurred edges, and with that trend goes a loss of significance. This loss of respect or loss of stature is perhaps most obvious with news, where important issues come and go without proper resolution, mutilated into the shape and schedule of news bulletins and dressed up as attention grabbing soundbites, only to drift off into oblivion when the next story comes along.

Whatever the exact figures for information growth the conclusion is the same: recorded knowledge has far outgrown man's ability and availability of time to assimilate it and make use of it. We can perhaps learn how to be more intelligent, certainly we can improve our techniques for learning, but there is no real substitute for the hard slog of learning the facts about the world, without which intelligent manipulation and the creative cross-fertilisations that arise from comparison and analogy are likely to be of doubtful value. We each need to attain a critical mass of solid data input before these processes can begin. We will be lucky if we can get an overall grasp of the arts and sciences, of geography and history, to have a skeletal understanding of what, where, who, why and how, and to be able to select the best bits for our study and enjoyment. It is true that the growth in the volume of literature has coincided with developments in computer and communications technologies, now fused as information technology, and they can offer us some help with our problem, as we shall see, but they can only take us so far: we have to do the rest. Offloading onto storage media is fine, but we ourselves still want to know things for a variety of reasons. We want to know details, we want an overall picture, we want the profound and the trivial, we still have Wolfean cravings, all of which are difficult to shrug off onto electromechanical or optical storage devices, onto IT peripherals.

As children or teenagers we may think it is bad enough having to rote learn the things we have to - spellings, multiplication tables, foreign vocabularies - as well as those essential facts which enable us to make sense of the history and organisation of the world and all its contents. But it is ironic that as adults we cannot even keep up with information about ourselves. For there is a growth of personal information too, not just our autobiographical histories, and our collection of self-related documentation (diaries, letters, photographs, home videos), but ever more in the way of identity numbers (phone, fax, PIN numbers) and addresses, financial records, society memberships, and all the myriad facets of life in a society increasingly operating in a 'world as information'. Some may say that we are becoming a race of self-obsessed narcissists and we only have ourselves to blame. Well, maybe, but that is how it has become.

If we achieve fame we also accumulate externally produced information about ourselves which surely we ought to know about. An example of this is provided by the late Buckminster Fuller, a man ahead of his time, a true visionary and icon of 20th century technological imagination. Fuller's lasting claims to fame may well turn out to be the geodesic dome and a chemical named after him (buckminsterfullerene, because of its geodesic-like shape and in 1996 the subject of the Nobel prize for chemistry for its discoverers), and whose modernist technical jargon now sounds strangely dated, with concepts like 'synergetics', 'tensegrity' and 'Spaceship Earth'. Fuller kept a file of press cuttings and publications about himself, which characteristically he called the Dymaxion Chronofile, something which always reminds me of one of Professor Stanley Unwin's gobbledy-gook inventions. This included some 37,000 unique items since 1917, plus about 100 radio and TV broadcasts per annum[23] in his later years. Lesser mortals than Buckminster Fuller can also have personal information retrieval problems, albeit of a lesser magnitude. Let's hope that their memories or their filing skills are up to it.

Outsiders and Infopaths

For a certain type of child, a 'clever child', there is an awareness that he can achieve vastly more than is expected of him, tempting him to believe that he is a special case, able to rise above his circumstances and to escape to better things. This is a kind of development of the trainspotter attitude we encountered in Chapter 2. Given sufficient intelligence, self-awareness, the ability to absorb information like a sponge, and to be interested in most things - which are the blessings of that stage between true childhood and adolescence - the brighter than average child may make several interesting observations. Among these is the fact that in some fields he can absorb and understand far more, and far more quickly, than adults believe possible and than his parents and teachers expect of him; that there are short cuts to knowledge (wisdom or low cunning) which no one else seems to know about and which depend upon some odd and highly subjective aspects of thought and perception; and that the rate at which he is supposed to learn at school is ridiculously slow. He may therefore strike out on his own, and because of his enthusiasm and the rate at which he can progress he may conclude that omniscience can be his in a relatively short while.

This seems to have happened to Colin Wilson, surely one of the most remarkable digesters and disseminators of information in modern times, a one man knowledge industry, regarded by some as a genius and by most of the literary Establishment as some sort of contemptible charlatan. Unusual in England, he soon acquired the reputation of being an intellectual, and (unfairly) not a particularly modest one, something not generally approved of, and other reasons why he has not achieved the acclaim he deserves perhaps include his interest in sadism and in the paranormal, and the repetitiveness of the subject content of many of his books. He is not quite respectable. However, his hunger for life borders on the obsessive, on the Wolfean, but unlike Wolfe he is an expert at consuming information and repackaging it with his own stamp. For all his perceived faults, he is a symbol of modern Wolfean man: his appetite is superhuman. Since the publication of his first book, *The Outsider*, in 1956, he has written over 100 books - many of them of considerable length - plus a large number of articles, reviews, and prefaces. Kai Falkman writes of Wilson's demonic passion for work: '... he loves what he is doing, but he also feels an inner compulsion to do it; it is his duty. It is also, in the sense that it gives meaning to his life, his *life's work*, his *vitalizing activity*'[24]. In 1969, in his autobiographical *Voyage to a Beginning*, Wilson wrote:

> 'I have written twenty-two books in ten years: eight novels, seven volumes of philosophy, and various essays and studies. I have written at this speed because I felt I had too much to say, and that I would explode if I didn't get it said. I write as a dog with fleas scratches'[25].

Despite a perfunctory formal education and a series of dismal manual and clerical jobs before he achieved early success as a writer, his hunger for knowledge goes back to childhood. Since the age of 16 he has kept a daily journal of his thoughts. More recently he has written of how, during the summer holidays of 1943, when he was twelve, he started a notebook in which he hoped to summarise all the basic laws of physics, which in turn led him on to attempt the same for chemistry, astronomy, geology and biology - way beyond what was taught at school. Not satisfied with this, he decided that his book ought to include mathematics, philosophy and zoology.

> 'The original idea went on expanding until it filled seven notebooks; what began as a scheme for occupying the summer holiday turned into a task that was still unfinished eighteen months later ... My *Manual of General Science* was never finished; but the attempt turned me into a writer'[26].

The challenge of the total, of multiple possibilities, was there, perceived at an early age, stimulating and taunting the adolescent Wilson in dreary Leicester. His recognition of this challenge resulted in the crystallisation of a concept, or a character type, which he brought before the public with *The Outsider*. It was hardly a new idea. Kierkegaard among others had essentially described it with his 'introvert', but it is a type which perennially appeals: one of its more recent versions is Peter York's 'neurotic boy outsider'. So at the age of 25 Wilson was famous - and soon notorious - and labelled as one of the 'Angry Young Men'. Since then, in many books, Wilson has developed his idea of the outsider personality, aided by his interests in existential and phenomenological psychology and in particular in the development of 'third force' psychology, popularised by Abraham Maslow and Carl Rogers.

So what is the outsider and how does he concern us here? The outsider is fundamentally dissatisfied with his situation and with the restrictions on life, and cannot accept that the rules are unchangeable or unbreakable. By feeling different or apart from others and by trying to act differently he hopes to escape the mundane reality of daily life, and because of his aversion to 'ordinary life' he suffers from feelings of alienation and inadequacy. He may feel like an observer, a tourist in the land of human affairs. Actually, the outsider condition is only the extreme form of a spectrum of feelings which must occur to all people to a greater or lesser extent. By the time we have completed a long and often strange childhood we must all feel unique and separate.

The outsider asks the fundamental questions about life, about his role, about what to select from life's opportunities, which so many people apparently do not, and throughout his life he is seeking the answers. He doesn't give up the search when he grows up, and in a sense he never does grow up. For him there are no easy, ready-made solutions. Because he has an acute awareness of the transiency and preciousness of life he is peculiarly vulnerable to being overwhelmed by life's volume of activity, by information overload, and his perceptions are likely to be coloured by an almost religious sense of sacredness of everything he encounters and with a sense of duty to the world. He is aware of the total informational potential of the world, and his responsibility to it, and so he is likely to be a Wolfean, with a predictable thirst for knowledge. Wilson writes: 'The passion for knowledge replaces the need for faith, and purpose becomes an *internal drive*. In that moment, man glimpses the possibility of becoming truly human ...'[27].

Wilson himself certainly possessed this passion for knowledge. Interviewed in 1978 on the BBC radio programme *Desert Island Discs*[28] he claimed to own 15,000 records, and even in 1969 he said he had some 5,000 albums, including 300 or so complete operas, which would take two months, non-stop, to listen to. At the same time he reckoned that his private library would take ten years to read at the rate of one book per day[29]. By 1988 his book collection numbered about 30,000, as did his records and tapes[30], and with a growing library of videotapes too. He evidently collects more than he ingests.

The outsider suffers from a kind of informational wanderlust, intellectual, possessional, and sometimes geographical. This postmodern wanderlust springs from every High Street travel agents, but more significantly from every home and college and workplace, from every PC attached to a node on the Internet, and from every TV screen. It involves informational versatility, knowing as much as possible about everything, or at the very least 'checking it out', dipping one's toes into all kinds of life experiences and creative pursuits and travelling around the world with a rapidity and a frequency (and often a superficiality) which 100 years ago would have seemed both impossible and absurd. The world as oyster is no longer the privilege of just the few. The whole planet is for many quite ordinary folks well within ransacking range - for places, information, lifestyles, collectables, clothes, food, music, anything. The choice of what to do or what information to access becomes increasingly our own, and less a matter of being restricted by the imposed arbitrary conditions of birth, location, language, education, status, or economic circumstances.

With this freedom there comes choice, and with it, responsibility. For some, it is genuinely liberating, but for others it leads to the downsides of overweening ambition. Ambition is pathological and doomed to disappointment when it is merely a need for the trappings of success or for superiority; often it stems from feelings of inadequacy and inferiority. Francis Fukuyama[31] has written extensively about what he calls 'thymos', the urge for recognition, and how unhappiness arises from failure to satisfy this, and notes how the gap between desire and fulfilment constantly grows wider, and how modern consumer economies exacerbate this. And yet not to have ambition - in the Wolfean or Wilsonian outsider sense - is somehow failing in one's duty to existence. The desire for success is natural.

For most people, success means success within a single field of activity, say a business or a sport or some well-defined area of science or the arts, and the same goes for the acquisition of knowledge. For the Faustian, Wolfe-like outsider no such pedestrian ambition is anywhere near adequate, and certainly for anyone wishing to acquire what might be called wisdom, a restriction of activities to only one area of behaviour is unsatisfactory or even counterproductive. As Heraclitus remarked, to be wise one must enquire into many things. One needs to be able to see parallels and analogies, to make connections and cross-fertilisations. It has been observed by Patrick Wilson[32] that cross-disciplinary studies impose a particularly heavy informational burden on their practitioners. At present, when information overload is so serious and so few of us can glimpse an overall picture, we need divergent thinkers and generalists, synopticians and polymaths and Renaissance men, who can synthesise a world picture. In order to create such people we need to develop a wide range of interests and abilities in childhood and to delay specialisation and the scleroses of professionalism, to resist conformity and to retain a sense of awe and mystery about our predicament.

It may be that to fulfill ourselves we must have as large an appetite for life as we can, and if we are true Wolfeans we will know that the boundary conditions of life are unacceptable. Luke Rhinehart suggests that 'our deepest desire is to be multiple: to play many roles'[33] and so it is perhaps not surprising in a society characterised by pluralism, eclecticism and the fragmentation which glories in the names of postmodernism and multiculturalism, that the personality should want to go the same way, while retaining some central driving purpose and control. Perhaps this is what postmodernism really represents: the craving for all.

For most people this is not a realistic expectation, but there are people in the public eye who act as Wolfean role models for the masses, and they appear hugely attractive, because of the vicarious way in which they satisfy our lust for experience and achievement. By being hyperactive multiply talented superstars, self-driven Wilsonian outsiders, they use their creativity and public influence via the mass media to achieve something that might be seen as a fulfilment of the Wolfean urge. These are the contemporary heroes to whom many ordinary people look with admiration, sometimes with envy, figures who, for many, provide the measure of the mismatch between an ideal of self-fulfilment and an unsatisfactory day-to-day reality. The popular media are only too happy to cater for, indeed in some cases to create, this fascination with the superstar 'multiple personality'. The example that these glamour figures offer can urge one on to self-improvement; or to resentment. They remind one that anything short of multiple achievement is, for some people at least, a failure to adequately come to terms with the world, a failure of one's life challenge. Probably the most extraordinary example from the 20th century is Churchill; a more current role model of this sort is David Bowie.

Aldous Huxley, who knew more about most things than do most mortals, neatly summed up our predicament:

'Science is not enough, religion is not enough, art is not enough, politics and economics are not enough, nor is love, nor is duty, nor is action however disinterested, nor, however sublime, is contemplation. Nothing short of everything will really do'[34].

If this is so, we need to know how to efficiently access and assimilate information. The remainder of this chapter, and the following chapter, will look at some of the methods used.

Taming World 3

The organisation of World 3 (however named) has long been recognised to be a central concern of information science, and of its practically oriented predecessor library science (or more prosaically, library indexing). The best way to organise World 3 materials has been the subject of debate for as long as such materials have been systematically collected, although it is only in comparatively recent times that this has become the subject of detailed study, perhaps because it is only recently that the issue has threatened to become unmanageable. Nevertheless, we should not underestimate the size of very early collections of literature. The famous library of Alexandria, which was planned by Ptolemy I Soter and actually established and enlarged by his son Ptolemy II Philadelphus, contained over half a million scrolls, with an information content comparable to 100,000 modern books, and these were classified on 120 scrolls[35] which were the responsibility of scholars and scribes. Although Alexandria was the largest and the most famous of the ancient libraries there were other significant collections in classical times, for example at Pergamum in Asia Minor, Rome, Herculaneum, and Byzantium. During the Middle Ages libraries tended to be more diversely scattered, and became the province of monasteries and of the very rich. During this era monks began the process that we today call abstracting, the summarising of the contents of documents for a particular purpose, in this case, for authorities such as monarchs or the Vatican.

It was not until the 17th century that scientific journals as we know them first began to appear, with the advent in 1665 of *Le Journal des sçavans* from the French Academy of Sciences and the *Philosophical Transactions* of the Royal Society in London. Both of these journals carried abstracts of other publications, as did many of the hundreds of similar (but usually ephemeral) journals that sprang up across Europe during the next century. At the beginning of the 18th century it was recognised that journals were the most useful medium for the rapid dissemination of new ideas, replacing ordinary books or encyclopaedias for this purpose.

With the growth of scientific journals came an increased need for indexes and abstracts. The first scientific journals, as one might expect, tended to be universal in ambition, attempting to cover all subject areas, but as the volume of literature increased they inevitably had to become more specialised. This trend has been with us ever since. So, for example, we have the German publication popularly known as *Crell's Chemical Journal* dating from 1778, the first journal wholly devoted to chemistry, and including original articles as well as abstracts or extracts of other significant publications[36]. In the early 19th century the number of chemistry journals grew rapidly, and in 1830 the first abstracting journal devoted entirely to chemistry was introduced by Gustav Fechner in Hamburg, with the stated objective of covering the journal literature in pure chemistry with concise and accurate abstracts of the relevant scientific facts.

From such early beginnings developed the huge abstracting journals which were to play so prominent a role in mid-20th century scientific research, journals such as *Chemical Abstracts* and *Index Medicus*. By the end of the 1960s there were over 1500 abstracting and indexing journals produced worldwide reflecting the growth of the primary literature. However, the growth of that primary literature was so immense that not even the most ambitious of the abstracting services such as *Chemical Abstracts* with its monitoring of about 9,000 journals could cover all the relevant information for some subject areas. These services have been superceded by, but not yet entirely replaced by, commercial on-line databases.

In one respect the journal literature is easy to index; its contents are broken up into articles usually of only a few pages in length and of highly focussed subject matter. Using a number of descriptors, either in the form of an index or as search terms in an electronic database it is usually possible to characterise and subsequently to identify the relevant material, and in most cases an adequate abstract indicative of the contents of the article can be written without too much difficulty. For books, however, the situation is not so straightforward, because their contents are greater in length, more complex and intangible in subject matter, and because they cannot be classified by being members of a series of publications in the way that a journal issue can be cited. An abstract of necessity loses much of the information content of the original document to which it refers, and in the case of a book this loss of information is excessive to the point of being unreasonable. A book is not normally susceptible to this kind of treatment. It is a one off.

If we think of a library as being a place where we go to find books, i.e. our familiar public libraries, rather than in the specialist sense of providing storage for journals, then the needs of library classification can be seen to be quite different from those of the academic journal repository. Some of the requirements for library classifications are that they should be inclusive of all fields of knowledge, that separate subjects should be distinguished in such a way that relevant and related books can easily be found on the library shelves, that books dealing with similar topics should be located near to each other, that allowance should be made for rapidly evolving or entirely new areas of knowledge ('infinite hospitality'), and that differences between classificatory terms should be meaningful, allowing for a unique and significant distinction between items[37]. Obvious and necessary requirements though these are, they are easier to specify than to achieve.

Over the last 100 years or so classification schemes have been evolved which have tried, more or less successfully, to accommodate these requirements, and typically these schemes have made use of numerical or alphabetical coding systems to identify subject areas. The assumption has always been that it is possible to devise such systems, adequate to the demands of the era, even though 'presently, our factual knowledge, has by far outdistanced the capacities of learning and of synthesizing of any individual intellect'[38]. In other words, not only does no one person have the expert knowledge necessary to devise such a scheme in detail, but also there never will be an answer to the fantasy which Thomas Wolfe entertained in Cologne, of 'finding in a bookstore one volume that would summarize all the other books that had ever been written'[39]. A number of library classification schemes have been devised, some of the better known ones being the Dewey Decimal Classification of 1876, the Universal Decimal Classification, and the Library of Congress Classification. These all have their strengths and weaknesses; the Library of Congress scheme, for instance, reflects more the administrative policy and actual physical attributes of the book collection in the Library of Congress itself than 'a body of principle designed to respond to the epistemological complexities of the world of information today'[40], but is nevertheless extensive and powerful. Henry Evelyn Bliss was one of the first to recognise the distinction between 'natural' and 'artificial' schemes, in other words, he realised that the organisation of World 3 did not have to follow that of World 1, although it was preferable that it should. Probably the most significant development in library classification, pre-computer, was due to Shiyali Ramanarita Ranganathan (1892-1972), who devised the Colon Classification which allowed for the analysis of complex material and its description according to 'facets'[41]. This offered an escape from the rigidity of pre-established, ready-made classes, and permitted a modular and coded description to be devised which could be uniquely and accurately assigned to each book. He split the concept of classification into three layers, namely those of the ideas that literature contained, the 'verbal plane' or the words in which those ideas were expressed, and the 'notational plane', the symbolic system by which those ideas could be represented. All these developments, and others, provided ways forward from the restraints of systems such as Dewey.

The fact is that by the second half of the 20th century all the traditional forms of World 3 classification were beginning to creak. Their limitations included inconsistency of organisation, excessive complexity, and inflexibility in the face of evolving knowledge. When we are faced with new areas of knowledge like space research, chaos theory, genetic engineering, artificial intelligence, and the literature about AIDS or the Internet, we find that traditional systems can cope, but only in a clumsy, forced kind of way. Another problem that bedevils librarians trying to place books on their shelves is that there are some subjects which are closely similar but relate to different kinds of reader, or to different reader demands. A good example of this is the literature on places, which might be located in sections on geography, travel and tourism, the history of exploration, architecture, history, politics, or in other parts of the library. Assuming that a library does not wish to acquire and house multiple copies of books this means that one preferred location has to be chosen, and reliance placed on an appropriate indexing system to retrieve items if approached from 'non-preferred' trains of thought. As with an office filing system, we need multiple access routes into the information we require. The card index could cater for this, clumsily, but electronic systems offer us so much more power and flexibility.

Closely related to the work of the library classifiers but often forgotten is the achievement of Roget with his *Thesaurus of English Words and Phrases*, first published in 1851. This scheme classified the language, and hence - arguably - the world of ideas, not by alphabetical order as in a dictionary but by meaning, breaking this intellectual realm up into 1000 classes, and listing them in a sequence reflecting similarity and opposition of ideas. These days *Roget's Thesaurus* is perhaps most commonly thought of as a source of synonyms or near synonyms for jaded writers or crossword addicts, or poets in need of a rhyme, but its most astonishing achievement is this semantic classification of language. Coming as it did over a century before the creation of thesauri to support electronic databases it is quite remarkable and may even yet find valuable application in the design of more intelligent information retrieval systems.

If we now return to the problem of indexing the literature in the more general sense we can consider how there are a number of closely related problems and approaches which need to be taken care of, and which older systems, such as indexes and abstracts, did not entirely accommodate. There are several things that we may wish to do. We may want to identify literature that will answer a particular question or provide evidential support for some proposed action. This we may call document retrieval. A trivial instance of this is when we want to see a book or article which we can identify by one or more of its standard bibliographic descriptors, namely author, title, and journal reference or publisher. More demandingly, we may want to know a fact, such as the current population of Manchester, the atomic weight of uranium, or the date of birth of William of Normandy. This we might call fact retrieval. More demandingly still, we may want an answer to a more complex kind of question, such as, can taking aspirin cause Reye's Syndrome in children, is aluminium a suitable material for constructing a particular component of a washing machine, or what work is being done in French universities on the control of atmospheric pollution? This is a requirement for a question answering system, and it implies the transformation of isolated facts into evaluated and coherent knowledge structures. For the most part we have to supply the intelligent evaluation-in-context ourselves.

If we are even more optimistic about what an information retrieval system can offer us we may say, we have a chemical X, which we want to convert to chemical Y. What is the best synthetic route? Or, if we are a doctor, we might say we have a patient here, Mrs. Smith, who has a blood pressure reading of so and so, complains of certain symptoms, had a parent who died of so and so, and whose laboratory tests on her liver enzymes have just come back and say such and such. What is likely to be the matter with Mrs. Smith ? If it is possible to devise an algorithm which can cater for all the possible inferences to be drawn from these facts we may be in luck with an expert system. All these types of questions are trying to locate the specific among the general.

Yet another approach to information retrieval is the need to know 'about' something. I may be a research worker and I need to know 'everything' about metal fatigue in aircraft or about toxocara infection in dogs. Or I might be a student who wants to know quite a lot, but not everything, about the American constitution or about the physical properties of graphite. I might specify that I am only interested in articles published since 1970 and in English. Or, I might be a busy executive who wants to grasp the essentials of biotechnology in the time it takes me to fly from Chicago to Los Angeles. Or, I might want a 'topline' on the Malaysian consumer electronics industry to ingest while travelling up to town on the morning commuter train. Or, I might be a child of eight doing a school project on the solar system. In each case what I need is a painless summary of the relevant information, put together by others who have done the leg-work on the details. And I need it in my own native language, at a level of detail I can use, not too much, not too little, and at a level I can understand. What I need is, in essence, a map (or the description of a map) of a domain of knowledge, perhaps with a few punchy facts and figures that I can quote.

From all the examples above we can see that there are really two approaches to finding information, which we might choose to call the analytic and the synthetic approaches, or convergent and divergent approaches. The analytic approaches are those that try to home in on a particular question, looking for a specific fact or some other kind of answer. The synthetic approach is required when we need to know 'about' something to any level of detail and exhaustivity. Over the years there has been much confusion over these two roles, as regards the design of systems, and of course it is often necessary to design systems that can supply both kinds of information either for different audiences or for the same people but at different times. Analytical and synthetic needs will often combine in a single request for information.

The synthetic approach is the way we might begin to tackle the Wolfean problem, and I will defer that until the next chapter. Here, I want to consider briefly the ways in which we can accommodate the analytical requirement for information and some of the difficulties and limitations, in other words, the currently conventional approaches to information retrieval.

The keys to information retrieval are meaning and relationality. In order to search for information relevant to our needs we have to match that intellectual requirement with the content of literary items, and given the complexity of our language (English especially, but any developed natural language) it means we have to in some way convert the varied ways in which ideas can be expressed into some commonality of expression. Somehow the deep structure pattern of the answer has to match the deep structure pattern of the question. The words may not matter, but the underlying ideas do. This means the development of a more or less structured thesaurus, whereby words of identical meaning can be linked together, words that are not identical but have some degree of meaning or association in common can be cross-referenced, broader and narrower concepts can be related to each other, and appropriate foreign language versions and spelling variants (singulars, plurals, other grammatical derivatives, British and American orthographies) can be linked. The need to extract meaning implies the development of search strategies which are immune to the surface peculiarities of everyday language. We must be able to match our search need, our understanding of the question, with the way it is likely to be described in the literature, without being diverted and misled by the vagaries of that description.

Relationality, the other key component of information retrieval, refers to the fact that often we want to look for an idea in the context of other ideas. So, for example, we want to find information published in French in the last 20 years on viral infections in children in West Africa where particular drugs had been tried, but not in communities where schistosomiasis was endemic. Or it may be that we need information on legislation for packaging materials for foods, but only solid foods, not semi-solid or liquid ones, and that we are unconcerned with polymeric materials. The idea of a relational database (though maybe disguised by the videotext-style menu presentations which they often employ) is perhaps most familiar to us from the travel business where a flight, a hotel or a complete holiday may be booked by relating together concepts such as dates, locations, price ranges, availability and all kinds of other specifications. Or in a health centre or general practice environment we might use it to identify patients who have not been screened for cervical cancer in the last three years. What we are doing is finding the intersections of common factors, and where that intersection of commonality occurs, we may choose to act.

With information retrieval in the more literary sense we are essentially doing the same kind of thing, looking for concepts in relation to other concepts, but for convenience this is known as text retrieval. At the present time there is a gradual convergence of relational database and text retrieval systems. The types of relations between terms are many and complex, relationships involving, for example, possession, movement, causation or purpose. Systems have been devised to accommodate this, such as the relational indexing of Jason Farradane[42], but more usually one ignores this and relies instead on the simple concurrence of terms in a text, searching according to so-called Boolean logic or Boolean algebra, named after the mathematician George Boole who developed the idea more than a century ago. The essence of this is that any search can be specified by combinations of the logical AND, OR, and NOT relationships. For instance we might want to search for literature on bacteria or viruses in the context of meningitis in children living in England or Wales, which in the Boolean way might be expressed as '(bacteria OR viruses) AND meningitis AND children AND (England OR Wales)'. A search result indicating a mass of relevant literature references might persuade us to look only at the most recent data, and so we might take the previous search and combine it with, for example, the request to ignore references before 1985, by putting in something like 'NOT year<1985'. We might further refine the search by putting in, for example, 'AND Gloucestershire'. And so on, until we reach a manageable result which we hope is relevant to our needs, containing only what we are interested in and missing nothing that we should be aware of. Clearly, it often falls short of that ideal.

Boolean logic is the power behind major public databases such as Medline, Embase, Lexis, or Chemical Abstracts On-Line, held on host systems like Dialog or DataStar, permitting one to zoom in on a highly specific and manageable selection of relevant literature from among the millions of possible documents. Some of these databases retrieve article abstracts only; increasingly they offer full text. In a so-far relatively crude way it is also used by some Internet search engines; rapid improvements are occurring here almost daily. This highly analytical approach to information retrieval, using so-called inverted indexes of search terms, is also that taken by do-it-yourself software such as BASIS-plus, CAIRS, Fulcrum, Topic and Search '97 from Verity, which allow the creation of text databases catering for one's own specific needs. The structure of such databases, unlike that of conventional library classifications, is sufficiently free and open-ended so as not to be bound by artificial constraints as subjects grow and sub-divide into new specialities and as they undergo fission and fusion in unforseen ways. Subject areas, well-understood or novel, can be indexed to any depth of detail required, without strain, so long as the requirements of indexing vocabulary and the semantic relationships between terms are looked after in an adequate and consistent manner. Computing power has increased such that it is now possible to search all the words in a document, rather than just a string of keywords or a short abstract, as was the case formerly.

The electronic equivalents of old established ventures like *Chemical Abstracts* and *Index Medicus* are essentially hierarchical in inspiration but since each reference will be indexed under at least several - and probably many - keywords, the hierarchy cannot be entirely characterised two-dimensionally. It is more of a multi-dimensional matrix, and in a somewhat paradoxical manner the user may be said to be at least partly responsible for creating the state-of-the-art structure of knowledge in these systems. The systems originators provide the choice of keywords and the facets of publications that are deemed worthy of indexing, but it is the user, with his particular cluster of search parameters, who crystallises and pulls together the relevant references for each selection of subject matter. The final structure of the World 3 map as such remains hidden and incomplete, in fact it remains in a potential rather than an actual state. It is subject to variable interpretation according to the requirements and search strategies of the user; it is dynamic, ever changing, evolving and growing, and the key to its structure lies in the questions asked of it. Authors such as Foucault and Eco have explored the idea of how the labyrinthine structure of the library and the potential hyperconnectivity of its contents can lead to almost infinite possibilities for new correlations and for the generation of new knowledge; this applies very much more obviously in the on-line and Internet environments than in the manual indexes of yesteryear, and has obvious parallels with the concepts of data mining and 'knowledge discovery' mentioned in Chapter 4.

Many people are unhappy about using Boolean logic, although it is less fearsome than it might appear at first sight. It does, undoubtedly, pose its own problems such as the fact that it is easy to confuse the AND and the OR relationships (which to some appear to be counter-intuitive, at least until illustrated in a Venn diagram), to some people it seems a totally artificial way of thinking, it allows no weighting of search terms so as to make one term more significant than others in a search, and it is very much of an all or nothing approach. It does little to encourage the chance serendipity of browsing - but then, it is not intended for that purpose. Information retrieval - especially in the context of providing Internet search tools for non-specialists - is crying out to go 'beyond Boolean', but most systems still use it, albeit sometimes in disguise. There are other practical problems too. Quite often when conducting a Boolean search, putting in all the relevant parameters to limit the answer appropriately results in zero hits being obtained. The usual strategy then is to make a rapid and intuitive assumption about what is the least important term, and to drop that one in the hope of obtaining at least some results. The reliability of this approach may be suspect. Conversely, all too often the result obtained is unmanageably large, which means again that a more or less arbitrary and instant decision is made to discard certain of the references, or to restrict the search parameters in a way that may not be justified or desirable. Ways round these difficulties have been proposed, mostly by adopting strategies to weight search terms according to their perceived importance, by ranking of retrieved references according to recency or by number of occurrences of the search terms, by proximity searching, that is, by specifying that key words must occur within the same paragraph or sentence or within so many words of each other, by the use of pre-coordinate indexing or fuzzy logic, or by other techniques[43, 44]. Retrieval of this sort is definitely more of an art than a science, but is the best we have at present. Getting a usable result is satisfying; whether it is the correct result, the complete result, the same result as someone else would get, or we would ourselves get tomorrow, is something else.

We are still a little way from having any kind of automatic indexing system that would allow us to literally pour the contents of a book or a magazine article into a computer and for us then to be able easily to interrogate that computer with questions posed in the kind of language that we would use naturally. Such systems are getting closer. In practice this would imply having an optical character recognition device for scanning items in, and not only storing them as a bit-mapped image (and also of course being able to include photographs, diagrams and other graphical material as well as text) but also in intelligently machine readable form, i.e. with the scanned characters converted into one of the standard digital codes such as ASCII. This can already be done, with considerable accuracy, depending on the type font and the quality of the original document, to produce an alphabetical index of all the words to be found in that item. These words can then be related to others, as synonyms or according to other standard thesaurus relationships. Systems such as Pix Tex (and its successors) from Excalibur go one stage further, and use fuzzy matching to identify words which are, for whatever reason, not perfectly formed in the original. Use of neural network techniques allows such systems to 'learn' new terms and new fonts, with minimal human intervention. This is a significant achievement, but it disguises other difficulties that lie ahead. These difficulties are in the linguistic interpretation of the given material, involving a solution of the problem of how to electronically parse sentences, indeed, whole works, to a degree of sophistication which has not yet been achieved.

The increase in the power and capacity of computers to crunch data has not been matched by theoretical understanding of syntax and semantics, but both statistical number crunching and more subtle linguistic approaches are developing apace. It may even be that, with some ingenuity, the hard linguistic problems can in many cases be bypassed. As William Black[45] of the Centre for Computational Linguistics at the University of Manchester Institute of Science and Technology (UMIST) pointed out in 1990: 'automatic abstracting is one of the earliest computer applications ... yet we have not reached the point where the problem can be said to have been solved'. Effort in this area is being increased significantly, stimulated by the growth of the World Wide Web and its accompanying almost unmanageable glut of documents, and there are systems around now which claim to précis or summarise texts. Bruce Schatz[46], Director of the Digital Library Research Program at the University of Illinois at Urbana-Champaign has recently reviewed the developments in information retrieval techniques from the 'grand visions' of the 1960s through to semantics-based concept searching of the 1990s and beyond, and refers to the Interspace project with which he is involved. He comments that 'automatic indexing with scalable semantics will be necessary in the world of a billion repositories in the next century'. By 2010, he claims, concept searching will enable semantic retrieval across large collections. My guess is that this will be the case well before that date. Currently, developments from many companies including Oracle, Muscat, Xerox and Verity are addressing these problems on all fronts, using a mixture of techniques to offer a more powerful approach to intelligent searching.

The crucial problem that we are now talking about is the abstraction of knowledge as opposed to computer recognition of strings of alphabetic characters. This implies that the computer needs to be able to mimic the human understanding of natural language. The human mechanisms, whatever they are, need to be paralleled - faked if you like - within the software. Some major difficulties inherent in machine 'comprehension' of text result from the fact that texts are generally embedded in an overall implicit understanding of the world, so that much can be assumed without having to be stated; because of linguistic ambiguity and multiple meanings of words; from the fact that parts of a text can refer to other, very distant parts of the same text, or maybe even to other works with which some familiarity is assumed; and because of the problem known as anaphoric reference, whereby many of the concepts which one might wish to search for are in fact disguised in unexpected ways, not only by referring to them by pronouns such as 'he', 'it' or 'they', but in all kinds of other ways, for instance by starting a phrase 'similarly ...' or by the use of expressions like 'the latter'. This makes the analysis of text extremely difficult for the computer, whereas for the human reader - provided the text is not complicated to the point of ambiguity - anaphora permits a speeded-up and abbreviated form of sentence construction, avoiding clumsy repetition and encouraging stylistic creativity. The problem of anaphora is especially pertinent if we are trying to use weighting techniques to improve the relevancy of retrieved items; the concepts searched for may be referred to many times, anaphorically, but unless explicitly present they will not be detected, without some very sophisticated parsing[47].

If we can overcome the linguistic problems of full text analysis and automatic parsing then there is every chance that the electronic gobbling up of information and automated retrieval may be achieved. The difficulties are very great though, and beyond the fundamental linguistic problems there is the whole area of meaning, of ideas and concepts which are not explicitly stated in the text, but which the human mind can extract without effort. There is no way at present that a machine can learn - with any degree of reliability - to code what the 'aboutness' of a piece of text is, if it does not happen to use certain words which we might expect it to[48]. But this difficulty ought not to be impossible to overcome, especially for straightfoward scientific or business texts. The concept of 'idea retrieval'[49] is one which has been around for some time without very much progress being made, but it will need considerable development if automatic indexing is ever to become a reality. More problematic still is the whole area of fiction indexing, where little has been done. One can imagine that it might be possible, although labour intensive, to index novels by the names of characters, places, even certain incidents, as has been done for some of the classics or for long and difficult works, but other important attributes of the novel, like genres, plots and sub-plots, moods and atmospheres, which can contribute so much to the appeal of a work, are that much more resistant to tangible analysis, despite work by narratologists such as Genette, Greimas, Propp and Todorov. How do you identify 'suspense' or 'horror' or 'romance' or 'humour', let alone 'parody or 'irony or 'allegory', or the cosy snugness of 221B Baker Street on a foggy November evening, when they are not explicitly labelled as such? Nevertheless, following the seminal work of Robert Collison in 1962 some progress in fiction indexing has been made, and is reviewed by Ambrose Ransley[50].

As a final ingredient in the automatic analysis and indexing of texts in a global sense, there would need to be effective machine translation between natural languages, and this can only happen once the electronic parsing of any one language (not necessarily English) has been adequately achieved. The needs of the European Community and of growing economic and scientific exchanges with such countries as Japan, China, the former USSR, and the Arab nations will provide motivation for research into better machine translation systems. The first automatic translation devices grew largely out of the perceived needs of the Cold War years; early examples gloried in such names as Systran, Spanam, Engspan, Susy, Socatra, Winger 92, Globalink, and Gigatext[51, 52]. Reasonable success rates are now possible, especially with non-idiomatic texts, in automatic translation between major languages, and software for doing this has now started to appear commercially.

In time - perhaps only a few years - information retrieval will cease to be an activity involving much intellectual activity on the part of users or system creators; it will become as transparent and obvious as using language itself. Meanwhile we will see the growth and proliferation of individual databases designed to provide a way into particular domains within the mass of literature - which will continue to pour forth unabated. Information retrieval techniques, perhaps based on artificial neural networks and fuzzy pattern matching, are starting to appear for non-linguistic 'texts', for pictorial images, maps and diagrams and video sequences, and for speech and music. We will also see more and more in the way of full text databases which will ease document supply problems. All of these developments will, however, have little effect on the fundamental human problem of the information explosion, namely that of trying to assimilate everything that, for whatever reason, we feel as individuals we should. We will be able to find what we need more easily, but we will still struggle to take it all on board.

We started this chapter with an attempt at quantifying World 3 and its growth rate, an attempt which could only be wildly inaccurate and - because it is way beyond the capacity of any individual to cope with such huge amounts of data - to a large extent meaningless, 'academic'. We have gone on to consider how over the years tactics have been evolved in order to identify and pinpoint what is known on any one topic, so as to be able to extract the benefit from what one might call the paper record of man's intellectual endeavours. This analytical approach is extremely valuable and is the one which has excited most interest in recent years.

Useful though all of this is, trying to find the wood for the trees is only one way of approaching the realm of information. There is another way, a way which might appeal more to Wolfean man, and which - to extend the metaphor - implies mapping out the extent of the forest and making sure that we know about every single tree as well. This might be called the encyclopaedic or synthetic approach to the information explosion, and this is the subject of the next chapter.

8. From Akasha to Xanadu: Towards the World Brain

There is a concept known to parapsychologists as the Akashic record, which is the archive of every event, thought and emotion which has occurred to all beings and all things throughout time. The ultimate in information resources, this record is supposed to exist in a spiritual plane, imprinted on astral light (Akasha), and is accessible only to those with the requisite paranormal powers. Because it is outside the dimensions of space and time it can provide a convenient explanation for a variety of paranormal phenomena as well as being a warning for us that even our innermost secrets and darkest thoughts are on record, waiting to be used in evidence as part of the karmic judgement process. Such a record, if it exists, would certainly qualify as a contender for the title of World Brain. Unfortunately, it might not be a very practical device to use, at least, not in this life. Without invoking (or necessarily dismissing) such occult extremes I think it is true to say that we could develop, if we wish, an informational realm which bears certain akashic-like features, beyond the informational realm that already exists. Indeed, the process has already started, albeit somewhat uncertainly.

Until now, World 3 has consisted largely of documents and artefacts produced as unselfconscious things in themselves, that is, as relatively isolated productions with little attempt made to relate them to each other or to a grand overall scheme of things. Now, because of information overload and thanks to recently developed technologies, we may need to consider exactly how World 3 information can best be fitted together for maximal usefulness and to make the most sense. What I am referring to is the world of knowledge *as it is in itself*, not as chopped up into discrete books, newspaper reports, journal articles, and so on. The separation of meaning from given texts. Pure, integrated knowledge.

Another World

In many creative, educational, and commercial activities there is often a need to transfer a miscellany of isolated and partially overlapping or duplicated (and hence redundant) fragments of information lying around in various representations in World 3 to a centralised, coordinated database having low redundancy and a usefully structured organisation. In its simplest form we are talking here about the writing of a comprehensive review article, with all the relevant sections pulled together into a coherent structure, shaped according to meaning and association of ideas. This concept can then be extended to databases as a whole, and to knowledge as a whole. Though easiest to visualise as a two-dimensional data structure, in reality the links between subject areas and between facts are multi-dimensional; therefore they do not have an easily imaginable geometry or topology.

This is where we need Popper again. Suppose we had a vast, multiply coordinated database, a rationalised realm of information in which every independent fact or 'conceptual byte' (as Ted Nelson would call it) occurred only once - 'in the right place' - and was linked appropriately according to meaning and association. I will call this realm World 4. This could include - thanks to technologies such as hypermedia and virtual reality - representations of World 1 objects, expressions of our subjective (World 2) views, as well as integrated, synthesised data in World 3. Very few parts of this realm at present exist in any systematic sense, although the ultimate goal hovering in the background, when taken to its extreme form, is an old and powerful one - that of the World Brain. For that is what it could lead too. Whether this is desirable or feasible remains to be seen.

A less Popperian name would be better, for World 4 suggests something ontologically different. In Popper's terminology we are still firmly in World 3, but I think it is useful to have a convenient shorthand for this semantically seamless noetic domain[1], whether hypothetical or actual. In fact it is just a grandiose extension of World 3, but a new synthesis of digested, integrated, and evaluated knowledge brought together as a comprehensive, electronic representation in multimedia. It is the logical progression of encyclopaedias, reviews, and on-line sources of data into the realm of cyberspace. Let us slow down and see why this might be useful for us.

The sort of information retrieval which has been practised until recently, and as was examined in the previous chapter, can be summarised as: 'give me the bibliographic references to papers or books which contain the following selection of indexing keywords ...'. Having been given the references we have to read, absorb, interpret and understand, possibly dismissing huge chunks as being irrelevant to our current needs. The demand we really want to make is, of course, 'tell me the answer to my problem'. One of the ultimate aims of a practical information science must be the development of workable question-answering systems, employing techniques of artificial intelligence, knowledge engineering, report generation, automatic translation, and heuristic problem-solving approaches. It goes without saying that a very important ingredient in all this will be the facility to make use of the information that already exists, and to bring everything relevant to bear on a given issue. That isn't easy when information is scattered around myriads of documents in a multitude of styles and formats.

Such an advanced capability involves the proactive or ad hoc integration of current information into coherent bodies of knowledge, and the derivation of evaluative techniques which approximate to a kind of deliberate synthetic wisdom - if that is not an abuse of terminology. It involves an appreciation of the relativities of truth and untruth, an understanding of how people really think, especially with respect to memory, organisation and word association - and a much more subtle approach to the subjective pliability of language. Much of this understanding occurs naturally, tacitly, without very much detailed awareness of what actually happens and without any theoretical basis. Sorting it all out, laying it bare, of course, is one of the central concerns of artificial intelligence research and cognitive science in general.

To devise a question-answering system involves correlating knowledge about the physical world, about how people think, and about the way that what is already known is actually formatted in the literature; in other words this endeavour is concerned with all three of Popper's Worlds. The end product is something resembling H. G. Wells' 'world brain', or at least small sections of it. Technologically this is not unfeasible now, but the intellectual foundations are trickier. The initial component must be a kind of map which incorporates the known linkages as they occur in Worlds 1, 2 and 3, and which attempts to put together again a total picture of reality, at present fragmented between the three Worlds. What in fact we are talking about, amongst other things, is a practical solution to Thomas Wolfe's craving - to the extent that there can be any answer to such an obsession. It is a way of visualising one's entire world, actual and mental.

The current narcissistic trend of our media saturated society is towards the wholly recorded world, thankfully still a long way off, but already in the little way we have gone in this direction there is an urgent need for structuring and for evaluating the World 3 material which we already have. Pulling references off an on-line database or pages off the Web is not the answer, although no doubt it helps. Locating potential sources of information is not the same thing as retrieving useful information specific to our current needs; strangely, this is not always appreciated. Although I am sure we do not really believe it, there is a tendency to regard anything which appears in print as being true, and for all printed matter to be of equal value. There is certainly a trend to credit print with greater validity than the ephemeral spoken word. If a computer is involved in our search for information this tendency is reinforced. Often, if asked to find some information on a given topic, the more references we can find on a database the happier we are; the assumption is that more information equals better information. For some people, information retrieval is one of those instances where size is important. Sometimes this is reasonable: if we have to make a difficult decision and we haven't got much to go on, any extra information may help. But all too often a surfeit of information actually hinders us because it is repetitive, irrelevant, misleading, or of low quality. At this point the T. S. Eliot quotation from Chapter 3 finds its place: 'Where is the wisdom we have lost in knowledge? Where is the knowledge we have lost in information?' We need help with quality control of information, and most importantly we need a structure for it, a framework upon which to hang the details. We will come to the structure later. Let us first consider some aspects of quality control.

If we must record and preserve material the validity of which is uncertain we ought to at least have some way of recognising and labelling that uncertainty. We cannot go on pretending for ever that everything that appears in print is true or of equal value. But this is enormously difficult, because it implies the application of value judgements which for the most part we are in no position to make. Some kind of quality ranking system, even where an objective one can be devised (and as is being used by at least one major drug information publishing company to grade clinical trials), may be unacceptable when it appears to be critical of work performed or published. Who would determine the standards? What happens when standards change over time? What happens to minority interests, to truly novel ideas, to the first seeds of a paradigm shift? What happens to the unpopular voice, the individual who would rock the boat and unseat a staid and complacent Establishment? Politically this would be a very tricky area, and yet such a system could be so useful.

Generally speaking we want the truth, although this must often remain relative; we can, for example, have local truths which are valid within the constraints of one paradigm or at a certain time in history or in a particular geographical or cultural setting, but for which we cannot make any wider claims with certainty. Truth - or at least some types of it - can change. Any global database must recognise this difficulty - and that sometimes the truth, to the extent that it can be known, is unpopular. Without necessarily going overboard into the value-denying relativism of postmodernist pluralism and multiculturalism, information science has to allow for levels of truth and certainty and must recognise that in the literature there are bound to be contradictory or even seemingly incompatible facts and statements. While literature existed in the form of isolated books and papers scattered across the world, with not very good communications and not much interest in forming a comprehensive picture, this was not a problem, and library science could afford to be value-blind, but it becomes a problem when we try to put everything together in a coherently organised database. Truth is truth everywhere, and yet identifying it is not so easy, and in places that truth may be denied or rejected. Even within the so-called 'hard' sciences there can be a problem. Ziman has commented: 'the physics of undergraduate text-books is 90% true; the content of the primary research journals of physics is 90% false'[2]. For so-called softer sciences the figures must be even more depressing, and for philosophy, politics, religion, and the arts few 'truths' at all will be found.

So our hypothetical World 4 database will have to double as a truth machine or allow incompatibles to sit side by side. It could be used as a final court of appeal, in the same way that we make recourse to a dictionary or an encyclopaedia and accept as true what it has to say. New information is generally presented in good faith as being true even though posterity may come to judge otherwise. This cannot be helped. What then are we supposed to do ? Reject everything other than very old, well-established data from the most august sources? That would not be very useful, but we have no ultimate external authority - even to judge the veracity or otherwise of scientific papers. Ziman complains that there is 'no *Encyclopaedia* where *all* well-established science, and only well-established science, may be consulted'[2], an encyclopaedia that would be constantly modified as new information became available with new facts added and erroneous assertions deleted.

Any total, world-brain system must take into consideration different paradigms or world views, in other words it must have some capacity for being outside or above paradigms, operating as a metaparadigm, as it were, and it must be able to meaningfully accommodate ranges of intentional validity from lies, propaganda, fiction, journalistic sensationalism, artistic and poetic licence, subjective anomaly, and so on right through to consensus science, historical and biographical fact, the daily practicalities of finance, business, travel and so on, to as close to objectivity as possible. It will capture aspects of Worlds 1 and 2 - although they cannot be incorporated directly or in toto - as well as World 3, undoubtedly its major contributing source. A World Brain, by definition, will be a pretty ambitious undertaking.

We are now a world community; informationally there is nowhere left to hide. No assertion is an island; everything interrelates and is judged against everything else. Difficult and controversial though it will be, World 4 must be able to incorporate differing perspectives, which means putting together items and ideas which will provoke comments as to value and usefulness. It will be a database in which we can find Darwinism and creationism, Islam and Judaism, parapsychology and particle physics. Not in separate places as in an encyclopaedia, protected from each other by thick wodges of paper, but in logically mapped out knowledge structures. Mutual incompatibilities will be very visible. We may already be worried by the notion that Beethoven and gangsta rap are both classed as music, that Monet and dead sheep both qualify as art, and that Proust, the Pittsburgh telephone directory, the *Sunday Sport*, the back of a cornflakes packet, and the rantings/pronouncements of a terrorist/freedom fighter or misfit/persecuted minority or pervert/person-of-alternative-sexual-orientation all qualify as literature suitable for academic scrutiny; to have them all stacked up next to each other in a database will really begin to beg some questions. It does not mean that these things *are* of equal value, but it does have the advantage that, putting them side by side, we are in a better position to judge. Cultural relativity will become a major issue if such a project is tackled seriously, globally. World 4 will have to cater for all this, as it will also have to for novelty, that is, for the relative attractions and drawbacks of old versus new information, for different educational and linguistic abilities, providing information at different levels of difficulty and detail to meet a range of user needs and abilities.

These are some of the essential features which must be considered in the design of anything resembling a World Brain. Already, however, in the absence of a reliable, accepted, overall theoretical background structure, we are putting more and more into World 3 and into partial, mini-World 4s. Whether we realise it or not we are working, piecemeal, in this direction, in conventional literature and on the Web. Unfortunately, the structures we are creating may be far from ideal. They are incomplete, overlapping and incompatible. Without any kind of centralised direction and control they will always be like this. Quite likely this is the reality of our informational future.

The Early History of the World Brain

In 1933, in *The Shape of Things to Come*[3], H. G. Wells referred to a 'Fundamental Knowledge System', based - for some reason - in Barcelona, with regional centres, employing 17 million workers and 5 million correspondents and reserve engineers. As Wells put it, this system 'accumulates, sorts, keeps in order and renders available everything that is known'; it would be the 'Memory of Mankind'. Wells followed this up in 1936 with a proposal to the Royal Institution for a 'World Encyclopaedia', and this was issued in print as 'World Brain' in 1938, and has since been reprinted, in 1967, in Manfred Kochen's *The Growth of Knowledge*[4].

This Wellsian 'world encyclopaedia' or 'world brain' would be a series of volumes kept at home, and in schools, colleges and libraries, where one could find 'in clear understandable language, and kept up to date, the ruling concepts of our social order, the outlines and main particulars in all fields of knowledge, an exact and reasonably detailed picture of our universe, a general history of the world' and if one wanted to pursue a question into its ultimate detail, 'a trustworthy and complete system of reference to primary sources of knowledge. In fields where wide varieties of method and opinion existed, [one] would find, not casual summaries of opinions, but very carefully chosen and correlated statements and arguments'.

This database would consist of authoritative items, carefully collated and assembled. 'It would not be a miscellany, but a concentration, a clarification and a synthesis'. Wells continued: 'This World Encyclopaedia would be the mental background of every intelligent man in the world. It would be alive and growing and changing continually under revision, extension and replacement from the original thinkers in the world everywhere. Every university and research institution should be feeding it.' So like the World Wide Web and yet so unlike it, but astonishingly relevant to the present day, and a reflection of Wells's scientific optimism and foresight.

Anticipating the need for such a database to include contrary opinions and controversial data Wells went on to say: 'Such an Encyclopaedia would play the role of an undogmatic Bible to a world culture. It would do just what our scattered and disoriented intellectual organizations of today fall short of doing. It would hold the world together mentally'.

Wells believed that the World Brain was necessary 'to hold men's minds together in something like a common interpretation of reality'[5]. Since the 1930s we have experienced the information explosion and a general decentralisation and pluralism of thought, and some hard knocks to the scientific optimism of the earlier part of the century, yet it may appear that the World Brain is even more necessary now than it was in Wells' time. Equally, it may appear both logistically impossible and anachronistically unfashionable, a product of the mindset of intellectual imperialism and WASP-ish elitism, and a laughable no-hoper given the current rate of information proliferation.

Be that as it may, the idea of a World Brain, if not so explicitly named, had been around for a long time before H. G. Wells. A historical perspective of this idea, in the sense of restructuring and mobilising information in documents, for increased accessibility and utility, is provided by Boyd Rayward[6]. The World Brain idea is quite different from our focus of the last chapter, and of the thrust of many recent efforts in information retrieval, namely the attempt to home in on a particular fact or document among a vast collection of currently irrelevant facts or documents - in other words an analytic approach. What we are contemplating now is a synthetic approach, whereby we want to put knowledge together independently of its documentary origins, so that all the relevant facts about one subject are in one place, and so that the connections between subject areas are appropriately configured. What we are after is knowledge freed from its textual sources.

When Wells made his proposals, before the construction of even the most primitive valve-based computer, the practical means of achieving his idea involved the use of bound paper volumes. Now, the growth of literature has made that proposal a non-starter, but we also have technologies to handle the problem much more effectively. In our synthetic approach we now realise that the problem of the information explosion is not so much finding the wood for the trees - we have more or less tackled that one via on-line databases - but in having an overview of the forest with, if necessary the capability to swoop down and examine small clumps of trees, or individual trees, or branches, roots, or leaves, to swing from tree to tree, and to group together similar kinds of trees. The problem is not so much that of finding as of structuring, putting together, making sense of it all. This is central to the Wolfean situation too. Information has to connect together to be of much use, to become knowledge. Ted Nelson, the visionary behind the Xanadu project, to be considered shortly, has recognised that literature is 'a system of interconnected writings'[7] and that all documents are interconnected, or potentially interconnected. With the development of global telecommunication networks, media for storing terabytes of information, and the digitisation of text, images, sound and motion pictures it would seem that we should be able to bring about any necessary interconnections. In theory we could put it all together into a logical knowledge structure - if only we could determine what that structure should be. Yet Nelson fears that '... the reality is that currently we are developing ... 'docu-islands' of knowledge that are incompatible with one another'[8]. The World Brain must conceptually and technologically overcome this difficulty with a great many multidirectional interconnections and constant updating, in a way that computers can cope with but which Wells' bound volumes could not permit.

As I say, the idea is not new, and is reflected in the desire, throughout history, to accumulate knowledge in vast libraries or in encyclopaedias, arranged alphabetically or by subject matter. The idea was certainly around in 600 B.C. at the time of the Confucian encyclopaedia, in the words of Plato as compiled by his nephew Speusippos in about 370 B.C., and in various libraries in existence between 300 and 200 B.C. around the eastern shores of the Mediterranean, for example at Alexandria and Pergamum, giving birth to the notion of 'a comprehensive planetary library'[9]. Aristotle's writings were arranged in a logical way - subsequently modified by Porphyry, Boethius and Cassiodorus[10] - that might be viewed as the encyclopaedia of the times. The *Historia naturalis* of Pliny the Elder, written in 77 A.D., divided the realm of knowledge up into 2500 chapters arranged in 37 books. Chinese and Arab encyclopaedias developed in parallel. We see the same motive much later, in the early 17th century, in Francis Bacon's *Novum Organum*, which attempted to synthesise much of what was known in a single work, in a seamless realm of knowledge.

In the 16th century Conrad Gesner (1516-1565), a physician and naturalist from Zürich, produced a 20 volume encyclopaedia of all knowledge (except for medicine), with other volumes describing animal and plant life, and languages, and in 1545 he published his *Bibliotheca universalis*, the first bibliography of its kind, covering the works of about 1,800 authors. Gesner compiled an alphabetical index of more than ten thousand works in Latin, Greek and Hebrew, but besides merely indexing them in this way, was also concerned with the overall structure of knowledge, the topology of knowledge as it were, providing cross references to the concepts occurring in these texts. The *Bibliotheca universalis* acted as a role model for later bibliographic ventures and provided a classification system used by some major libraries for more than two centuries. An early proponent of what might be called the multimedia approach to the

World Brain, and an acknowledged source of inspiration to H. G. Wells, was the 17th century Czech scholar and Protestant bishop, John Amos Comenius, otherwise Jan Amos Komensky. His vision of a world encyclopaedia included pictures and realia (i.e. World 1 objects themselves) as well as texts collected and created by a 'Pansophic College' of European scholars with Comenius adopting an editorial role. Comenius received encouragement and support from Charles I of England, but following the king's execution the venture foundered. Nevertheless, Comenius may be regarded as one of the grandfathers of information science[9] and of the World Brain idea.

In the 17th century Leibniz had plans 'to develop a comprehensive calculus and an encyclopaedia for representing the state of all the sciences and their progress'[5]. Unfortunately only the first ambition was achieved, and even the development of the calculus he had to share with Newton, who was working on it independently at the same time. Then, in the 18th century there were several major projects for encyclopaedias, the most famous one being the 35 volume *Grand Encyclopaedia* of Diderot and d'Alembert. At this time it was still realistic to attempt to encompass the world's knowledge in reasonable detail in book form, and this led on to the great Victorian and early 20th century encyclopaedias, such as the *Encyclopaedia Britannica* and *Brockhaus*, and other great national endeavours, such as the *Enciclopedia italiana* first published in Rome in 1929 and the *Espasa*, first published in Barcelona in 1905. The first edition of the *Encyclopaedia Britannica* was published in 1771, but the greatest editions were the ninth, in 1888, with 24 volumes comprising 16,000 articles and 20,000 pages, and the eleventh (1910-1911) with 29 volumes[10]. The same ideal of logically structured knowledge led, albeit in a slightly different way, to *Roget's Thesaurus*, a work very much ahead of its time. Another major 19th century influence was that of Anthony Panizzi, responsible for much of the organisation and cataloguing of the British Museum and library.

Towards the end of the 19th century two Belgian senators, Henri LaFontaine and Paul Otlet, backed by their government, oversaw the development of the International Institute of Bibliography (founded in 1895 in Brussels), which contained the Universal Bibliographical Repertory. This Repertory, which was housed in the so-called Mondaneum in Brussels, was intended, eventually, to provide a reference source to indicate the location of at least one copy of every printed work in the world. Before the outbreak of the Second World War it housed some fourteen million index cards, or twice as many as were held at that time by the Library of Congress in Washington[9]. This attempt at universal bibliographical control failed ultimately because of political difficulties and because of the primitive manual technology which was all that was available. Through the 20th century the dream of the unification of all knowledge continued against all odds. Some of these efforts pre-empt the concept of hypertext, to be considered shortly, but it is worth mentioning Neurath and colleagues at the University of Chicago with their idea for an *International Encyclopedia of Unified Science*; recent editions of the *Encyclopaedia Britannica*, with its Propaedia, Micropaedia and Macropaedia, which constitutes a sort of prototype paper-bound, hypertext-linked knowledge base system; the *ISI Atlas of Science*; and Manfred Kochen with his *World Information Synthesis and Encyclopaedia*. This last project, with the appropriate acronym

WISE, suggested by K. W. Deutsch, anticipates later hypertext-based schemes, with its hierarchical structure 'in the sense that the decision-maker can quickly and conveniently zoom from a perspective that gives him a bird's eye view of his problem to one enabling him to penetrate toward a solution with a worm-eye view'[5], and allowing simultaneous viewing of different levels of detail.

However the World Brain is realised, if it ever is realised in usable form, one of the major difficulties in its construction is going to be in deciding how to link together the component subject matter. One approach may be to follow how the literature feeds off itself. Retrospectively one can show graphically how literature interconnects using co-citation analysis, a procedure developed by Eugene Garfield, Belver Griffith, Henry Small and coworkers at the Institute for Scientific Information (ISI) in Philadelphia. This bibliometric technique, mentioned in Chapter 6, examines the degree to which scientific papers cite from each other, the existence of such a citation suggesting some kind of close conceptual link. There are some confounding factors in all this, and the procedure has been criticised, but it can be used to produce maps showing how the literature clusters. Using this method it is possible to identify significant publications, groups of workers, paradigms and paradigm shifts and changes in consensus, and leading edges of knowledge. It has been used quite successfully, for example, to study the development of understanding of the physics and mathematics of chaos. Of especial interest here is Garfield's attempt to produce an atlas of knowledge spaces showing the territorial scope of the various sub-disciplines of science (although as we shall see later on, and as Ted Nelson pointed out, when you get down to it all subjects are interconnected), which first appeared in practical form as the *ISI Atlas of Science: Biochemistry and Molecular Biology 1978-80*. As a modest start this used co-citation cluster analysis to produce maps of the connections within 102 biochemical specialities, a process dubbed 'scientography' by George Vladutz, one of Garfield's colleagues. Extended to the whole of science this would provide one method of building an associative and encyclopedic map of the entire field, and it might incidentally be useful for identifying what Belkin termed 'anomalous states of knowledge', areas of ignorance which might be profitably researched. But it is not the World Brain itself, merely a kind of wiring diagram.

However we go about devising a supporting structure, what we really need is a facility for accommodating a 'universal viewpoint', as Ivar Hoel [11] has called it. This would permit the maximum possible freedom for divergence of opinion and would attempt to be comprehensive and omniscient. As Hoel points out, this can only be done in a 'library-based' structure, in other words, using World 3 materials. Decisions would have to be made as to what, if anything, would be excluded in principle. Would there be controls on input, or would we use quality control filters at output to suppress the seemingly less worthy contributions? Who are we to judge who or what has the right of entry into an elitist World Brain, even though judgements are made all the time by those who want to use information? As we noted in the last chapter, it is a fact that '... very much of the scientific literature is not cited, not read, not sought, and not useful'[12]. At the US National Library of Medicine 300 out of 22,000 serial titles satisfy 70 per cent of all interlibrary loans requested. The survival of the fittest applies to information sources too. It would be tempting, but - I suspect - wrong, to apply the same sort of criteria to the World Brain.

For our World Brain to be useful it must provide facilities way beyond what we are used to, and it should address commonplace problems of knowledge generation. Typically, when we are gathering information together on a particular topic, there are always certain irritations we encounter. To start with, we find that much of the information we need is scattered around different sources, so that collecting it can be time-consuming, inefficient and expensive. Then when we finally get hold of the potential sources we discover that much of the material is irrelevant, is repeated redundantly from one item to the next, contains much in the way of background or context that may be superfluous to our needs, is lacking in sufficient detail, is out of date, is incoherently presented so that it is difficult to read and to make sense of, or is just simply bad[13]. Additionally it may be written in a language we cannot read, or in a style too technical for us to manage. It may demand a background education in a subject which we are lacking, and there may be facts which we cannot connect together meaningfully because of a deficient contextual background. Our synthetic World Brain will, we hope, overcome these difficulties.

In the sense of tackling all knowledge, such demands must seem over-ambitious, utopian to the point of impossibility. The World Brain could hardly be anything less. However, more modestly, we can consider a development which is a useful, indeed vital, step in the right direction, namely that of the domain-specific knowledge base, the World Brain in miniature, what I referred to a while back as mini-World 4s, restricted to a small subject area. An early and illustrative example of what I mean is provided by the Hepatitis Knowledge Base established at the National Library of Medicine in Bethesda, Maryland. Here it was recognised, in the early 1970s, that information retrieval from the biomedical literature was becoming increasingly difficult, not simply because of the quantity and rate of growth of publications, but because much of the literature was of poor quality. The feeling was that it should be possible to extract the important work, even if some of it was contradictory or controversial, and to present it in a format something like a cross between an on-line database and an encyclopaedia, with frequent updating to produce 'new state-of-knowledge synthesis statements'[12]. Starting from just 40 major review articles plus the references cited in them, out of 16,000 publications on hepatitis appearing in English in the preceding ten years and indexed on MEDLINE, a team of experts extracted the significant information and, using a hierarchical format for arranging concepts, plus text editing facilities, digested this information into a single document and fed it into a minicomputer.

For each concept area in the Hepatitis Knowledge Base there would be a heading, a heading statement (a synthesis of knowledge to date), and then one or more 'data element paragraphs' providing more detailed evidence to support the heading statement and citing original documentation. Searching could thus be performed at three levels of detail, and was by a hierarchical menu, in a manner highly reminiscent of that outlined by Wells. Consensus opinion as to the conclusions to be incorporated within the database was obtained from a panel of experts, either by correspondence or by computer conferencing. If consensus could not be agreed or if there was an acknowledged area of ignorance or doubt, this was recorded in the system. The intention was not to dismiss data simply because it was unusual or difficult to integrate into the existing knowledge structure.

Knowledge bases of this sort seem to work particularly well if the subject matter is limited and well defined. Similar ventures in the field of medicine are PDQ and the Lithium Index. PDQ, or the Physicians' Data Query, produced by the US National Cancer Institute, was intended to promote the diffusion of information about cancer treatment, to facilitate access to current clinical trials, and to accelerate the practical application of advances in research[14]. This followed a menu system, with citations of source material. The Lithium Index was produced by the Lithium Information Center, located in the Department of Psychiatry at the University of Wisconsin Health Sciences Center in Madison, Wisconsin. Lithium has a highly specific medical role in the management of mania, hypomania, and the manic phase of manic depressive psychosis. Its mode of action is incompletely understood. The Lithium Index was set up in 1975 to organise and disseminate information about lithium, and within its first ten years had indexed and stored over 12,000 relevant publications[15]. As with the Hepatitis Knowledge Base, the Lithium Index consisted of summaries produced on a text editor (as early word processing systems were called), frequently updated, and with cross references to more detailed information (as cited publications embedded within the text). A similar endeavour was the AIDS knowledge base produced by the San Francisco General Hospital and searchable on CD-ROM.

Projects such as the Hepatitis Knowledge Base and the Lithium Index were prototype forays into the creation of small parts of World 4. The structure being aimed at is the structure of knowledge as it is, divorced from its supporting texts (but referring to them), a synthesis deeper than all the pre-existing presentations in various disparate publications, with their various peculiarities and agendas, deficiencies and use of different natural languages. A fully developed World Brain would be able to accommodate paradigm shifts and alternative perspectives and world views. As more knowledge is 'made', so the World 4 map will become both more extensive and more detailed, more finely grained, so that its finest structures represent the 'quanta' of knowledge. By analogy with Noam Chomsky's deep and surface structures of language, the World 4 map, the integrated record of knowledge, might be regarded as the deep structure of knowledge, with the variety of accounts in World 3, in a range of sources in different media - in books, journals, computer memories and elsewhere - constituting the surface structure, rendering a fundamental speech in many different voices and dialects. With the development of digitisation and multimedia this World 4 is able to cater for not just textual material but graphics, video and sound as well. It might also be able to include within itself some kind of replica of original artefacts (the realia of World 1) and statements expressive of World 2. For instance, using techniques of virtual reality simulation something like the Hepatitis Knowledge Base could include an electronic representation of the liver down to the finest level of histological detail, or the Lithium Index could include subjective accounts of how manic patients feel before and after they take lithium salts. But it must be stressed that though this

World 4 could capture aspects of Worlds 1, 2 and 3, it is strictly speaking, in the Popperian sense, just another item in World 3.

This may all sound rather far-fetched, and we must be careful not to confuse true World 4 with run-of-the-mill multimedia or even with some of the excellent, comprehensive and extensively cross-referenced multimedia encyclopedias available on CD-ROM, like *Britannica, Encarta* and *World Book,* or the Library of Congress *American Memory* project or the multimedia version of *The Guinness Book of Records.* However, though they may fall short of full-blown World 4 status, in all these endeavours the aim is to make knowledge more accessible, more 'visible, like food on the shelves of a supermarket'[16]. The structure being aimed at is the natural structure of information whatever that is, the quasi-Chomskyan deep structure. The crucial difficulty is deciding what that structure should be. Fragments of data do not have convenient one-to-one, or even two-dimensional interrelationships and they can be related and interpreted in all kinds of ways. Information sources have different levels of organisation and complexity. One approach to tackling such difficulties is afforded by the access possibilities of hypertext.

Hypertext

Literature is traditionally conditioned by the fact that it has to be presented in a book. You start at page 1, turn over to page 2, and keep on going until the last page. All right, there have been books produced which rather self-consciously offer alternative endings, there are self-tuition manuals which allow one to progress along different channels, and there are people who like to read books back to front, to find out what happens - 'who did it', but none of these exceptions are really very satisfactory, and for many works of literature we transit predictably from front cover to back. An important exception, though, is that group of books whose logical structure is not dictated by the physical structure of print and page, and including encyclopaedias, dictionaries, thesauri and other reference works. It would be unusual to read such books from start to finish. Normally we plunge in somewhere in the middle, according to the word or idea we are looking for, and we expect to be led to cross references elsewhere in the book, to follow up ideas or to pursue related information. Often in these sort of books we even expect a certain amount of graphical material with logical links between them - maps, diagrams and photographs - and footnotes or other links to more detailed primary sources of information. So from our long experience of reference works which involve non-sequential patterns of information display we can say that we were already familiar in principle with the concept of hypertext by the time it arrived electronically. Even more fundamentally still, hypertext emulates the way we (and the Thomas Wolfes of this world) think, that is, by association - usually, but not always, because of obviously related meaning and relevance.

Hypertext is the development of the footnote and the cross-reference to a potentially unlimited degree, aided by the power of the computer. The word 'hypertext' was coined in the 1960s by Ted Nelson, who went on to define it as '*non-sequential writing -* text that branches and allows choices to the reader, best read at an interactive screen. As popularly conceived, this is a series of text chunks connected by links which offer the reader different pathways', and he went on to note that hypertext 'can include sequential text, and is thus the most general form of writing'[17]. It is writing freed from the straightjacket of the linearity of continuous narrative and the speed restrictions imposed by grammar, by pronouns and prepositions; consequently it has properties for the writer and the reader which are very different from conventional script. Since Nelson's early theorisings as to what hypertext actually is, the idea has come a long way, so that now there are many commercially available and practical hypertext systems in existence, by far the most ambitious of which is the World Wide Web.

In its simplest form hypertext may be thought of as a breed of software which allows information to be stored in discrete chunks, at nodes which are connected to each other by electronic links, the links being chosen to represent some kind of purposive or meaningful connection between the ideas expressed in the nodes. Although there is no natural, God-given topology for information space it is quite usual to visualise concepts as being related to each other spatially, most easily in two dimensions as in the co-citation cluster maps produced by the Institute for Scientific Information, but more realistically in many dimensions. The computer power behind hypertext allows for this multi-dimensionality, which is beyond the human mind to grasp properly. It follows that the sort of networks which are built up in hypertext systems are similar to maps which may be made of mental associations and that they have properties not dissimilar from the mental maps which we encountered earlier, including those of geographical perception. The associations are based (usually, but not necessarily) on meaning: 'hypertext is isomorphic to the knowledge representation scheme of semantic network'[18]. Advocates of hypertext point out that natural thought processes are not sequential but associative, and thus hypertext should be a more natural metaphor for database construction.

In order to create a hypertext system, therefore, we need to convert literary material from its existing sequential format into smaller modules, each one representative of a discrete idea, and then to consider how these should be linked together. Better still, we can create a system from scratch, building in the appropriate level of granularity or modularity of ideas according to how detailed the system needs to be. There may well be a need to create modules for chunks of information which have no obvious name and which had not previously been thought of as stand-alone information units. Deciding on the appropriate size for such units, and where to draw the boundaries, may be difficult, but the exercise should clarify our understanding of the structure of knowledge. This will be a familiar concern to anyone who has designed a Web page. Our total hypertext system, probably derived from many sources, but with connections built in (and in some versions allowing other connections to be established by users) may be considered to be a 'hyperdocument'. This might be the complete collection of reports and correspondence accumulated by a company or a government department, a private collection of documents used by a writer or researcher, or - in the case of Nelson's Xanadu project - the entire realm of published literature. It could even be a representation of the world as perceived and ached for by Thomas Wolfe.

If we translate the idea of hypertext to schemes like the Hepatitis Knowledge Base we can see how this approach can be used to structure information in a flexible, multifaceted way. Starting from a high level of overviews, of broad sweeps of subject matter, there can be links, or pointers, to summaries and brief reviews, in turn leading on to more detailed information and ultimately right down to the level of original documentation. There can be links to definitions, comments, references, footnotes of all kinds, and to non-textual materials (at which point hypertext becomes hypermedia).

Most importantly, any hypertext system must be easy to navigate around. There should be some kind of overall map, and preferably local area maps of detailed parts of the database so that one can easily zoom in and out of topics of particular interest. It must always be possible to backtrack from the depths of an information mineshaft, say after skipping between several hyperlinked Web sites, back along the way one has come, and to be able to return easily to screens viewed previously. It is vital that the structure is highly visible - again, making explicit use of the spatial metaphor for information structure.

If hypertext is combined with traditional methods of information retrieval, using key words and Boolean logic, a very powerful retrieval tool results, and this we discover when browsing the Web with the aid of a search engine like Alta Vista or Lycos. Browsing through hypertext can lead to useful discoveries, but it still may be more desirable and quicker to home in on concepts identified by coincidence of search terms. The question of vocabulary control then comes in. Should a hypertext system use a rigidly controlled vocabulary or should it support a hidden thesaurus of term inter-relationships? If the latter, should this be at the morphological level (so that grammatical variants of terms are picked up appropriately), the synonymic level (so that words meaning the same thing are conceptually linked, leading to more complete retrieval), or the semantic level, so that terms broader or narrower in concept, or related by meaning in some other way, can be involved in the search strategy? System design needs to consider such issues, and the situation with respect to the Web is developing all the time.

It is true that hypertext 'can represent *all* the interconnections an author can think of'[17] and this has been compared to the Hindu concept of 'bhasha', an approach to learning 'in which each question asked is pursued to its final answer, regardless of how long it takes'[19].   On occasion this may be desirable, but there will be many times when it is not. Many people would say that they learn best from the linear sequence of a book, and being able to jump off at tangents all the time is of no great benefit. At least you know when you have finished a book; with hypertext you may never be totally sure that you have exhausted all the relevant pathways, and this is certainly true when browsing the Web. It can be a most inefficient way of displaying quite mundane information. 'Hypertext walks a thin line between order and chaos'[20], writes Torrey Byles. The thin line is that between the controlled but possibly restrictive approach to retrieval that we have become used to in existing databases, and the full Wolfean wallowing in the interconnectedness of everything. As Ted Nelson says: 'There are no 'subjects', everything is deeply intertwingled'[21], and this frightens some people, who are happier with things being just so, in watertight compartments. Stephen Manes[22] wrote a highly sceptical review of hypertext in which he referred to an article[19] which showed how 'with four simple clicks anyone could whiz from an article on indoor lighting to a totally unrelated piece on diamonds; what the author omitted to say was why in the world anyone might want to'. Such scepticism is not new. There are many notorious predictions by luminaries who should have known better, proposing extremely modest futures for, say, the telephone or the computer. The common link between the four items was in fact carbon, as found in the carbonised cotton tried by Thomas Edison as a filament for light bulbs. Once again, this is the process of mental association at work. Whether it is silly or profound depends entirely on the circumstances and the application intended. The example referred to meant to illustrate this power of association; it is not necessarily trivial, but clearly it could be a huge time waster. Since Manes' article was written such apparent absurdities of association have become a commonplace discovery when surfing the Internet.

Returning once again to the World Brain idea, hypertext has the advantage that, if properly designed, it can accommodate concepts which are mutually incompatible or inconsistent. This requirement is not handled so easily in conventional, flat, linear text. You can't really say two completely opposing things at once. In dynamic, as opposed to static, hypertext, users can create their own links between nodes, according to their own needs and interests, and there may also be options for personalised display modes, thus fulfilling one aspect of Nicholas Negroponte's concept of 'idiosyncratic systems'[23]. As Byles[20] has noted, hypertext can accept heterogeneous viewpoints, but he asks the question whether hypertext can also produce heterogeneous viewpoints, and whether it can dissolve the consensus that appears to exist within given fields of knowledge. It may quite effectively destroy or negate any sense of reliable meaning. Experience with the Web sometimes tends to support this assessment. For the World Brain ideal, and for the structure of information lying deep beneath the surface of literary representation, these are pertinent issues.

Hypertext leads naturally to the more general concept of hypermedia, which can accommodate any information that can be digitised and stored in magnetic or optical media. Hypermedia can include text, graphics, audio, animations and video sequences all interrelated according to some kind of meaningful link. We can expect graphical and sound 'documents' to grow in importance relative to conventional text over the next few years. The theoretical scope is there for creating a logical structure of information which until now has been impossible because of the separate media required to 'play' text, sound, or vision. Hypermedia has thus been described as 'a seamless carpet of knowledge'[19] and evidently has the capability of being the foundation for what I have called World 4, for the World Brain. Undoubtedly it 'may profoundly alter the way in which we retrieve, manipulate, and store information'[24]. Adding a depth and a richness to information as traditionally perceived, its possibilities for interactive and educational use remain to be fully explored. Given that some people learn better by reading, some from looking at visual or spatially arrayed material, and some from receiving verbal instruction, there may be potential here for more effective learning aids.

Hypertext and hypermedia, two related technologies which have come to practical fruition since the late 1980s, and which until the take-off of the World Wide Web in the mid-1990s were employed in rather limited projects, for example for travel and tourism information (e.g. Glasgow On-line and Hypertour on Tyneside), historically have their roots in the grand vision of the World Brain. As we have seen, there are a number of contenders for the title of 'father' of the World Brain - H. G. Wells being the most obvious, with perhaps Comenius as one of the 'grandfathers'. For the specific invention of hypertext as a solution to the World Brain problem it is equally difficult to assign responsibility; probably Vannevar Bush would get the vote for a 'grandfather' role, for suggesting the possibility and for highlighting the need, whereas Ted Nelson would most probably qualify for the 'father' figure. But there are many other important figures too. Revealingly, while the World Brain was historically European in conception the more recent practical development of hypertext has been primarily an American affair.

Vannevar Bush (1890-1974) was appointed the first Director of the United States Office of Scientific Research and Development in 1941, and as such was scientific adviser to F. D. Roosevelt. In 1945 he published an article entitled *As We May Think* in the *Atlantic Monthly* magazine, an article which is usually cited as the first description of hypertext. In fact the ideas for this had been developed in 1932 and 1933, ahead of Wells' World Brain or World Encyclopaedia pronouncements, and a draft paper had been written in 1939, but never published. In the *Atlantic Monthly* piece Bush described what he called a 'memex', short for 'memory extender'. This was a theoretical device, never built, but it anticipated hypertext in the style of the technology then available. The memex was to consist of a very large library supplemented with personal notes, photographs and sketches (thus anticipating multimedia and hypermedia), and its crucial feature was that it would provide links between any two items, according to the requirements of meaning and association. Items would be viewed on screens. Computers were not then available, of course, apart from a handful of unreliable prototypes, and the memex was to be constructed using microfilm and photocells. There would be several projectors involved so that multiple images could be viewed simultaneously, in a manner crudely analogous to the windows on a modern computer screen. Most importantly the structure of the memex was associative according to the way we think, thus providing the title for Bush's article. Bush developed the idea because of his concern, even then, that the growth of information was making it difficult for specialists to follow their subject.

By far the most spectacular development of hypertext, however, has been the World Wide Web. Originally developed at CERN, the European high energy physics laboratory outside Geneva, in 1989, and the brainchild of Tim Berners-Lee, it was intended as an international network of hypertext linked documents relating to high energy physics, initially just for use within the physics community. However, in 1991 it went public, and became much more popular in 1993 following the application of the Mosaic graphical browser, developed by the National Center for Supercomputing Applications. Growth has been phenomenal, so that estimates of the size of the Web in terms of host sites or documents, or numbers of users, are likely to be extremely inaccurate and immediately way out of date. A January 1997 review of the number of Web hosts suggested a figure of 16.1 million, more than 800,000 domains, and users in the tens of millions[25]. By April 1998 the number of Web pages was quoted at 320 million[26] on 2,215,195 sites[27], but these are just snapshots of a rapidly moving target.

Even with such impressive statistics, the Web falls short of the ideal that motivated visionaries like H. G. Wells, Vannevar Bush, Douglas Engelbart and Ted Nelson. Nelson's Xanadu project has been the only serious attempt at World 4 to date.

Xanadu and the Alternative

Ted Nelson, or more formally Theodor Holm Nelson, is something of an oddball outsider figure. Born in 1937 and educated at Swarthmore College and Harvard, his published output, some of it produced privately, is eccentric in format and use of neologisms. His original ideas are many and often quirky and humorous. His lecturing style is informal and experimental, with frequent asides - the oratorical equivalents of 'Post-It' notes or hypertext itself - enthused with a subversive grin and with tossings of his unruly blond mane. He is one of the few charismatic figures in the otherwise largely dull and nerdish ranks of information technologists; he reputedly tapes every conversation in case something memorable is said, and keeps a video camera handy too.

For all the colour of his projected persona Nelson's ideas are provocative and profound. He has been criticised because his 'goal seems to be putting all human experience on-line so that humans need never do anything but stare at screens'[22]. Even so, Nelson was one of the first to be thinking in a big way about how to synthesise information and to extract meaning from it, to recognise the value of putting information together from different media, and to worry about the incompatibilities and obsolescence of hardware and software and of the resulting disastrous implications for the long term storage of data. Unfortunately there is as yet no product, and he has been beaten to the punch by the Internet and the World Wide Web in the capture of the public imagination, and by Bill Gates as the unimaginably wealthy telegenic guru of IT. What Nelson has to say, however, is of great importance.

Nelson's starting point is the enormous value of text; he states that 'text is the self-portrait of human thought; more precisely, it is the ordered presentation of the results of that thought'[7]. He goes on to say that 'there are not many text problems but one problem, *the* text problem, which is the grand interplay of written materials, their interconnections, and the minds that play on these interconnections like harp-strings'. He is acutely cognisant of the feedback loops between Worlds 2 and 3, of the needs of creative users and producers of literature, and of the way that ideas bounce off texts and works of art and feed off each other. But he is aware too of the need to have harmonised access to materials in a variety of media, and is worried by the incompatibility between systems that already exist or are under development. In his studiedly off-the-wall *Literary Machines* he writes[17]:

> 'The world of paper is at least unified and compatible. Objects can be easily mixed and matched. Books, manuscripts and notes can be stored on the same shelf, opened on the same desk. You need not start up, initialize or insert a disk before opening a magazine'.

Not so with computer systems, or indeed with films, video or audiotape. A common system with stable indexing and storage is required. Nelson's answer is Xanadu.

Xanadu was named after 'the magic place of literary memory' in Samuel Taylor Coleridge's poem *Kubla Khan*, and is intended to be nothing less than a dynamic repository for all the world's literary media, all interrelated by meaning and by other links deemed to be useful. The basic ideas for the project supposedly 'came to' Nelson in 1960, while on a humanities computer course at Harvard. Never one to be untruthfully modest Nelson says that 'Xanadu is a whole world: a way of thinking, a way of relating to documents, a way of creating and delivering a whole new literature'[28]. And indeed it is a whole new world, a unified data structure that is the closest we have yet come to World 4. As Nelson continues '... it is a universal approach to the creation, melding and delivery of vast numbers of documents with different points of view, eventually merging them all into a new electronic literature for much of the planet'. The crucial word in this sentence is 'melding', for Nelson intends that the system will escape from the wastefulness of duplication and irrelevance that characterises existing information sources, and that Xanadu will approximate to the World 4 map of information 'as it is'. 'Such a system', he writes[17], 'will represent at last the true structure of information (rather than Procrustean mappings of it), with all its intrinsic complexity and controversy, and provide a universal archival standard worthy of our heritage of freedom and pluralism.' The 'Procrustean mappings' are World 3; Xanadu is World 4.

In its ultimate form Xanadu is the repository for the world's cultural efforts which are amenable to digital capture and storage, but it also offers private or semi-private archive facilities for individuals or organisations, in a manner analogous to the relationship between Intranets and the Internet. Provision would be made for multi-authoring, for the retrieval of documents in their original form, and for the collection and payment of royalties to authors each time their creations were accessed - a welcome advance on today's unwieldy copyright legislation. The key to this is what Nelson calls transclusion or xanalogical storage (some of Nelson's neologisms have a whiff of Buckminster Fuller - another visionary American one-off - about them). Xanalogical storage means that the components of documents are only stored once, and if these components happen to be quoted in other documents or are revised into different versions, then they are retrieved via quotation links or revision links, i.e. hyperlinks, with just the alterations added as separate material and without the redundancy and storage overheads which multiple copying would imply. There is thus only one copy in the system of each 'conceptual byte'. Nelson says that xanalogical storage 'makes it possible easily to *make new things out of old*, sharing material between units'[17]. This is now a commonplace feature of document management systems.

As the ultimate macro-literary hypertext system (to use a term employed by Conklin in an early review of the subject[29]) Xanadu explicitly caters for the need to provide information in context, and here, the concept of xanalogical storage finds its place. Much of the information in print is redundant in the sense that it is setting the background context in which to display a relatively small new piece of information.

This introductory context tends to get repeated many times throughout the associated literature. With xanalogical storage it is held just once, and appropriately related to other material. The same technique allows for multiple versions of documents to exist as they go through phases of creation and update, without having to include entire copies of each document with only minor alterations. Just the original, the alterations, and the connecting links are held on Xanadu.

Several types of links are envisaged by Nelson, some of the more obvious ones being for comment, correction, translation and quotation. Nelson believes that his system allows documents to be increasingly better organised, and that as the system develops the degree of order will be cumulatively enhanced whereas with most existing computer systems progressive disorder is more usual.

Xanadu is a complete hyperworld, and it is quite likely that - even with sufficient financial backing - it will never be realised. It may be just too radical, too ambitious, and - more lethally - too inflexible. Steinberg[30] is critical, stating that 'the dream of organising all knowledge has been thoroughly discredited' and that schemes such as Xanadu 'are widely seen as laughable in our relativist, postmodern era'. The thinking behind Xanadu does seem to come from the Victorian 'imperial archive' tendency, to use Thomas Richard's expression[31], from the currently unfashionable and politically incorrect realist assumption that there is a single version of 'the truth' which can be consistently mapped, although Nelson specifically refers to the system's ability to contain alternative viewpoints.

Perhaps with appropriate irony, Xanadu has been the subject of considerable hype, with release promised several times ... 1976, 1988, 1991 ... but not yet delivered. It has become the kind of offering that gets labelled sarcastically as 'vapourware', and Nelson has often been put on the defensive. Programming began in 1979 at the Xanadu Operating Company in San Jose and subsequently continued from 1988 under the auspices of Autodesk Inc., a major supplier of computer-aided design systems based in Sausalito, California, who reputedly pumped $5 million into the project. In August 1992 Autodesk withdrew practical support from the project. From time to time, though, Nelson still promises roll-out of the product, and there have been tentative developments, particularly in Japan and Australia, and as a more modest publishing system, but nothing like the real thing as envisaged. Taking McDonald's as his role model, Nelson proposed having roadside Xanadu stands for access to this global literature resource with such facilities operated under franchise agreements. Ironically, parallels to this have been emerging for some time in the way of public access to the Internet, from cybercafés and cyberpubs, and increasingly from kiosks installed in shopping malls, airport terminals, and so on. The final irony would be the opening of the first Cyber-McDonald's.

So far, sadly, and somewhat surprisingly, there has been no hint of even the beginnings of the massive collection and structuring of data which would have to be the starting point for the system. Nelson has been more concerned with the technology and with issues like copyright and royalty collection than with content. If Xanadu ever develops according to Nelson's punningly described 2020 vision (referring to the year by which he expects it to be operating as the planetary information retrieval system), we will have a unified digital hypermedia, a memex, a World 4, a World Brain. If the Xanadu project fails then maybe the ideal of a World Brain will never be realised, and information disorder will spiral ever more out of control. As regards knowledge synthesis, at present there is nothing else remotely as ambitious as Xanadu in sight. It looks very much as though we will not have a World Brain, a 'Novum Organum', in place as the new Millennium begins. Maybe this was never a realistic possibility. All the same, it seems a pity. So when T. S. Eliot asks 'Where is the knowledge we have lost in information?' the answer might well be 'Xanadu'.

Exactly how World 4 develops, whether systematically and omnisciently as per Xanadu, or as small, discrete knowledge bases or summary pages on the Web, only time will tell. From the point of view of information overload on the individual some digestion of knowledge and reduction of redundancy would seem to be highly desirable, and in this respect the present on-line systems, the Internet, and CD-ROM will never be entirely adequate. Indeed, they might in the long run make matters worse. Unless or until Xanadu succeeds to its fullest potential we can expect that many organisations and individuals will develop their own private 'mini World 4s' to cater for their own needs, in ways which might be quite wasteful and redundant in an overall sense. These would be developments of current knowledge base designs, using hypermedia and intranet technology, and possibly some home-grown brand of 'xanalogical' storage, but significantly less ambitious in scope than the Xanadu project. A search of closely related documents on the Web rapidly reveals how much wasted effort is going into the creation of broadly similar - and often similarly poor quality - syntheses of knowledge in particular domains. Licklider, writing way back in 1965 on 'Libraries of the Future'[32] said that we must 'accept the notion that, for many years at least, we shall not achieve a complete integration of knowledge, that we shall have to content ourselves with diverse partial models of the universe. It may not be elegant to base some of the models in geometry, some in logic, and others in natural language, but that may be the most practicable solution'. Regrettably, I think Licklider's prognosis might still stand, three decades on, and more.

The idea of Xanadu and World 4 extends to the individual, even - or especially - to the individual with Wolfean obsessions, because it permits the structuring of knowledge according to one's own habits of association and the annotation of existing public domain information with one's own comments. The crucial problem for Wolfean man is that he cannot recall everything at once, cannot remember very much, cannot concentrate on much at any one time, cannot explore all the possible ramifications of every idea. The Xanadu idea, with its hyperlinks by association and its overall maps of the territory it covers, is the nearest we can get at present to an answer for the Wolfean urge, for it can carry representations of World 1 (as hypermedia), World 2 (as our own comments), and World 3, the entire contents of the world's cultural archive - stripped of unnecessary duplication, thanks to Ted Nelson's xanalogical storage. Alas, it is no more than an idea.

For those so inclined, access to Xanadu might go some way towards relieving the Wolfean problem. This could be as personalised as one liked, or as one had the patience and the time to create. In the true Wolfean sense one's private file on Xanadu might even be used to establish a permanent record of longings and nostalgias - and of the details of the stains on hotel ceilings! Arguably it might increase feelings of alienation and unreality. There is no substitute for having one's own thoughts inside one's own head, but since information overload and the pinpoint of conscious awareness limit one's capacity so drastically, to set up a personalised 'extrasomatic brain' might be no bad thing.

Xanadu notwithstanding, any World 4 type of project is bound to have great limitations for some time to come, and it will still be true that - whether or not we as individuals are tormented by Wolfean hungers to have the whole universe constantly before our eyes - we do need more help to enable us to cope with information overload. The realm of what we constitute as knowledge always exceeds our own knowledge and we need help in orienting ourselves. Synthetic approaches to knowledge engineering will become increasingly necessary. At present we are hindered by lack of cooperation and coordination between commercial databases, despite techniques for 'de-duplication', by the lack of quality control and structure on the Web, and by incompatibilities between systems, a traditional problem that has bedevilled many developments in information technology (programming languages, TV transmission standards, computer operating systems, video formats, protocols for multimedia and data networking) and about which Ted Nelson has warned us. A recent example of the situation is provided by Canadian health workers[33] who commented - in an article sub-titled *Navigating to Knowledge or to Babel?* - that 'many incompletely developed instruments to evaluate health information exist on the Internet. It is unclear, however, whether they should exist in the first place, whether they measure what they claim to measure, or whether they lead to more good than harm'. In this and many other ways seamless synthesis still eludes us.

Another potentially serious difficulty awaiting us is that of navigation and retrieval of manageable quantities of relevant data within the very large information spaces ('cyberspaces') inevitably to be encountered within World 4. This may have to wait for developments in the creation of the so-called virtual library, before a really elegant solution is found, a 'walk-in' repository with domains of information presented in a highly visual way to us. However, we are already witnessing interesting advances in some of the search aids being produced for the Internet.

So why isn't the Internet the World Brain? The Internet allows hyperlinking between documents, distributed processing, easy browsing of document titles and opening up of document contents without concern as to their format or geographical location, very often it offers the full text of documents, and - most important of all - it permits access to (potentially) everyone. The main reason why it isn't the World Brain, in the way that I have described it, is lack of organisation, lack of knowledge synthesis, and lack of overall quality control and content control. Despite all the hype and despite the astonishing rapidity of its take-off, the Internet is a natural - though comprehensively unpredicted - outcome of the uncontrolled progression of World 3 as an unstructured global mish-mash of 'information'. It is interesting to speculate how it would have developed if Xanadu had got there first. Would it have happened at all? That it might not seems unthinkable now. As things are, the success of the Internet has probably killed off Xanadu, yet

Xanadu-like features will increasingly need to be developed for the Internet. It may never be possible to proactively create syntheses of knowledge à la Xanadu, we may have missed that particular boat. Instead, powerful search engines and meta-search engines working on the Web will enable us to identify all the data relevant to a particular issue, so that syntheses can be created on demand, on the fly, or pointed to where they already exist. This is probably the way that this need will be satisfied.

The Internet is a highly dynamic environment with astonishing statistics for growth of numbers of sites, documents, and users, inviting constantly changing perspectives on available information, new ways of slicing through it and interrelating different kinds of material. This is valuable, and its instability excites some people, particularly those who reject the notion of centrally organised knowledge, and who can benefit from the serendipitous potential inherent in unstructured browsing, but as we have seen it does mean that there is a risk that information becomes increasingly uncontrollable. It means that unreliable, highly selective, biased, or just plain wrong misinformation can masquerade as objective fact. The Web was never intended to serve as the planetary data repository; one may say that its development has been essentially accidental. The natural desire for quality control of the Web, and indeed for any kind of control of it, goes against the spirit in which the beast was conceived, but some sort of compromise solution will have to be achieved, and it will be interesting to see how this works out over the next few years.

Synthesis from isolated fact to coherent knowledge remains the most difficult task. It may be argued that for too long information has been the focus of attention, rather than organised knowledge, but this is a stage that has had to be gone through. According to A. L. Dick in the Department of Information Science at the University of South Africa, in Pretoria, 'Knowledge needs to be restored to its former status as a legitimate and serious theoretical focus in the education of information professionals'[34]. Or as Roberto Refinetti of the University of São Paulo puts it, 'a whole class of information managers is necessary to perform the highest function in the progress of knowledge - namely, the integration of disconnected data into a coherent whole'[35]. Initially this implies the use of techniques for extracting information from texts[36]. This is the most pressing goal for information science, and if we cannot find a way of doing it proactively we will need techniques for doing it on demand.

The development of anything like World 4 - whether via Xanadu, the Internet, or anything else - will not reduce the psychological pressures suffered by the Thomas Wolfes of this world; rather, it may exacerbate them while simultaneously offering practical help, in terms of information retrieval, semantic linking, and visualisation. The Wolfean urge will be untouched by technology but the wallowing indulgence in information overload which Wolfe so masochistically enjoyed in the Widener Library and elsewhere will become more comprehensively available to all. A doubtful blessing indeed.

The most valuable outcome of any attempt at creating World 4, other than practical advances in information retrieval, may be in the way we are spurred into a more realistic evaluation of and a more tolerant acceptance of the facts, opinions and partial truths we already have. Information is not always the value-neutral commodity it sometimes appears. Awareness of this begins to emerge even at the level of classification, when a librarian's point of view - political or otherwise, and probably held intuitively and in all innocence - if imposed on a collection of literature, may mean that an item cannot be found and retrieved by someone with a differing viewpoint. Classification is not always the objective, dry-as-dust activity that it may at first appear to be, and it is not immune from patches of cognitive turbulence, for it is inseparable from underlying philosophical principles which are not always universally agreed. Nor is knowledge synthesis without controversy. Indeed, encyclopaedias have, throughout their history, included unfashionable or subversive opinions, or acted as propaganda vehicles for fanatics and for totalitarian regimes of all persuasions. World Brain projects crank such issues up to a higher and more visible level - hopefully not to the level of 'cyber-warfare'. As the frankly untenable is thrown into sharper relief by the adjacency of more credible data, there will be plenty of scope for the exercise of intolerance and misrepresentation, yet there is just a chance that World 4 could become the one 'place' - the one 'cyberplace' - where conflicting viewpoints could peacefully co-exist.

9. Conclusion – Some Implications for the Information Age

Given the situation we are in, how can we best respond to an expansion of information which is too much for us to take in, and which threatens our individuality, while being taunted by needs to know more and more about everything, to keep up with the informational Joneses until we feel that we are going to explode? How do we reconcile ourselves to being nobodies while daily we have dangled in front of us evidently highly successful people able to develop and live with their 'multiple personalities', able to 'be' and to 'have' the world - to use Erich Fromm's terminology - all at the same time? How do we avoid the anger and resentment, and all the pathologies that flow from despair and defeat? As the information explosion carries on mushrooming how can we avoid becoming relatively more ignorant and, with the availability of new technologies, how can we avoid that ignorance becoming more apparent and less forgiveable? How do we live with the opposing forces pushing towards destructive information overload and the social disadvantage of information impoverishment? How do we cope with the fact that, beyond the basic need for consumption of experience and acquisition of new data input, there is a need for meaningfulness, for recognition of our yearning, for the chance to 'tell someone'? Andy Warhol promised us fame for 15 minutes: that is as inadequate as it is unlikely. These are some of the questions that the Age of Information must face.

No doubt there is a desire to 'tell someone' about one's feelings but except for the relatively very few who achieve conventional success, as artists or scientists or whatever, this prospect for communication does not exist. However, thanks to developments and convergences in computing power, storage media, telecommunications and the economics of the provision of data and entertainment, and especially with the advent of global data networks and hypermedia-based cyber-realms such as the World Wide Web (and Xanadu, if it eventually succeeds), it becomes increasingly feasible to enmesh oneself in World 3, to participate in what one might call the public record of mankind, to pootle out onto the infobahn, to venture out into the arena while cowering at the keyboard. Bill Gates writes[1]: 'The ease with which an individual, any individual, can share his opinions with the members of a huge electronic community is unprecedented'. This gives us new opportunities for creativity and for some of the satisfactions of published creativity - even if it is only a new version of vanity publishing. It offers us new perspectives on what we want to say and to have identified with us. It probably isn't enough, but it's a start. Given that you can put anything you like on to your home page on the Web, what would you put? Does it help you to define yourself, to develop as a person, or does it just massage your ego?

At the same time as we define our information territory, we need to be able to exclude that which is never going to be ours, to be able to deliberately ignore and say: 'that isn't for me'. We must be able to select, to fashion our own information spaces. The lesson to be learned is that it is the quality and personal meaningfulness of internalised information that are ultimately important, rather than the surface skimming of vast tranches of data and pseudo-experience and living-by-proxy which cannot be adequately assimilated. Information as a commodity becomes ever more the same sort of thing, of equal value and emotional weight, as transient news or fodder for entertainment - infotainment, edutainment, advertorials - just another interchangeable species of ambient noise. It fails to satisfy or to command affection. We - as self-determined individuals - can do better than this.

The whole concept of sacredness is one which merits careful examination in this age of mass data handling and in the context of what might be called the ecology of information, the protection of trivia as unique and endangered species, the stains on the ceiling and the ephemera of trainspotting. This is difficult: trivia often give us the greatest sense of reality and meaning and satisfaction, but they are nevertheless trivia. There is a knife edge between reverence and narcissism. Some time ago an unexpected and radical approach to this predicament was announced, and from an unlikely source. British Telecom have an 'artificial life' team based at their Martlesham Heath research laboratories in Suffolk, and they actually employ an 'official futurologist', Ian Pearson[2]. In July 1996 this team, fronted by a spokesman, Dr. Chris Winter, hit the headlines with their proposal for a 'soul catcher' microchip, a device implanted behind the eye which could record every thought and sensation throughout a person's life. 'This is the end of death', said Dr. Winter. He predicted that by the year 2025 it would be possible to relive other people's lives by playing back their experiences via a computer, a scenario anticipated in Dennis Potter's television series *Cold Lazarus*, in which a dead man's memory is revived. The BT team claimed that by combining this information with a record of the person's genes, it would be possible to recreate a person 'physically, emotionally and spiritually'; a 'soul catcher' chip implanted into a newborn baby could imbue the infant with a lifetime's experiences from a dead person. It was argued that the compression of data on to silicon is accelerating at such a pace that by the year 2025 a single chip would be able to handle this amount of data, said to be equivalent to 30 million books. I'm not sure how the 'lifetime's experiences' are to be extracted, or where they are to be found, but a few thousand words of French vocabulary or the London Underground map would be a useful leg-up in life! Watch this space ...

However, it is what we do with information that is important, not how much of it we have. We should remember the nutritional parable of Thomas Wolfe, as told by Wright Morris: 'A glutton for life, he actually died of impoverishment. He bolted both life and literature in such a manner he failed to get real nourishment from either. Nothing that he devoured, since it was not digested, satisfied his insatiable appetite. He was aware of that himself, and his now legendary hunger haunted him like the hound of heaven, and it became, in time, synonymous with life itself. *Appetite*'[3].

Information is a fundamental property of the universe as we know it, a property just like consciousness, or matter or energy[4]. And like matter or energy, it would be fair to assume that information has ecological needs of conservation, preservation, efficient utilisation, and avoidance of waste and pollution. Using our Popper's Worlds model it may be seen how information flow shows some parallels with more familiar ecosystems and how each World is interdependent on the others, either for its creation or for meaningful interpretation. It may even be said that everything we do is information processing of one sort or another, although that would be both to trivialise our activities and to render the term 'information' - in all its ubiquity - redundant and without real meaning. We have to be careful that the study of 'information' does not become as meaningless as studying 'things'.

Matter and energy cannot be created or destroyed according to their respective principles of conservation, although they can be interconverted. Information appears to act differently: it can be created and destroyed and converted into many different forms, but without man, without World 2, it loses all practical significance. While the universe in general terms tends towards entropy or heat death, towards a total randomness and sameness and lack of meaning, information can reverse this trend, and can negentropically create new structures and new meanings. Sometimes, though, in fact all too often, it can seem to be heading the same way as entropy.

Wolfe was much concerned with the sacred properties of information and felt that he had to record it for fear that it would be lost for all time, and in a more practical sense too we can be concerned with the ecological aspects of information. Let us consider a few of these issues in turn: the natural decay of information, the loss of information because of changes in the technology for accessing it, the wastefulness in the way that information is formatted and distributed, the boredom that could result from a more logical approach to information structuring, the sorts of problems that arise from not having a logical structure, and pollution by useless information.

First, the natural decay of information as an ecological issue. Information per se does vanish from time to time, often for the good reason that it is ephemeral anyway and no longer of any use, but both on the individual and societal levels knowledge can simply go out of fashion. Each age has its concerns, which are reliably documented in print for those who want to know, and though there is considerable evidence to the contrary, in general terms we believe we are making progress and that we can leave behind problems which concerned us in the past. In the terminology of Buckminster Fuller, there is an accelerating ephemeralisation in our activities. Detail gets reduced to general principles, the complex into slogans, and style into cliché. We feel that we have moved on. In a general societal sense that may be true, but as individual people we still have as much to learn as ever, in fact, vastly more. Otherwise we become vastly more ignorant and disadvantaged in many ways. The irony is that the more that is known at large the more relatively ignorant we as individuals are likely to be. Despite Thomas Wolfe, long gone is the time when an educated man could know 'everything'. But at least we are now able to tackle the problem at its real size; now we are drawing all the information in the world together and our technology gives us the chance of being able to manage it.

This is where the real ecological threat of the Age of Information comes in. To have any meaning or value, World 3 has to be accessed by World 2. If for any reason that cannot happen we have a problem in the local informational environment; it might be that the information is unavailable to us because it is presented in a foreign language or in too complex a form for us to understand, difficulties which can hopefully be overcome by education, but more seriously it might exist in a form which cannot be interpreted by present day equipment.

Technological obsolescence is a major component of information ecology. While World 3 exists in discrete forms as books, paintings, musical scores, and so on, though we as individuals might have difficulty reading, interpreting, or appreciating them, there are experts around who could. If the information exists in, shall we say, the Betamax format and we only have VHS equipment, then we are in trouble. Apart from panic about the so-called Millennium bug there has been relatively little said about the way that vital information which we are creating in ever larger quantities might in time be totally inaccessible and lost forever, because the software has been superceded, or the hardware is obsolete, because a worn out component cannot be replaced or because the data was stored on a medium which we hadn't realised would decay and turn to magnetic dust after 20, 50, 100, 1,000 years. The powerful protocols devised for the Internet ride roughshod over many earlier incompatibilities, but how long before we are onto the next thing? One of the few commentators to seriously address this problem of incompatibility and loss has been Ted Nelson, and that is one of the motivations behind his Xanadu project, with the whole of World 4 in one place but accessible from many locations. So we need to be aware that information has to be processed in a suitable form to keep it alive - it has to be future-proof.

We must also recognise that technical possibilities may go beyond what we are comfortable with, or may require significant cultural adjustments. Some people learn best by reading, some from diagrams or other visual aids, some from being taught; most people learn best by doing. Then again, some people are afraid of computers or as a matter of principle refuse to have anything to do with them. This will change as the generations pass on, but there will always be personal preferences and aversions, and there will always be relative Luddites and relative technophiles. The book may still be preferred to the laptop, the scent of the trail through dusty archives found to be more exciting than the point-and-click at the high definition VDU, similarly the mono 45 r.p.m. single may be preferred over the slick CD with accompanying video, or even the grainy black and white print over the glossy colour transparency. Subtle sensory qualities, smells and touches, the minutiae of aesthetics and kinaesthetics, imperfections even, matter to us at least as much as raw information content. We are a perverse species - thankfully.

Continuing with the ecological theme, and again invoking the insight of Ted Nelson, we need to consider how information might be produced less wastefully than at present. Rather than creating isolated documents which are reproduced and distributed in multiples of millions there could and perhaps should be a transition wherever practicable towards the generation of more integrated and comprehensive documents located centrally but with multiple remote electronic access. In other words a trend towards World 4. In an ecological sense this is both kinder to trees and avoids the side effects of physical distribution systems, and is conceptually a neater and more efficient way of handling information. Whether it would ever be generally acceptable is something else. Nelson has coined the expression the 'conceptual byte', meaning the smallest modular unit of a fact or idea. The ideal is that this conceptual byte should be stored once and once only, rather than cluttering up information space in the way that generally happens. By recognising that World 4 is a seamless multimedia hyperdocument with all conceptual bytes slotting into an overall structure and being 'intertwingled', Nelson has broken through a fundamental barrier which has existed within our culture ever since the invention of writing. Whether we will ever want to or be able to exploit this possibility for avoiding redundancy of information on a large scale is quite another matter. True multimedia is in its infancy and there is no sign in the general population of a drift away from the popularity of books, newspapers and magazines to screen-based media. Nor is there any indication that people would want to contribute to or read from an integrated 'book of all knowledge' rather than individual books or articles. The distinction between the idea of information as discrete documents and information as an abstract structure is reflected, however, in current notions of library science versus information science.

There are other problems with the idea of World 4. The standardisation of knowledge that it implies may well be thought of as threatening and sinister as well as boring. One could find oneself retreading the same stereotyped and well-worn paths - information chreodes, one might call them - through data realms time and time again. We all like to be different, to be free, to enjoy variety, and not infrequently we want to know things that others do not. A monolithic World 4 militates against such freedoms. The construction of World 4 poses worrying questions about control, judgement and standardisation. The openness and chaos of the Internet at least leaves us with more freedom. Anarchy can be a tricky beast to ride but although it is uncomfortable, arguably it is preferable to the sterility of a more controlled - and perhaps unworkable - system.

One of the main concerns of this book has been with the need to extract personal meaning from impersonal information and here we touch on another ecological concern, namely personal hygiene as applied to information. We are back with the question of what to allow into our minds and what to banish safely to Worlds 1 and 3. A frequent complaint is about the amount of junk mail we receive - junk faxes and junk e-mail too - and how wasteful it is. Normally we throw such items away unread and it does not cause us a major problem, other than wasting our time, but there are more insidious kinds of personal informational pollution. We recognise Bhopal, Seveso, Exxon Valdez or Chernobyl as environmental catastrophes; less dramatically there may be informational equivalents. We spend a lot of time roaming World 3 to little benefit - hours spent with newspapers, magazines or sat in front of the TV - being exposed to multiple versions of things that do not interest us at all. And that is quite apart from what we have to wade through in the workplace. This all adds to our personal overload. The media latch on to the latest trend and exploit it to death, with rampant redundancy and synchronised duplication of content across many sources. The scientific community at least tries to minimise the growth of literature by frowning upon multiple publication of single pieces of work, invoking the wonderfully named Ingelfinger rule, but this scarcely happens in other areas of activity.

Within conventional ecology we have learned to recognise pathogenic processes at work, from over-logging to over-fishing, from global warming to the dangerous elevation of atmospheric levels of radiation, CFCs, or sulphur dioxide. Information too has its pathologies - personally, organisationally and societally - and these will increasingly come to be recognised. Wurman[5] in his book *Information Anxiety* has characterised some of these, notably in the areas of difficulty of access to information, junk information and 'information bulimia', while the Reuters report[6], referred to earlier, has examined some of the features of information addiction in the workplace. We are used to the idea of the large company strangled in its own unusable data, or the Kafkaesque farce of the political bureaucracy, but we are not yet so aware of the personal information pathologies that may occur. We are starting to develop laws about freedom of information, data protection, and copyright, but we are hardly cognisant of the hazards that information availability imposes on World 2. This book has, amongst other things, highlighted some of these effects with the examples of Thomas Wolfe and other hoarders or cravers of Worlds 1 and 3 who failed to find satisfaction. Perhaps, as we move onwards through transitions in information handling, such concerns will come more to the fore.

In a world perceived increasingly as information, so people become increasingly to be seen as information processing beings, and we need to consider what that means to us. We are ever more in a position of being able to design our own personal information content, to specify what, in informational terms, we will be. That probably sounds far fetched given the reality of daily life for many people. Much was heard not so long ago about how we have left the industrial era behind and are now in the post-industrial age, even the leisure age. For many, this is a sick joke. In reality we are in an era of increasingly unsatisfying and stressful jobs and of unemployment which, if not actually rising, is contained only by the creation of jobs which don't actually produce anything real. At the same time people have greater expectations, greater awareness of possibilities and inequalities. In such difficult times the concept of an authentic and fulfilling lifestyle becomes more important than ever, and the available technology can both help and aggravate this problem. Within a few short years it may be a fact of life that some kind of World Brain exists, just possibly Ted Nelson's Xanadu with its roadside access points and McDonald's style franchises, or more likely some development of the Internet. The world's store of music, literature, films and visual art will be available from every terminal as will shopping, banking, all kinds of virtual reality simulations and many kinds of paid occupation. Recently, plans were announced in the UK for piping the Internet into every house along with the electricity supply[7]. Information retrieval, of a sort, will have become instant and trivially easy. An important consequence of this revolution in information handling, however it occurs, will be the way that a greater personal responsibility is thrust upon us for choosing, using, evaluating and re-synthesising information.

In the personal sphere, home computers and the databases and networks they can access will offer greater flexibility for personal exploration and for syntheses of knowledge in ways which centralised, commercial operations cannot accommodate. This may lead to unhealthy solitude, introspection, even a kind of electronic solipsism, but used wisely will enhance freedom of expression, communication, one's sphere of contacts - no longer limited by geography - and self-knowledge. The extended free time of the leisure age, if it ever comes, would allow us to gain more pleasure and enrichment from Worlds 1 and 2, as well as World 3. To live entirely by the demands of man-made media is paradoxically a denial of important aspects of our humanity, and we could usefully spend more time getting to know ourselves and our physical environment better.

As the informational realm becomes better organised and more widely accessible there is a danger that immersion in it will become an increasingly sterile pursuit; we still need the input of original thought that comes with the oddities of childhood perception and the peculiarities of the creative psyche. Probably most of us could benefit from a little more sensual wallowing and subjective waywardness, more feeling and less left-brained logical cleverness, but trying to escape the manic modern world is all too often stigmatised as personal failure.

So much that we call knowledge gives us little or no satisfaction. It has been said that we learn in order to forget: facts are discarded in favour of theories, details are replaced by generalities, items of data are chunked, painfully acquired skills are routinised, and knowledge becomes intuitive and automatic rather than consciously fabricated. Thomas Wolfe never understood this, and the conflict between the desire for the sacred detail versus the effort-liberating general concept was at the heart of his problem. Not that you can 'chunk' a yearning for a Bowery street scene into a generalised conceptual Manhattan - or whatever. But some kinds of knowledge are amenable to this kind of treatment, or to delegation onto machines. We are not very good, for example, at arithmetic, which may be one explanation for the popularity of pocket calculators[8]; of course there will always be calculating freaks and mathematical masochists but most of us are quite happy to off-load this kind of mental activity - and much else besides. Information technology can help us here. IT can also help us receive data in ways more congenial to us, which primarily means visualisation, allowing us to more readily detect correlations, significances and trends which would otherwise be lost in a sea of text or numerical data, and illustrating graphically how subjects or concept areas interrelate. It will also save us time by giving us speech input and output in our interactions with intelligent devices. Whether it will allow us to directly 'jack in' our minds to cyberspace, as envisaged by William Gibson, is more problematic. The connection of mind with electronics, as in the fully-fledged cyborg beloved of science fiction, implies solving a fundamental problem about the nature of consciousness - a problem as far away from solution as it ever was. For the time being, though, we should exploit the technology available to us.

Most of us are more at home with information tinged with human significance, some emotional content, some warmth and texture, some associational possibilities. The computer can help. We need to be able to free our minds from a clutter of tiresome facts which are more conveniently and efficiently stored elsewhere and consulted when necessary, without us feeling alienated from the data and without having to suffer impossible unsatisfiable Wolfean longings for it. We need to know what is the crucial material to incorporate in the minds of living, throbbing humanity - and to file the rest away, electronically or otherwise, in the 'conceptual Basingstoke' we encountered in Chapter 4. Cognitive, epistemological, ontological, digital Basingstoke.

The rapid development of information processing technology will soon bring to an end our comfortable era of information innocence. As we transit through the turn of the century, and as the latest advances in information technology gel and synergise, we can expect that developments in global databases will pose questions about the quality of information that we process and what it actually means, rather than its mere quantity. Until quite recently we have been happy enough to be doled out a large wad of printout or computerised gobbledegook as an alternative to having to think about the real problem at hand; from now on the quality, presentation and validity of that information starts to become more important. We are reaching a time, unique in human history, when facts will have to be reconciled, theories stacked up against each other, subjective opinions and evaluations deliberately collided with each other and something like a global truth - or a partial truth, a compromise or a proto-truth - extracted. This is a novel state of affairs in the intellectual world. Until now there has always been room - thanks to the inefficiency of global communications - for contradictory statements. Now, the truth has to be recognised for what it is, and the bogus rejected. In an intolerant, prejudiced, multicultural world where most of the time we don't know what the truth is, this will be extraordinarily difficult, but the creation of a genuine World 4, a full-blown Xanadu, is dependent on this happening. Information structures will act increasingly as provocations of discussion, as identifiers of zones of anomaly, conflict, doubt, and faith.

Computers can easily process large volumes of data, but the hard part is reconciling one piece of data with another. So far, only man can do that. Only man understands significance; only man knows the meaning of meaning. Computers can simulate and pretend, and increasingly will be doing so aided by neural networks and related technologies, and often we will have no idea how they are doing this, but in the beginning it is we who set them up and running and in the end it is we who judge. Once we begin to compile integrated databases or knowledge bases on a variety of subjects, paradigms and viewpoints will clash, or at the very least their disparity will be highlighted. Reductionist and holistic approaches will need to be reconciled as well as scientific and artistic, objective and subjective, rational and irrational; conflicting paradigms will need to be subsumed under an umbrella metaparadigm. Great philosophies and faiths will get shuffled uncomfortably next to each other in the 'universal viewpoint' of an electronic database. Growing up is hard to do. At some point Santa Claus has to go. Individual freedom of thought and expression will become very important issues when we want to reject what seems to be untrue or worthless for ever, and the responsibility for database management will assume some onerous aspects.

Up until now ideas and what seem to be factual truths have been able to hide within local cultures, protected from the wider world by barriers of geography, language and general impracticality of access, and if necessary by censorship - even by the building of walls. Inevitably such things will continue and some protection of vulnerable communities - such as children and 'primitive' societies - is desirable, but this kind of intellectual parochialism is less and less tenable. The collapse of communism in the Soviet Union and Eastern Europe is perhaps the most spectacular example of this trend. As data migrates from printed to electronic form, as international data networks proliferate, and as language ceases to be a barrier (because English becomes the world language and because, in time, machine translation becomes a workable reality), ideas increasingly will have to stand or fall in the world marketplace of critical evaluation. Constraints such as nationality, ethnicity, class and language become increasingly irrelevant in the world information marketplace. Although alliteration can be highly irritating, what is true in Bournemouth or Brighton will also have to be true in Bradford or Bethnal Green or Belfast - and in Berlin, Bucharest, Baltimore, Beijing, Baghdad, Brasilia, Brisbane, Bulawayo and Bangkok. And Basingstoke. In this hard-edged, realist, no-nonsense approach to the integration of information there will be great temptations to suppress unfashionable minority opinions and controversial or inconvenient data. How this would work out in practice remains to be seen, but one would hope that the usual human democratic institutions of whistle-blowing, covert communication and subversion would rectify any such intolerances.

This loss of innocence, this emergence from the protection afforded by invisible walls of enforced ignorance, affects not just society at large. A parallel situation arises in the life of the individual. Until now, the information a person could be expected to know or to consult has been limited by personal circumstances. Now, or very soon, there will be fewer limits, and this holds important consequences. Until now a person's input has been artificially restricted, by geographical location, general availability of material, education, language, and cost. The fact that for a long time man has been unable to cope with the volume of information in existence has been obscured because circumstances provided natural protection against information overload. These restrictions are now being removed, for good or ill, and before long almost all significant information will be equally available throughout the industrialised world. Making the excuse that the local library didn't have the book or that the article was too difficult or was written in Japanese or that the thesis could only be consulted in a university archive in Texas will no longer do. Thanks to the networked virtual library it will be right here, in the office, the classroom or the living room, at low cost, in a form which can be understood. The onus is transferred onto the individual to search out all the relevant material, to select, interpret, evaluate and use it. We are now leaving the local trainspotting era behind; now we all have full time access to the big black book at rail headquarters, the book with all the numbers. Sad perhaps, extremely boring to some, but true. The full personal consequences of this are yet to be seen.

Features of our lives long dictated to us in subtle ways are starting to open up. Access to information is one of these, with responsibility for finding and using it being decentralised and devolved onto the individual. As we increasingly demand instant availability and immediate gratification in other areas of our lives, spoiled impatient children that we have become ('Want it now!'), so it will be with respect to information.

And the onus will be on us to pull information from readily available sources, rather than having it pushed at us and force fed to us like TV schedules or the contents of daily newspapers. Some may find this disturbing, for it encourages us to examine our personal needs and tastes - and paradoxically this might give us a better chance of expressing our true individuality. It will certainly enable us to do and to experience more - albeit via the intermediary of the IT or VR device. That could be very useful in the work environment, but the increased pressures it implies could be more problematical in other situations.

One of the major trends characterising the late 20th century has been the culling of sacred cows and the erosion of artificial restrictions previously imposed by ignorance, technical inability and social constructs. This trend has affected access to information as much as anything else. Latterly, the power of computing, electronic communications and allied technologies has permitted a freedom to manipulate information - in the widest sense of the word - going way beyond anything known hitherto. One only has to consider the way that technology has freed information from being a rigid, static, paper-bound, labour-intensive, difficult-to-communicate commodity accessible only to the select few into a plastic, dynamic, infinitely malleable, multimedia, available-to-all, ubiquitously present feature of our daily lives, to see what a major change has taken place within a single generation. Computing, digitisation and telecommunications have permitted a kind of electronic eclecticism, a coming together of possibilities and with it a capacity to interconvert one kind of information into another. Video imagery, morphing, sound synthesis and sampling, machine translation of language, spreadsheets and graphical displays, and text manipulation are just some aspects of this new ability to handle information as a plastic medium, an ability scarcely yet recognised as such, but an ability accessible to anyone of modest intelligence and average skills. Soon we will demand any or all information to be delivered to us in any appropriate medium at any time and anywhere in the world, and at low cost. Information will be ubiquitous and omnipresent, on tap just like water or electricity, not just from the desktop PC or laptop, but from our domestic TV, on our wrist, in our wallet, in the car, on the plane. There will be no escape from it - or at least, no excuse. But it won't happen by magic, and - if we are to get it right - it won't happen without huge intellectual effort. As in other areas where deeper understanding permits the removal of limitations imposed by empirical techniques - as in drug design, architecture and civil engineering, food production and biotechnology[9] - this new found elevation of information as an artefact in its own right poses many problems concerned with choice, notions of the sacred, meaningfulness, aesthetics, identity and the boredom which results from an excess of freedom. The final outcome of the Age of Information has yet to emerge.

Prominent among the concerns of the Age of Information must be structure, organisation, and the fact that information has no limits in the ways that it can be put together and interpreted. Anyone's opinion is as good as anyone else's in the postmodern world - at least, for those who choose to believe it. There is no definitive structure of information. If there was, we could build it, and we would know what we were about, with no scope for argument. But there isn't, and we can't, and we don't.

What we can do is build our own structure, that personalised thread through impersonal information space that reflects our own peculiar interests and concerns. Creativity is encouraged by this trend.

As Xanadu hiccups its way to an uncertain future[10] and the Internet threatens to race away out of control, it is not clear whether an organised global knowledge structure, a true World 4, will develop, with either the capacity for supreme intolerance[11] or for permitting and evaluating the existence of all varieties of fact, thought and belief, side by side. Maybe the plurality of our belief systems, commercial pressures, vested interests, and the sheer size and logistic difficulty of the problem will preclude realisation of an integrated structure. I guess that will be the case. Maybe - and despite everything that has gone before - it really isn't that important. Maybe it isn't the information that is so important; maybe it is us. What is surely more important is to learn to choose, to learn what it means to be a person, what the essence of being alive as oneself is, and how to cope with the limitations of mortality and the given conditions of life. When choice becomes impossibly wide, when informed decision is fraught because there are too many facts and variables to digest, and when access to information vastly beyond one's coping abilities is routine, then one is forced to re-examine one's true needs, and to investigate more deliberately - or create - one's identity. These will be issues for the 21st century to grapple with. They are issues that children could usefully be exposed to early on.

In the 20th century we were in a sense getting our act together, finding out what really works, acquiring a scientific understanding of the universe and rejecting a lot of tired old myths and inefficient ways of doing things. And we came an extraordinarily long way. This will continue in the new century, but of increasing importance will be the problem of what to do as an individual in a complex world in which so much is already cut and dried, in other words, how to maintain our interest when someone else - or something else, such as a computer - is looking after all the engine numbers for us.

It is hard enough deciding who you are when you don't have much choice in the matter; when you can choose many aspects of this it becomes infinitely harder. Hence the words of Joe Jackson's song in the introductory chapter. What to do, what to search for, when we all have easy access to all the world's literature, TV and radio output, art and music, even to virtual reality simulations of museums or faraway places. The choices will be ours alone. How do we make them? It gets worse. There is the further prospect of 'agents' or 'knowbots' fed a profile of our interests, combing the data highways to bring us items likely to be useful to us, perhaps in the form of a personalised newspaper, the *Daily Me*, as envisaged by Nicholas Negroponte[12]. They could throw away the info-junk for us as well, but the idea that they might decide what we should read or view or listen to is, for many people, vaguely minatory. Or what about Internet-accessible software such as Firefly[13], a program which can select music and films on the basis of one's preferences? This system asks the individual to rate a handful of artists, and then compares these ratings with those made by other people. In this way it can build up a profile of one's tastes, and make recommendations on the basis of the likes and dislikes of people with similar declared tastes. It has been described as 'automated word of mouth'[14]. In so doing, theoretically, it can increase one's exposure to other artists, and it is claimed that the more users who enter their preferences the more accurate the system will become. Presumably it cannot accommodate sudden whims and changes of taste, the sudden appetite for hard core or Hollywood spectacular, the manic lunge from string quartet to hip-hop after a bad day at the office. In its early stages it could recommend up to 300,000 CDs, but clearly the principle could extend into other areas of personal choice, such as books, restaurants, food, or cars. What then of the collecting habits of a Colin Wilson or the unsatisfied cravings of a Thomas Wolfe? And anyway, who has the time? This becomes a matter of personal design, of personal ecology.

To specify one's profile for the *Daily Me* could be quite a challenge, unless it was limited to just a handful of core professional interests. This sort of service is already available, from companies such as the NewsEdge Corporation and the Financial Times, who can scan raw news services (Dow Jones, AFX, Reuters, PR Newswire and so forth) according to personal or corporate interest profiles, and then present them very rapidly via an Internet link. For particularly significant items the system can be set up so as to break through as an e-mail alert. This sort of push technology is becoming commonplace in business, but is less usual on an individual basis. Recent criticisms of the *Daily Me* concept suggest that not only is it by definition solipsistic, satisfying the interests of a community of one, but that 'such communities exist only in the imagination', and that the premise that people's tastes and interests are so different that each would demand unique menus is false. 'The image of billions of readers with distinct, customised newspapers is techno-fiction'[15]. Probably so, but the technical possibility does raise the question of personal choice, and offers us the chance of deliberature exposure to new ideas and areas of information which might encourage serendipity[16]. Nevertheless, most people, I imagine, are quite happy to go out and buy the *Telegraph* or the *Guardian*, the *Sun* or the *Mirror,* and don't particularly want to have to think about what might interest them. Primarily they want to be entertained rather than informed, or they want the subtle reassurance of a familiar habit. The whole point of news, after all, is that it is unexpected. If it could be anticipated it wouldn't *be* news. More practically, intelligent agents would roam the networks and databases alerting us to items of potential interest to our professional, academic or cultural lives, items recognised from a frequently updated personal profile as being relevant to our core interests and life projects, to our deepest sense of identity.

In time electronic assistants will be able to put together coherent summaries of developments in areas of interest, fully searchable, with access to original documents, complete personal libraries, individualised miniature World 4s in effect. This is not so far off, given the demand for such systems, and is perhaps the ultimate goal of information retrieval in the way that it can be visualised from the present day. This would be an automated aide to what we do already, namely to navigate our way through information space along a thread of our interests, an information 'line of life' or 'throughline', not just our professional interests but much more personal matters including our perceptions and sensory enjoyment, cultural input, hobbies, and so forth. Electronic assistance in this sense could be extremely useful, but we shouldn't go overboard with the idea. How and where do we start? Could the very act of profile specification narrow our experiences and life-projects, rather than broadening them? Could it rapidly drain everything of interest, destroy our motivation, obviate purpose and the pleasures of the search?

Let us return finally to Thomas Wolfe, our troubled hero. Trying to grapple with the painful longings of the type he expressed could be a useful exercise for future man, for man as information processor. The successful resolution of the predicament he described ought to lead to happier, fuller and more satisfying lives. It may even be possible to learn to enjoy the unsatisfied Wolfean ache in its own right, as the emotional bedrock of being alive, without trying to ignore or resist it, without transcending it or distancing or decentering ourselves from it. Perhaps we should even try to develop it, as a core emotion or as an ambient mood. Pamela Hansford Johnson wrote about Wolfe that he was 'young, and an amateur in living; his profound appeal is to the young, and to the amateurs in living'[17]. Maybe this youthful amateurism should be encouraged: keeping alive something of the trainspotter mentality into adult life can only be enriching and enhancing of meaning. We will still have to note down the engine numbers, or memorise the timetable, or learn the route map or the sequence of stations - whichever metaphor of enthusiasm for interactions between World 2 and Worlds 1 and 3 we choose - in order to have meaningful lives. And we have to do this ourselves; no one can do it for us.

Yes, let us not forget the trainspotter. Surprisingly, it could just be that the trainspotter is in for a renaissance. In November 1996 the London *Times*[18] reported on a £20,000 campaign organised by the National Railway Museum in York to try and improve the image of rail enthusiasts and to free them from ridicule. Under the wonderfully punning headline 'Trainspotters try new line to shed nerdy look' the article declared that: 'They [trainspotters] are fashionable, they are romantic and they are definitely not the sort of people who follow the nerd'. The campaign was to include posters, new fashions, support by celebrities and a social survey of Britain's two million spotters, to highlight the fact that perfectly normal people can have a healthy interest in trains, and that the hobby is no more ridiculous than angling or golf. Maybe it could lead to further in-depth analyses of the trainspotting mentality and motivation.

Rather than the IT revolution permitting a reduction in what we have to learn we can expect instead that it will free us to learn more significant and rewarding things, warmer things, more human things. We still cannot answer the fundamental question: 'What should we put into our minds?', but at least we are more aware of the question and can use our technological resources to help us. If there is an answer it is one which everyone must work out for themselves, and it is hugely difficult, so closely tied in as it is with questions of personal identity, development and ambition, but in the Age of Information we should be more conscious of this issue, and be given the means for answering it more efficiently. The trend from the single subject specialisations and single employment roles which were prevalent until recently, to multiple roles and wider education, either simultaneously or sequentially throughout life, should - whether we are outsider personalities or not - both enrich us and satisfy some of the more obscure longings which we have been discussing. At the same time, the heavy glut of information overload and the burn-out of meaning which derives from the devaluing relativism of postmodern culture, should reinforce the desirability of an individually thought out answer to our fundamental question.

In the 20th century, for good reasons, we tended to emphasise the importance of World 3 knowledge at the expense of acquaintance with the real physical world and exploration of the subjective realm. The current fascination with the possibilities of cyberspace is an extension of this emphasis. Correctives to this trend have often been extreme and wrong-headed, but I believe that for a more meaningful existence - and meaninglessness was one of the hallmarks of the 20th-century developed-world psyche - there has to be more attention paid to one's perceived inner needs, including some of the fundamental feelings of being alive that I have been discussing. But let us not get too self-centred or unbalanced about this. There is much more that we should be doing to improve the lot of our fellow humans and the well-being of our planet. Without attending to these issues many of our ventures into the world as information can be rightly judged as selfish indulgences. A truly tolerant pluralistic society must also care for and accommodate those - perhaps the majority - who do not want to, or who cannot, play its most intensive games, whether driven by politics, economics, technology, by the acquisition or deployment of information, or whatever; games which are often pretty meaningless when seen in perspective from outside.

This book has looked at the world from the Popperian perspective, and at the individual as an information processing being, taking information in from Worlds 1 and 3, ruminating over it in World 2, spitting it out again into World 1 and sometimes into World 3, and - because of the problems of overload and the quest for meaning - into what I have called World 4. I believe that this is a valid model of what we do, but it is a very skeletal and shallow one. It *is* possible to see the world as information, but we may choose not to. There are other ways of seeing, other ways of being. Most importantly we need to rediscover the miraculous in our daily lives, and marvel at the strangeness of being alive, as did Dorothy Richardson. In so doing, we may be inspired to creativity and spirituality and to a greater love of the world and of life. Being alive is, for all we know, a highly unusual, precious and rare condition to be in, amongst the sterile vastnesses of space and time, and it is the strangest, most unlikely, most sacred, most wonderful thing that we - or anything at all - should exist.

References

1. Introduction

[1]   The Reuters Guide to Good Information Strategy ; Reuters Ltd., London, 1997, p.8

[2]   Clark, S. ; Stop the world ; Sunday Times, 23rd March 1997

[3]   Midgley, M. ; Wisdom, Information, and Wonder : What is knowledge for ? ; Routledge, London, 1989, p.53

[4]   Pirsig, R. M. ; Lila : an inquiry into morals ; Bantam Press, 1991, p.24

[5]   Wurman, R. S. ; Information Anxiety ; Doubleday, New York, 1989, p.294

[6]   Peacocke, A. R. ; Creation and the World of Science. The Bampton Lectures, 1978. Clarendon Press, Oxford, 1979, pp.181-182

[7]   Lewis, C. S. ; Surprised by Joy. The Shape of My Early Life ; Collins-Fount Paperbacks, Glasgow, 1981, p.20 (first published 1955)

[8]   Brooke, R. ; Collected Poems, with a Memoir ; Sidgwick and Jackson, London, 1929, p. lxxviii

[9]   Glued to the Screen : An investigation into information addiction worldwide ; Reuters Limited, London, 1997

[10] Manchester, W. ; The Last Lion : Winston Spencer Churchill, Visions of Glory 1874-1932 ; Sphere, London, 1984, p.29

[11] Rowe, D. ; Wanting Everything : The Art of Happiness ; Fontana, London, 1992, p.10

[12] Brown, P. and Gaines, S. ; The Love You Make : An Insider's Story of The Beatles ; Macmillan, London, 1983, p.88

[13] Jackson, J. ; Pokazuka Ltd. and Virgin Records America Inc., 1991

2. Railway Analogies

[1]   Whittaker, N. ; Platform Souls : The Trainspotter as Twentieth-Century Hero ; Victor Gollancz, London, 1995, p. 11

[2]   as [1], p.52

[3]   Kegan, R. ; The Evolving Self : Problem and Process in Human Development ; Harvard University Press, Cambridge, Mass., and London, 1982, p.33

[4]   as [1], p.16

[5]   as [1], p.252

[6]   Humphrey, N. ; Consciousness Regained : Chapters in the Development of Mind ; Oxford University Press, Oxford, 1983, pp.143-145

[7]   Gould, S. J. and Purcell, R. W. ; Finders, Keepers : Eight Collectors ; W. W. Norton, New York, 1992

[8]   Dittmar, H. ; The Social Psychology of Material Possessions : To Have is To Be ; Harvester Wheatsheaf, Hemel Hempstead, 1992

[9]   as [1], p.241

[10] The Guinness Book of Records 1997 ; Guinness Books, London, 1996

[11] Meades, J. ; Pompey ; Vintage, London, 1994, p.24

[12] as [1], p.234

[13] as [1], p.243

[14] Greene, G. ; A Sort of Life ; The Bodley Head, London, 1971, p.11

[15] Langer, S. K. ; Feeling and Form ; Routledge and Kegan Paul, London, 1953, p.390

[16] as [1], p.231

[17] Tart, C. T. (ed.) ; Altered States of Consciousness : A Book of Readings ; Wiley, New York, 1969, p.345

[18] Boursin, F. ; Stemming the Flood of Paper ; Chemistry and Industry, 1995, 4th December, 992

[19] Handy, C. ; The Hungry Spirit : Beyond Capitalism - A Quest for Purpose in the Modern World ; Hutchinson, London, 1997, p. 217
[20] Smith, A. ; The Mind ; Hodder and Stoughton, London, 1984, p.164
[21] Pask, G. and Curran, S. ; Micro Man : Living and Growing with Computers ; Century, London, 1982, p.46
[22] Kington, M. ; Miles and Miles ; Hamish Hamilton, London, 1982, p.135
[23] Cohen, S. and Taylor, L. ; Escape Attempts : The Theory and Practice of Resistance to Everyday Life ; Penguin, Harmondsworth, 1978, pp.212-213
[24] Churchill, W. S. ; If I Lived My Life Again ; complied and edited by Jack Fishman ; W. H. Allen, London, 1974, p.107
[25] de Unamuno, M. ; Tragic Sense of Life (translated by J. E. Crawford Flitch) ; Dover Publications Inc., New York, 1954, p.213 (first published 1921)

3. The Pain of Everything
[1] Smith, A. C. ; Opening Lines and others ; British Medical Journal, 1981, **283**, 1596
[2] Turnbull, A. ; Thomas Wolfe, a Biography ; The Bodley Head, London, 1968, p.277
[3] as [2], p.54
[4] Clarke, A. C. ; Profiles of the Future : an Inquiry into the Limits of the Possible ; newly revised edition, Victor Gollancz, London, 1982, p.215
[5] Wolfe, T. ; Of Time and the River ; Heinemann, London, 1969, p.150 (first published 1935)
[6] as [5], p.89
[7] as [5], p.137
[8] Field, L. A. (ed.) ; Thomas Wolfe - Three Decades of Criticism ; University of London Press Ltd., 1969, p.159
[9] as [2], p.53
[10] Wolfe, T. ; The Web and the Rock ; Heinemann, London, 1969, p.419 (first published 1947)
[11] as [5], p.160
[12] as [8], p.88
[13] Ghiselin, B. ; The Creative Process : A Symposium ; Mentor, New York, 1952, p.189
[14] as [5], p.137
[15] as [2], p.44
[16] as [5], p.31
[17] as [8], p.98
[18] as [5], p.150
[19] as [8], p.162
[20] Powys, J. C. ; Autobiography ; Picador, Pan Books, London, 1982, p.184 (first published 1934)
[21] Paffard, M. ; Inglorious Wordsworths : A study of some transcendental experiences in childhood and adolescence ; Hodder and Stoughton, London, 1973, p.61
[22] as [8], p.133
[23] as [8], p.166
[24] Donald, D. H. ; Look Homeward : A Life of Thomas Wolfe ; Little, Brown and Company, Boston, Massachusetts, 1987, p.15
[25] Haule, J. R. ; Divine Madness : Archetypes of Romantic Love ; Shambhala Publications, Boulder, Colorado, 1990

4. Popper's Worlds
[1] Eigen, M. and Winkler, R. ; Laws of the Game : How the Principles of Nature Govern Chance. Translated by Robert and Rita Kimber ; Penguin, Harmondsworth, 1983, p.252
[2] Fuller, R. B. ; Critical Path ; Hutchinson, London, 1983, p.27
[3] Popper, K. R. ; Objective Knowledge, An Evolutionary Approach ; Clarendon Press, Oxford, 1972, p.73
[4] Kemp, D.A. ;The Nature of Knowledge : an introduction for librarians ; Clive Bingley, London, and Linnet Books, Hamden, Conn., 1976, p.77

[5] Miller, D. (ed.); A Pocket Popper ; Fontana Paperbacks, 1983, p.67

[6] Bloor, D. ; Essay Review : Popper's Mystification of Objective Knowledge ; Science Studies, 1974, **4**, 65-76

[7] Grove, J. W. ; Popper 'Demystified' : The Curious Ideas of Bloor (and some others) about World 3 ; Phil. Soc. Sci., 1980, **10**, 173-180

[8] Bohm, D. ; Wholeness and the Implicate Order ; Routledge and Kegan Paul, London, 1980

[9] Talbot, M. ; The Holographic Universe ; Harper Collins, New York, 1991

[10] Minai, A. T. ; Emergence, a Domain where the Distinction between Conception in Arts and Sciences is meaningless ; Cybernetics and Human Knowing, 1995, **3**, (3), 25-39

[11] Wilson, C. ; Access to Inner Worlds : The Story of Brad Absetz ; Rider, London, 1983, p.128

[12] Kuhn, T. S. ; The Structure of Scientific Revolutions ; Chicago University Press, Chicago, 1962

[13] as [3], p.121

[14] Pratt, A. D. ; Information and Emmorphosis : An Attempt at Definition. In : Harbo, O. and Kajberg, L. (eds.) ; Theory and Application of Information Research. Proceedings of the Second International Research Forum on Information Science, Copenhagen, 1977 ; Mansell, London, 1980

[15] as [3], p.74

[16] as [3], p.159

[17] as [3], p.147

[18] Humphrey, N. ; Consciousness Regained : Chapters in the Development of Mind ; Oxford University Press, Oxford, 1983, p.37

[19] as [3], p.148

[20] Popper, K. R. and Eccles, J. C. ; The Self and its Brain, An Argument for Interactionism ; Springer International, Berlin, Heidelberg, London, and New York, 1977, p.504

[21] Fayyad, U. M., et al (eds.) ; Advances in Knowledge Discovery and Data Mining ; AAAI Press / MIT Press, Menlo Park, Cambridge (Massachusetts) and London, 1996

[22] Matthews, R. ; Panning for Data ; New Scientist, 1996, 25th May, 30-33

5. Dürrenmatt's Absent Lemur

[1] Stewart, D. and Mickunas, A. ; Exploring Phenomenology : a guide to the field and its literature ; American Library Association, Chicago, 1974, p.108

[2] Vickery, B. C. ; Classification and Indexing in Science ; Third Edition, Butterworths, London, 1975, pp.147-180

[3] as [2], p.162

[4] Körner, S. ; Classification Theory ; Intern. Classificat., 1976, **3**, (1), 3-6

[5] The Natural History Museum 1881-1981 ; Endeavour, 1981, **5**, (4), 139-140

[6] as [4], p.5

[7] Mayr, E. ; Biological Classification : Towards a Synthesis of Opposing Methodologies ; Science, 1981, **214**, 510-516

[8] as [2], pp.163-164

[9] Allen, E. L. ; Existentialism from within ; Greenwood Press, Westport, Conn., 1953, p.56

[10] Whittaker, N. ; Platform Souls : The Trainspotter as Twentieth-Century Hero ; Victor Gollancz, London, 1995, p.167

[11] MacCannell, D. ; The Tourist. A New Theory of the Leisure Class ; Macmillan, London, 1976, p.115

[12] Kington, M. ; Let's Parlez Franglais Again ; Penguin, Harmondsworth, 1982, p.85

[13] Dittmar, H. ; The Social Psychology of Material Possessions : To Have is To Be ; Harvester Wheatsheaf, Hemel Hempstead, 1992

[14] Fuller, R. B. ; Critical Path ; Hutchinson, London, 1983, p.131

[15] Eccles, J. C. ; Facing Reality : Philosophical Adventures by a Brain Scientist ; Longman and Springer Verlag, 1970, p.1

[16] Proust, M. ; Remembrance of Things Past, Translated by C. K. Scott-Moncrieff and T. Kilmartin ; Penguin Books, Harmondsworth, 1983, Volume 1, pp.530-531

[17] Weschler, L. ; Seeing is Forgetting the Name of the Thing One Sees : A Life of Contemporary Artist Robert Irwin ; University of California Press, Berkeley, Los Angeles and London, 1982, p.3

[18] Paffard, M. ; Inglorious Wordsworths : a study of some transcendental experiences in childhood and adolescence ; Hodder and Stoughton, London, 1973, p.32

[19] Hopkins, K. ; The Powys Brothers ; Phoenix House, London, 1967, p.177

[20] Powys, J. C. ; Weymouth Sands ; Macdonald, London, 1963, p.48

[21] Powys, J. C. and Powys, L. ; Confessions of Two brothers ; Sinclair Browne, London, 1982, p.169 (first published 1916)

[22] Powys, J. C. ; Wolf Solent ; Penguin, Harmondsworth, 1976, p. 571 (first published 1929)

[23] Salaman, E. ; A collection of moments - a study of involuntary memories ; Longman, London, 1970, p.134

[24] Mein, M. ; A Foretaste of Proust : A study of Proust and his precursors ; Saxon House, Farnborough, Hants., 1974, p.61

[25] Rosenberg, J. ; Dorothy Richardson, the genius they forgot ; Duckworth, London, 1973, p.71

[26] Richardson, D. M. ; Pilgrimage, Volume 1 ; Dent, London, 1967, p. 177

6. The Universe Within

[1] Walker, K. ; The Conscious Mind : A Commentary on the Mystics ; Rider, London, 1962, p.46

[2] Becker, E. ; The Denial of Death ; The Free Press (Macmillan), New York, 1973, p.171

[3] Ayer, A. J. ; Philosophy in the Twentieth Century ; Weidenfeld and Nicolson, London, 1982, p.230

[4] Jung, C. G. ; The Undiscovered Self. Translated by R. F. C. Hull ; Routledge and Kegan Paul, London, 1958, p.60

[5] Norton, G. P. ; Montaigne and the Introspective Mind ; Mouton, The Hague, 1975, p.57

[6] as [5], p.59

[7] Davy, M. M. ; Nicolas Berdyaev, Man of the Eighth Day. Translated by Leonora Siepman ; Geoffrey Bles, London, 1967, p.72

[8] Edward Hopper 1882-1967 ; Catalogue for exhibition at the Hayward Gallery, London, 11th February - 29th March 1981 ; Arts Council of Great Britain, 1981, p.23

[9] Hopkin, K. ; Dot Dot Dot Dash Dash Dash ; New Scientist, 1996, 18th May, 40-43

[10] Wilson, J. R. and the editors of Time-Life Books ; The Mind ; Time-Life Books, Alexandria, Virginia, 1980, p.16

[11] Restak, R. M. ; The Brain, The Last Frontier ; Doubleday, Garden City, New York, 1979, p.6

[12] Taylor, D. A. ; Mind : A Scientists's View of How the Mind Works - and how to make it work for you ; Century Publishing, London, 1983, p.32

[13] Loftus, E. ; Memory : surprising new insights into how we remember and why we forget ; Addison-Wesley Publishing Company, Reading, Mass., 1980, p.15

[14] as [10], p.159

[15] Rucker, R. ; Mind Tools ; Houghton Mifflin, Boston, 1987, p.81

[16] Editorial ; Drugs and Memory ; The Lancet, 1982, 2, 474 (28th August)

[17] Baddeley, A. D. ; The Psychology of Memory ; Basic Books, New York, 1976, p.366

[18] Pelton, J. N. ; Global Talk : The Marriage of the Computer, World Communications and Man ; The Harvester Press, Brighton, 1981, p.3

[19] Uhlig, R. ; Death has had its chips, say computer scientists ; Daily Telegraph, 1996, 18th July

[20] Gardner, H. ; The Shattered Mind : The Person After Brain Damage ; Routledge and Kegan Paul, London and Henley, 1977, p.453

[21] Lewin, R. ; Is Your Brain Really Necessary ? ; Science, 1980, 210, 1232

[22] Lorimer, D. ; Whole in One : The Near-death Experience and the Ethic of Interconnectedness ; Arkana / Penguin, London, 1990

[23] Dossey, L. ; Space, Time and Medicine ; Shambhala, Boulder, Colorado, and London, 1982, p.217

[24] Underhill, E. ; Mysticism : A Study in the Nature and Development of Man's Spiritual Consciousness ; Methuen, London, 1967, p.56 (first published 1911)

[25] Jaynes, J. ;   The Origin of Consciousness in the Breakdown of the Bicameral Mind ; Allen Lane, London, 1979, p.39

[26] Buzan, T. and Dixon, T. ; The Evolving Brain ; David and Charles, Vancouver, British Columbia, p.112

[27] as[23], p.23

[28] Murchie, G. ; The Seven Mysteries of Life : An Exploration in Science and Philosophy ; Rider / Hutchinson, London, 1979, p.278

[29] Hofstadter, D. R. and Dennett, D. C. ; The Mind's I : Fantasies and Reflections on Self and Soul ; The Harvester Press, Brighton, 1981, p.13

[30] Hilgard, E. R. ; Divided Consciousness : Multiple Controls in Human Thought and Action ; Wiley - Interscience, New York, 1977, p.1

[31] as [18], p.326

[32] Shattuck, R. ; Proust ; Fontana Modern Masters, London, 1974, p.13

[33] Treffert, D. A. ; The Idiot Savant ; Am. J. Psychiat., 1988, **145**, 563-572

[34] Treffert, D. A. ; Extraordinary People : An Exploration of the Savant Syndrome ; Bantam Press, London, 1989

[35] as [12], p.2

[36] Wilson, C. ; Access to Inner Worlds : The Story of Brad Absetz ; Rider, London, 1989

[37] McDermott, W. V. ; Endorphins, I Presume ; The Lancet, 1980, **2**, 1353

[38] as [9], p.10

[39] Abbott, R. ; Information transfer and cognitive mismatch : a Popperian model for studies of public understanding ; Journal of Information Science, 1997, **23**, (2), 129-137

[40] Lynch, K. ; The Image of the City ; The M.I.T. Press, Cambridge, Mass., 1960

[41] Shum, S. ; Real and virtual spaces : mapping from spatial cognition to hypertext ; Hypermedia, 1990, **2**, (2), 133-158

[42] Wainright, M. ; English examinees prove a class divided by common clangers ; Guardian, 1996, 15th July

[43] McCloskey, M. ; Intuitive Physics ; Scientific American ; 1983, **248**, April, 114

[44] Driver, R. : Culture clash : children and science ; New Scientist, 1991, 29 June, 46-48

[45] Abbott, R. ; Food and nutrition information : a study of sources, uses and understanding; British Food Journal, 1997, **99**, (2), 43-49

[46] Chiari, J. ; Art and Knowledge ; Paul Elek, London, 1977

7. World 3

[1]   Evans, C. ; The Mighty Micro : The Impact of the Computer Revolution ; Gollancz, London, 1979, p.67

[2]   Woodward, K. ; in : The Myths of Information Technology and Postindustrial Culture, edited by Kathleen Woodward ; Routledge and Kegan Paul, London and Henley, 1980, p.xv

[3]   Medawar, P. ; The Limits of Science ; Oxford University Press, Oxford, 1984, p.71

[4]   Lévy-Leblond, J-M. ; About misunderstandings about misunderstandings ; Public Understanding of Science, 1992, **1**, (1), 17-21

[5]   Dupuy, J. P. ; in [2], p.3

[6]   Murchie, G. ; The Seven Mysteries of Life : An Exploration in Science and Philosophy ; Rider / Hutchinson, London, 1979, pp.573-574

[7]   de Solla Price, D. J. ; Little Science, Big Science ; Columbia University Press, New York and London, 1963

[8]   Lonergan, B. J. F. ; Insight : A Study of Human Understanding ; Darton, Longman and Todd, 1983, p.xviii (first published 1957)

[9]   Bryan, H. ; The explosion in published information - myth or reality ; Australian Library Journal, 1968, (12), 389-401

[10] Senders, J. W. ; Information storage requirements for the contents of the world's libraries ; Science, 1963, **141**, 1067

[11] McGarry, K. J. ; The Changing Context of Information : an introductory analysis ; Clive Bingley, London, 1981

[12] Durack, D. T. ; The weight of medical knowledge ; New Engl. J. Med., 1978, **298**, 773

[13] Madlon-Kay, D. J. ; The weight of medical knowledge : still gaining ; New Engl. J. Med., 1989, **321**, 908

[14] Martin, J. ; The Wired Society ; Prentice-Hall Inc., Englewood Cliffs, New Jersey, 1978, pp.116-117

[15] Knight, D. ; Ordering the World ; Burnett Books, London, 1981, p.132

[16] Ziman, J. H. ; The Proliferation of Scientific Literature : A Natural Process ; Science, 1979, **203**, 143

[17] Boursin, F. ; Stemming the Flood of Paper ; Chemistry and Industry, 1995, 4th December, 992

[18] Branscomb, L. M. ; Information : The Ultimate Frontier ; Science, 1979, **203**, 143

[19] The Guinness Book of Records 1997 ; Guinness Books, London, 1996

[20] Steinberg, S. G. ; Seek and Ye Shall Find ; Wired, 1996, May, 60-66, 97-103

[21] Galinski, C. ; Information - the basis of Japan's forecast technological and economic development ; Aslib Proceedings, 1984, **36**, (1), 24

[22] Short Cited ; New Scientist, 1998, 2nd May, 21

[23] Fuller, R. B. ; Critical Path ; Hutchinson, London, 1983, p.134

[24] Falkman, K. ; Robot and Meaning ; Bachman and Turner, Maidstone, 1982, p. 31

[25] Wilson, C. ; Voyage to a Beginning : an autobiography ; Cecil and Amelia Woolf, London, 1969, p. 176

[26] Wilson, C. and Grant, J. (eds.) ; The Directory of Possibilities ; Webb and Bower, Exeter, 1981, p. 16

[27] Wilson, C. ; Beyond the Outsider ; Pan, London, 1966, p. 148

[28] Colin Wilson on "Desert Island Discs", BBC Radio 4, 24th October, 1978

[29] as [25], p. 3

[30] Seaman, D., in : Colin Wilson, a Celebration : Essays and Recollections, ed. Colin Stanley ; Cecil Woolf, London, 1988, p. 28

[31] Fukuyama, F. ; The End of History and the Last Man ; Penguin Books, London, 1992

[32] Wilson, P. ; Interdisciplinary Research and Information Overload ; Library Trends, 996, **45**, (2), Fall, 192-203

[33] Rhinehart, L. ; The Dice Man ; Panther, London, 1972, p. 251

[34] Huxley, A. ; Island ; Penguin Books, Harmondsworth, 1971, p. 136 (first published 1962)

[35] Skolnik, H. ; Historical Development of Abstracting ; J. Chem. Inf. Comput. Sci., 1979, **19**, (4), 215-218

[36] Ash, R. ; The Top 10 of Everything 1993 ; Headline, London, 1992, p.216

[37] Mayne, A. J. ; Some Modern Approaches to the Classification of Knowledge ; Classification Society Bulletin, 1968, **1**, (4), 12-17

[38] Wojciechowski, J. A. ; The philosophical relevance of the problem of the classification of knowledge; in: Conceptual Basis of the Classification of Knowledge, Proceedings of the Ottawa Conference 1971, Verlag Dokumentation, Pullach / Munich, 1974, p.15

[39] Donald, D. H. ; Look Homeward : A Life of Thomas Wolfe ; Little, Brown and Company, Boston, Mass., 1987, p.183

[40] Batty, D. ; Library Classification : One Hundred Years After Dewey ; in : Major Classification Systems, The Dewey Centennial, ed. K. L. Henderson ; Papers presented at the Allerton Park Institute, Allerton Park, Monticello, Illinois, 9-12 November, 1975, University of Illinois, 1976, pp.1-31

[41] Dahlberg, I. ; Classification Theory, Yesterday and Today ; Intern. Classificat., 1976, **3**, (2), 85-90

[42] Farradane, J. ; Relational Indexing. Part 1 ; J. Inf. Sci., 1980, (1), 267-276

[43] Cooper, W. S. ; Getting Beyond Boole ; Information Processing and Management, 1988, **24**, (3), 243-248

[44] Salton, G. ; Developments in Automatic Text Retrieval ; Science, 1991, **253**, 974-980

[45] Black, W. J. ; Knowledge-based abstracting ; Online Review, 1990, **14**, (5), 327-340

[46] Schatz, B. R. ; Information Retrieval in Digital Libraries : Bringing Search to the Net ; Science, 1997, **275**, 17th January, 327-334

[47] Bonzi, S. and Liddy, E. D. ; Testing the assumption underlying use of anaphora in natural language tests ; Proceedings of the 51st ASIS Annual Meeting, Atlanta, Georgia, October 23-27, 1988, **25**, 23-30

[48] Abbott, R. ; "Aboutness" and other problems of text retrieval in the pharmaceutical industry ; Drug Information Journal, 1997, **31**, 1, 125-135

[49] Shively, D. ; Idea Retrieval ; Technical Services Quarterly, 1988, **6**, (1), 23-30

[50] Ransley, A. ; Towards a Fiction Index. Part One ; Australian Library Journal, 1987, February, 44-53

[51] Kinscott, G. ; Applications of Machine Translation ; Study for the Commission of the European Communities, 1989

[52] Benton, P. M. ; The Multilingual Edge ; Byte, 1991, March, 124-132

8. From Akasha to Xanadu : Towards the World Brain

[1]   Abbott, R. ; Worlds 1, 2, 3 ... and 4 ? ; Journal of Information Science, 1983, **6**, (4), 143-144

[2]   Ziman, J. ; Reliable Knowledge : an exploration of the grounds for belief in science; Cambridge University Press, Cambridge, 1978

[3]   Wells, H. G. ; The Shape of Things to Come ; Hutchinson, London, 1933, p.129

[4]   Wells, H. G. ; World Encyclopaedia, in : The Growth of Knowledge : Readings on Organization and Retrieval of Information, ed. Manfred Kochen, Wiley, New York, 1967

[5]   Kochen, M. ; WISE : A World Information Synthesis and Encyclopaedia ; Journal of Documentation, 1972, **28**, (4), 322-343

[6]   Boyd Rayward, W. ; Restructuring and mobilising information in documents : a historical perspective ; in : Conceptions of Library and Information Science : Historical, empirical and theoretical perspectives, Vakkari, P. and Cronin, B. (eds.) ; Taylor Graham, London and Los Angeles, 1992, 50-68

[7]   Nelson, T. H. ; Replacing the Printed World : A Complete Literary System ; Information Processing '80, North-Holland Publishing Company, 1980, 1013-1023

[8]   Bevilacqua, A. F. ; Hypertext : behind the hype ; American Libraries, 1989, **20**, 158-162

[9]   Goodman, H. J. A. ; The "World Brain / World Encyclopaedia" Concept ; Proceedings of the 50th ASIS Annual Meeting, Boston, Mass., 1987, 91-98

[10] Collison, R. ; Encyclopaedias : Their History Throughout the Ages ; Hafner Publishing Company, London, 1964

[11] Hoel, I. A. L. ; On the concept of knowledge and its relation to information science, in : Harbo, O. and Kajberg, L. (eds.), Theory and Application of Information Research ; Proceedings of the Second International Research Forum on Information Science, Copenhagen, August, 1977 ; Mansell, London, 1980

[12] Bernstein, L. M., Siegel, E. R. and Goldstein, C. M. ; The Hepatitis Knowledge Base ; Ann. Intern. Med. 1980, **93**, (Part 2), 169-181

[13] Soergel, D. ; An Automated Encyclopaedia - a Solution of the Information Problem? (Part 1, Sections 1-4) ; Intern. Classificat., 1977, **4**, (1), 4-10

[14] Hubbard, S. M. et al ; A computer data base for information on cancer treatment ; New Engl. J. Med., 1987, **316**, 315-318

[15] Carroll, J. A. et al ; Lithium Information Center ; Arch. Gen. Psychiatry, 1986, **43**, 483-485

[16] de Bono, E. ; The Use of Lateral Thinking ; Penguin Books, Harmondsworth, 1971, p.71

[17] Nelson, T. H. ; Literary Machines, 1987

[18] Tsai, C. J. ; Hypertext : Technology, Applications, and Research Issues ; J. Educational Technology Systems, 1988-89, **17**, (1), 3-14

[19] Byers, T. J. ; Built by Association ; PC World, 1987, **5**, (4), 244-251

[20] Byles, T. ; A context for hypertext : some suggested elements of style ; Wilson Library Bulletin, 1988, **63**, (3), 60-62

[21] Nelson, T. H. ; A new home for the mind ; Datamation, 1982, **28**, (3), 169-180

[22] Manes, S. ; Hypertext : a breath of air freshener ; PC Magazine, 1987, **6**, (11), 91, 95

[23] Yankelovich, N., Meyrowitz, N. and van Dam, A. ; Reading and Writing the Electronic Book ; IEEE Computer, 1985, **18**, (10), 15-30

[24] Franklin, C. ; The Hypermedia Library ; Database, 1988, **11**, (3), 43-48

[25] Massie, B. ; The need for Mediated Information on the Internet ; Chemistry and Industry, 1997, August, Supplement

[26] The Internet : Untangling the Web ; The Economist, 1998, 25th April, 116

[27] The Netcraft Web Server Survey ; http://www.netcraft.com/survey/ ; April 1998

[28] Xanadu ™ Repository Publishing - publicity handout, September 1990

[29] Conklin, J. ; Hypertext : An Introduction and Survey ; IEEE Computer, 1987, **20**, (9), 17-41

[30] Steinberg, S. G. ; Seek and Ye Shall Find ; Wired, 1996, May, 60-66, 97-103

[31] Richards, T. ; The Imperial Archive : Knowledge and the Fantasy of Empire ; Verso, London, 1993

[32] Licklider, J. C. R. ; Libraries of the Future ; The M.I.T. Press, Cambridge, Mass., 1965, p.78

[33] Jadad, A. R. and Gagliardi, A. ; Rating Health Information on the Internet : Navigating to Knowledge or to Babel ? ; Journal of the American Medical Association, 1998, **279**,(8), 25th February, 611-614

[34] Dick, A. L. ; Restoring knowledge as a theoretical focus of library and information science ; S. Afr. J. Lib. Inf. Sci., 1995, **63**, (3), 99-106

[35] Refinetti, R. ; Information processing as a central issue in philosophy of science ; Information Processing and Management, 1989, **25**, (5), 583-584

[36] Gaizauskas, R. and Wilks, Y. ; Information Extraction : Beyond Document Retrieval; Journal of Documentation, 1998, **54**, (1), 70-105

9. Conclusion – Some Implications for the Information Age

[1] Gates, B. ; The Road Ahead ; Viking, London, 1995, p.161

[2] Uhlig, R. ; Death has had its chips, say computer scientists ; Daily Telegraph, 1996, 18th July

[3] Morris, W. ; The Function of Appetite ; in : Rubin, L. D. (ed.), Thomas Wolfe : A Collection of Critical Essays ; Prentice-Hall Inc., Englewood Cliffs, New Jersey, 1973, p.91

[4] Stonier, T. ; Towards a new theory of information ; Journal of Information Science, 1991, **17**, (5), 257-264

[5] Wurman, R. S. ; Information Anxiety ; Pan Books, London, 1991

[6] Glued to the Screen : An investigation into information addiction worldwide ; Reuters Limited, London, 1997

[7] Snoddy, R. ; Breakthrough will bring Internet on the mains ; The Times, 9th October 1997

[8] Gregory, R. L. ; Mind in Science : A History of Explanations in Psychology and Physics ; Cambridge University Press, 1981, p.58

[9] Stock, G. ; Metaman ; Bantam Press, London, 1993, p.13

[10] Wolf, G. ; The Curse of Xanadu ; Wired, June 1995, pp.70-85 and 112-113

[11] Skolimowski, H. ; Information - Yes, But Where Has All Our Wisdom Gone ? ; The Ecologist, 1984, **14**, 232-234

[12] Negroponte, N. ; Being Digital ; Hodder and Stoughton, London, 1995, p.153

[13] Central Intelligent Agents ; The Economist, 1996, 15th June, 109-110

[14] Judge, P. C. ; Why Firefly Has Mad Ave. Buzzing ; Business Week, 1996, 14th October

[15] My news or yours ? ; The Economist, 1996, 20th July, 13

[16] as [12], p.154

[17] Johnson, P. H. ; The Art of Thomas Wolfe ; Charles Scribner's Sons, New York, 1963, p. iv

[18] Prynn, J. and Whitworth, D. ; Trainspotters try new line to shed nerdy look ; The Times, 1996, 19th November

Index